A Series of Discourses Upon Architecture in England

I0153203

Also from Westphalia Press
westphaliapress.org

A Series of Discourses Upon Architecture in England

From the Norman Aera
to the Close of the
Reign of Queen Elizabeth

by Rev. James Dallaway

WESTPHALIA PRESS
An Imprint of Policy Studies Organization

A Series of Discourses Upon Architecture in England, From the
Norman Aera to the Close of the Reign of Queen Elizabeth
All Rights Reserved © 2018 by Policy Studies Organization

Westphalia Press
An imprint of Policy Studies Organization
1527 New Hampshire Ave. NW
Washington, D.C. 20036
info@ipsonet.org

ISBN-13: 978-1-63391-683-8
ISBN-10: 1-63391-683-9

Cover design by Jeffrey Barnes:
jbarnesbook.design

Daniel Gutierrez-Sandoval, Executive Director
PSO and Westphalia Press

Updated material and comments on this edition
can be found at the Westphalia Press website:
www.westphaliapress.org

A SERIES OF

DISCOURSES

UPON

Architecture

in

England

FROM THE NORMAN ÆRA TO THE CLOSE OF THE
REIGN OF QUEEN ELIZABETH,

WITH

AN APPENDIX OF NOTES AND ILLUSTRATIONS,

AND

AN HISTORICAL ACCOUNT OF

Master and Free Masons.

———

BY THE REV. JAMES DALLAWAY.

————————

LONDON:

JOHN WILLIAMS,

Library of Architecture,

10, CHARLES STREET, SOHO SQUARE.

1833.

CONTENTS.

Page 179 n. *for* 7000 tons *read* 7400 lbs.
—— 213, line 14, *for* Norwich *read* Chichester.

CORRIGENDA.

Page   3, n. *for* Denkmachler *read* Denkmahler.
—— ib. *for* Bankhunst *read* Baukhunst.
—— 99, line 7, *for* Wieseking *read* Chevalier Wiebeking.
—— 103, n. *for* Wheley *read* Rev. W. Whewell.
—— 179, n. *for* 7000 tons *read* 7400 lbs.
—— 213, line 14, *for* Norwich *read* Chichester.

DISCOURSES ON ARCHITECTURE

𝔈nglanð.

DISCOURSE I.

Iᴛ is a fact concerning which controversy
is no longer entertained, that the aboriginal
Goths had no share either in the invention or
perfection of that peculiar style of architecture
which bears their name. It is not worth the
dispute, whether the Gothick power was ever
annihilated in Europe, or whether they subsisted in the conquered countries as a separate
people. By the Goths, no individual nation
is alluded to, but the Northern conquerors in
general, before they were incorporated with
the people they had subdued. Gothick, therefore, should be considered merely as a term
to convey reproach to everything in literature
and arts, which was not strictly accordant with
the antique model, adopted and applied by

those who had introduced the restored Grecian. In Italy, the last mentioned had its origin, as appropriated to architecture, in the school of Palladio; and with us it was unknown in the present sense before the days of Jones and Wren.

The earliest Christian churches were not erected before the fourth century, which were very diminutive, and placed over crypts and caves, in which the Christians first assembled for public worship. One, dedicated to Saints Nazian and Celsus, at Ravenna, was built by Galla Placidia, the daughter of Theodosius. Those of St. Martin and St. Clement at Rome, were of the same age.*

The Goths were not inventive architects. The beginnings of that particular architecture, since called Gothick, are traceable in those buildings which were erected in Italy even before the arts had totally declined, and long before any Gothick invaders had established themselves there.† Neither the Goths nor Lombards were exclusively the inventors of the architecture which bears their name; for the ancient Paganism of the Northern nations had no influence upon church-building. The

* Cicognara, *Storia della Scultura, dal suo risorgimento in Italia, sino al Secolo di Napoleone.* 3 tom. fol. Venezia, 1813.

† Barry's Works, vol. i. p. 123—134.

churches constructed by Constantine and his immediate successors, were all of them formed upon the plan of the Roman Basilicæ.*

A total decay of the arts had even preceded the dissolution of the Roman empire; and the establishment of Christianity, with its privilege of building churches, was contemporary with the Gothick incursions. In this coincidence has originated a popular notion, that the barbarians annihilated the Grecian architecture in order to introduce a style peculiar to their own country, and that their edifices are called " Gothick" merely because they are as widely discriminated by their proportions and ornaments from the classical monuments of Athens, as the Goths were from the Greeks in their talents and national manners.

One of the chief causes of the substitution of the style we now call Gothick for the solidity of the Greek and Roman forms, was the scarcity in Germany, Flanders, or France, of columns or other members of architecture, which were so copiously supplied in Italy,

---

* Moller, *Denkmachler der Deutschen Bankunst*, &c. G. *Von Moller, Darmstadt,* fol. 1821. 72 plates in outline.

Heyné *(Comment. Göetenburg,* t. 13, p. 22) remarks, that the Gothick architects residing at Rome, were in reality the first who emigrated into France, and other Goths who professed the arts from Aquitain and Spain, and concludes " ita si artifices Gothos audias nequaquam necesse sit, arcessitos ex septentrione, statuere."

after the triumph of Christianity over the ruins of Paganism. In that country were found materials before used, and wrought into just proportions, which could be adapted; and that, with no great degree of skill. The Italian architects, therefore, did not trust to their imagination for their designs. But the Northern nations, possessing very few Roman remains, had a free and unconstrained recourse to their own conceptions. It was not in their power to employ precious materials. which they did not possess, nor to imitate models which they had never seen, so that they adopted every licence in their style; and their pillars and vaults created surprise, by exaggerated dimensions, which could impose an idea of magnificence or even elegance.*

At the beginning of the eighth century all Europe formed but one Gothick kingdom. Is there in any nation, a perfect church extant, which can make a just pretension to so early a date? In France and Italy there are very few

* *Cicognara.* The Monk Fridigode, who wrote the life of St. Ouen, observes, that his first church, built at Rouen in the sixth century, was constructed " manû Gothicâ;" but the authority admits of doubt. Certain, however, it is, that from all we can know, concerning the first efforts of architecture, after the fall of the Roman Empire, they were marked only by rudeness of execution, and a depraved application of classic materials.

really Gothick vestiges anterior to 800, the celebrated æra of Charlemagne.*

Upon no subject of antiquity have so many discordant opinions been maintained, as upon the origin of what is called Gothick architecture. It has given birth to bold conjecture and wide disquisition ; and where so many are ready to teach, few are satisfied with what they learn. Bentham, Gray, and T. Warton, were long held as the ablest discriminators of this question, and considered as having given the clearest idea of the regular progress of the Gothick, from barbarism to perfection.

Many idle cavils have been made about the time when the Goths ceased to exist as a nation. They probably introduced their rude manner of building into every country of which they had gained the possession : a circumstance evident in the peculiar styles of Italy, Germany, Spain, France, and England. In each of these there is an ostensible analogy without an exact resemblance. Considering the question as hitherto undecided, we may find no great difficulty in ascertaining the æra of its first intro-

---

* In the eighth century, Pepin began to rebuild the abbey church of St. Denis, which was completed by his son Charlemagne. The crypt is certainly a part of the original edifice. The capital of one of the columns bears a curious sculpture of the interior of a church in bas relief, with the emperor sitting in a curule chair.

duction into this country, when the manner of
building was changed or improved, when it
reached perfection, and when a love of exuberance finally effected its decline.

Gothick is said by Torré to have been first
applied as a designation by Cesare Cesariano,
the translator of Vitruvius, in his Commentary,
1521. He wrote likewise " *Saggio sopra l'Architettura Gottica, con più proposito, Germa-
nica dinominata.*" Cesariano was one of the
architects of the cathedral of Milan in 1491.

Maffeï, Muratori, and Tiraboschi have demonstrated that neither the Goths nor the
Lombards introduced any style in particular,
but employed the architects whom they found
in Italy.

The leading causes, therefore, which have
occasioned the disuse of Grecian architecture
in the first ages of Christianity, may be assigned to the ignorance and inability into
which the artists had fallen, before the Goths
had spread themselves over Europe. A knowledge of architectural elements was still preserved. The good taste of the ancients, both
in decoration and proportion, was indeed lost,
but certain principles of the art were known
and practised. They were not unacquainted
with the secret of arching a vault; but of all
the complicated forms adopted by the Greeks
and Romans, they retained that only which

is made upon cross-ribs rising from four angles, and intersecting each other at the common centre. Such a mode was universal in their structures, and is found in the smallest closets, as well as in the most spacious churches.*

Simple combinations — such as to raise a walled inclosure, and to place pillars in the length within, connected by an arcade or architrave, serving as a base to a second wall for the support of a roof of timber—were known and practised before the Goths had appeared in Italy.

The first Christian churches built at Rome, particularly that of St. Paul, by Constantine,† have been imitated as archetypes of the most ancient churches through Christendom. In the last mentioned, we have the earliest instance of arches constructed upon columns, instead of upon piers, which was universally the Roman method. The frequent resort of the bishops

* " Gibbon mentions the palace of Theodosius, as the oldest specimen of Gothick. Shrines for reliques were probably the real prototypes of this fine specimen of architecture. It was a most natural transition, for piety, to render a whole church, as it were, one shrine. The Gothick style seems to bespeak an amplification of the minute, not a diminution of the great. Warburton's groves are nonsense ; it was not a passage from barbarism to art, but from one species of the art to another. The style was first peculiar to shrines, and then became peculiar to churches."—*Lord Orford. Walpoliana.*

† *Temples Anciens et Modernes, par Mai.* 8vo. 1774, p. 122, where it is amply described.

of different nations to the Holy See, afforded them an opportunity of obtaining plans, which they adopted upon their return to their own country. The form of the Latin cross was at first simply followed in the ground-plan; that the distribution of its parts has been infinitely enriched and varied, may be traced through successive æras, as consonant to the genius of the several nations by whom it has been applied. We may discover, by comparison, differences in architecture, which are distinctly peculiar to the several countries of Europe, and as strongly marked as those of the Grecian orders;—let me be allowed, at least, to qualify this assertion, by confining it to a certain manner, analogous to the genius of the people who have used it;—so that the Gothick in Lombardy, in Spain, in Germany, in France, but especially in England, may be generically distinguished as decidedly as the Doric, the Ionic, or the Corinthian.

Those who have examined the superb edifices in Italy which are styled Gothick, as the cathedrals of Pisa, Orvietto, Sienna, &c. will find a bare resemblance of what they may have seen in other parts of Europe.* They must doubtless have remarked that circular

* Consult " Tempio Vaticano e suo origine da Carlo Fontana. Philippi Bonanni numismata Summorum Pontificum Templum Vaticani fabricam indicantia. Romæ, 1696." fol.

arcades and porticos are most frequent; which
if not composed of columns extracted and removed from Roman works, the deficiency was
supplied by pillars imperfectly imitated from
them;* and that the exuberance of style,
called by them 'Il Gottico-Tedesco,' very rarely
occurs in Italy. The *facciata*, or grand western
front, was the object of splendour to which all
the other parts of the fabric were subordinate.
It was in that part only that the artists strove
to surpass each other, by elevation and boldness, by the multitude and originality of their
sculptures. Cupolas† rise from the centre of
the transept, and the campanile is always detached from the main building. In a few instances, as in the exquisitely slender towers of
Florence and Venice, there is a certain species
of beauty; whilst those of brick, at Bologna,
are equally astonishing, but positively ugly.
The first-mentioned tower was designed and
built by Giotto in the thirteenth century, in
emulation of the stupendous spires which at
that æra were erecting in Germany and the

* When surveying the Duomo at Sienna, I remarked that
the capitals of the external pilasters which supported the
smaller arches, were composed chiefly of grotesque heads of
beasts and monsters, instead of foliage.

† The term " dome" is improperly used for " cupola"—
it applies merely to a cathedral church, and is not synonymous with an hemispherical roof, as at the Pantheon.

Low Countries. In Italy not a single spire of equal construction is now seen.

The æra of Charlemagne gave rise to many grand edifices dedicated to Christianity, the architects of which are not recorded. If we thus fix the epocha of Gothick architecture, though we cannot ascertain the first and most ancient specimen of it, we possess nearly all the rest of its history, when we know that it was adopted, with certain variations, all over Europe; that great cities contended for the honour of having the largest and the richest church; that the same style of architecture employed in the ecclesiastic, passed to other public edifices, and to the palaces of kings; and finally, that till the end of the fifteenth century, the Gothick reigned with a more extensive dominion than the most graceful or magnificent of the Grecian orders.

It is òf importance to remark, that the particular manner which has been denominated Gothick, in any of these countries, did not appear for five centuries after the first incursions of the Gothick nations into the south of Europe. The Goths themselves built upon a different model.

Of many opinions, lately published, concerning an intricate subject, some are plausible, some merely fanciful, or conjectural as to facts, and others replete with ingenious rather than conclusive reasonings, as being raised chiefly upon analogy. But I am unwilling to disturb the dreams of certain critics in architecture; and it might be therefore hazardous to offer any hypothesis of my own.

The several Italian authors on this subject describe this manner as " *la maniera vecchia, non antica, Greco-Goffa, Goffa, Tedesca, Gottica, Longobardica, Romanesca,* all which terms occur.* The last mentioned more especially applies to the architecture of the churches first dedicated to Christianity, by the Emperors Constantine, Theodosius, Justinian, and their successors. The dissatisfaction which has arisen respecting the term *Gothick,* as applied to architecture, within the last half century, has induced some writers on the subject to attempt an alteration, by which objections might be obviated. The Society of Antiquaries, in their accounts of cathedrals, introduced the term *English Architecture,* but as confined to the pointed style; and that not without controversy, for it was proved that its origin was derived from the French or Germans, and that we had, nationally, no exclusive right to that denomination. Lately, we have in a certain instance the term *Christian Architecture,* which is by no means discriminative, and

* *Frisi, " sull' architettura Gothica," Livorno,* with a treatise in German annexed to the translation of it.

therefore not likely to obtain a general usage. If it be applicable only to temples of Christianity, why are St. Peter's, St. Paul's, and St. Genevieve Grecian, or at least Roman temples? for they have nothing more in them of the earliest Christian churches, than the cruciform plan. None but a very distinguished author can hope to invent new terms in this science, which will either merit or obtain a general acceptation. Innovation is not always improvement.

Basilicæ were imitated by the first Christians in the construction of the first churches, who took the term from the Greeks, with whom they meant only the residence of the chief magistrate or king. The interior of them was formed upon the plan of the Greek *Cella*, especially of those in hypæthral temples, in which the Ionic and Corinthian orders were mainly employed, but the Doric, in the church of San Pietro *in vinculis*, at Rome. That of S. Paolo *fuori delle mura*, is the principal basilica as adapted to a church, which is now under an imperfect restoration, since the entire conflagration in 1822. It had a portico sustained by columns at the west end, and the nave was rounded off at the east end, or broken into angles, each having a large window, to remind the pious that Christianity had its origin in the East. There were six churches in Rome formed and adapted from ancient temples, and three others without the walls. But the largest temple, erected soon after the establishment of Christianity, by Constantine, was a perfect basilica, which remained nearly entire for almost eleven centuries, when it was taken down by Pope Nicholas V. in 1450.

To that early period of ecclesiastical architecture, succeeded three distinct styles. 1. That of the cathedral of Ravenna, built by Theodoric, king of the Ostro-Goths, in 526. If any regard should be paid to the assertions of Cassiodorus in his epistles,* a new description of architecture not only existed, but actually flourished, during his reign and those of his immediate successors in Italy. Whether that style were the true parent of one subsequently denominated Gothick, may be conjectured, but I am inclined to think not satisfactorily proved. The architecture common in Lombardy at that period, has a better though not a positive claim. 2. The lower Greek, or Byzantine, according to which churches were divided into from three to seven ailes of nearly equal dimensions, which style maintained itself to the beginning of the 13th century. It may be recognised by the many little pillars on the outside, by the cupolas and circular arches, by the small windows, the

* L. 3. *Epist.* 29.

triangles and ornaments in the cathedral of
Bologna, (where the old German is mixed with
the lower Greek,) at Cologn, and at Padua;
in the cathedral and baptistery at Pisa, &c.
3. This particular mode of building was entirely superseded by the works of Masaccio
and Brunelleschi.

It has been asserted by ingenious German
writers upon this subject, that *they* have the
best claim to the invention of the Gothick,
which existed before the reign of Charlemagne;
and this claim has been ably supported by a
late English anonymous author. This assumption admits of certain doubts. Even those
churches which remain the acknowledged works
of that emperor, are only " striking examples
of barbarous deformity. Little confidence can
be placed in the exaggerated accounts given
by historic monks, who extol these shapeless
edifices as beyond all praise, dwelling only on
unprofitable magnificence, the marbles and rich
materials, which had been subtracted from the
temples and palaces of the Romans." Clovis
and his immediate successors, kings of France,
were the magnificent patrons of church architecture at the very beginning of the sixth century. Structures of extreme expense were
erected from their treasures. But it appears,
that in all these primary buildings they employed no artists, but masons only; and that as

solidity was their chief object, they were most careful in procuring good materials. It is evident that no layman, at that time, deserved the name of an architect ; all science was left to the practice of ecclesiastics. Moller asserts that " neither the Goths nor the Lombards were the inventors of the architecture which takes their names, for the ancient Paganism of the Northern nations had no influence on the style of church building."

The cathedrals in Germany and France, like those in Italy, owe their effect to the façade, which is formed by a portico of pediments richly incrusted with the most minute ornament, an infinity of niches, statues, pedestals, and canopies, and one circular window of vast diameter between two towers of very elaborately clustered pinnacles, where not otherwise finished by a regular spire. This description applies in particular to St. Stephen's at Vienna, Strasburg, Nuremburg, Rheims, Amiens, Notre Dame, and St. Denis near Paris, Coutances, and Bayeux, not to multiply instances. These exhibit prodigies of sublimity, lightness, and patience of the constructors ; yet, as if the age of piety or wealth were passed away, most of them are left in an unfinished state.*

* The cathedral churches of Narbonne, Tours, Ulm, Strasburg, Cologn, Prague, and Mayence, have not yet been completed, in their façades or towers.

Even the sumptuous cathedrals of Florence, Sienna, and Bologna, built of brick, are as yet imperfectly incrusted with marble; and one only of the intended spires of St. Stephen's, Vienna, Strasburg, and Antwerp, has been conducted to its symmetrical height.

It is worthy remark, that in Italy the Gothick is most analogous to the lower Grecian architecture, in the early instances which I have cited. Yet the baptistery at Pisa, built by Dioti Salvi in 1152, exhibits a style called by the Italian architects, ' Il Arabo-Tedesco,' a mixture of Moorish or lower Greek with the German Gothick. It is a circular building with an arcade, in the second order, composed of pillars with rudely formed Corinthian capitals and plain round arches. Between each, there rises a Gothick pinnacle; and above, it is finished by sharp pediments, which are enriched with foliage, terminating in a trefoil. The conjecture I have hazarded, that some of the members of Gothick ornament originated with Italian architects, suggested itself at Pisa.* There, they were introduced in 1152; and many instances cannot be brought that they were common in France before 1220, at St. Denis; or in England in 1256, in the cathedral at Salisbury.

* See Note [A].

The square at Pisa,* which from its extent and scrupulous neatness gives to each edifice its complete effect, presents in the same view a most rich group of the Lombard-Gothick prevalent early in the thirteenth century; and the warmest admirer of that style, indulging his imagination, could scarcely form such an assemblage in idea as the cathedral, the falling tower, the baptistery, and the cloisters. They are indeed the first and most perfect in their peculiar manner, and, for august effect, unequalled in Europe. In the northern nations, a redundancy of ornament soon prevailed; whilst in France a more simple, and consequently a lighter style was observable: but in Spain the Gothick wore a gigantic air of extent and massiveness. From the Moors at the same time they borrowed or correctly imitated an excessive delicacy in the minute decorations of parts, from whence the term " Arabesque" is derived, and is nearly synonymous with "SARA-CENIC" as usually applied. The foregoing subjects are here introduced, merely for the purpose of a general analogy.

Sir Christopher Wren was the first who dissented from the general opinion, that the

* Consult "*Architecture of the Middle Ages,*—the Cathedral, Baptistery, Leaning Tower or Campanile, and Campo Santo at Pisa, by Edward Cresy and G. L. Taylor, Architects, F. S. A." fol. 1827, in which the subject is discussed and delineated, with accuracy and skill.

Goths were the inventors of the style which is so designated; for he ascribes the invention to the Saracens, from whom, as he conceived, it was adopted by the Croisaders of the West. His hypothesis is that of a man of genius, and he has been followed in it by others of great talent—by Warburton and T. Warton. Nevertheless, time and scrupulous investigation have revealed the error, for no such Saracenic works exist in Spain, Sicily, or any other place, to which the Arabian power extended.* It is a just remark of the late Mr. Kerrich, Librarian of Cambridge, that " the error has been, to suppose that this architecture came to us from some distant country, adult and in its full vigour, and that it was implicitly adopted and made use of, exactly, as received. And it was not till very lately, that these notions having been found not to be supported by facts, we began to look nearer home, to observe the buildings around them, and to consider the objects themselves with the abilities required for their production."† An author of equal talent has observed, " that Moorish architecture which has been thus hastily assimilated with Gothick, is connected only by a few slight and superficial circumstances."‡ The light Gothic was

* *Archæolog.* vol. viii. p. 191.   † *Ibid.* vol. xvi. p. 892.
‡ *"Architectural Notes on German Churches,"* 8vo. 1830.—
" *Kerrich, Archæolog.*"

called " *maniera Tedesca*," and the heavy style
" *Lombardica*."

Any farther observations I might make concerning Gothick architecture on the Continent,
are reserved for the next section, in which that
investigation will be confirmed by numerous
examples. And it may be here necessary to
premise, that every instance of the mode or
description of building under immediate consideration, will not be adduced in confirmation
of fact or opinion; but such only as are well
known and conclusive. It may possibly occur,
that certain readers may recollect other examples, with which the author may be equally
well acquainted, yet may not think them to be
more applicable.*

In Bishop Heber's late Travels over a great
part of the Hindoo and the Mohammedan provinces of India, we have very numerous examples of the prevalence of the acutely-pointed
arch, from its greatest to its smallest proportion, as applied in temples, mosques, and the
gateways of towns and castles.

Warburton, in his notes on Pope, has asserted, that Gothick architecture originated in
Spain, where Moorish architects were employed
or followed; and that it simply imitates an
avenue of lofty trees; the sharply pointed arch
being that formed by the intersecting branches;

* See Note [B].

and that the stems of a clump of trees are represented by columns split into distinct shafts. This observation is ingenious, but not wholly applicable, or original ; for the architecture styled Gothick in the northern parts of Italy, had a distinct origin and characteristicks ; and our own Gothick was not brought us from Spain, but from Normandy and France. He had overlooked chronological facts.*

From this summary view of architecture in the earlier centuries, since the establishment of Christianity in different parts of Europe, I proceed to that prevalent, at different periods, in England only. Our Saxon progenitors, from their intercourse with Rome upon ecclesiastical concerns, adopted, with however rude an imitation, the Roman plan of churches. We have likewise a fair presumption, that many temples and palaces of the Romans remained, at that period at least, undemolished in Britain.†

The western front of their churches‡ had a portico or ambulatory, and the eastern was

* See Note [C].

† *Gyraldus Cambrensis. Bedæ Hist. Ecclesiast.* l. v. cap. 21. That the Saxon small churches were mostly constructed of timber, is evident from the term used in the *Saxon Chronicle* relative to the building of Ripon, ᵹeᴛᴉmbꞃeᵭe.—*Ingram's edit.* p. 148.

‡ Ducarel (*Norman Antiq.* p. 106. fol.) is the first author by whom an enumeration is made of churches in England, which have a date, at least anterior to the Conquest ; and

semicircular, and resembled the tribune in Roman basilicæ. The principal door-case was
formed by pilasters with sculptured capitals;
and the semicircular head of the arch, above the
square of the door, which contained bas-reliefs,
was encircled by mouldings of great variety,
imitated, with imperfect success, from many
then existing at Rome, and, not without great
·probability, in England. These mouldings have
been more particularly specified and classed as
the indented—the zig-zag, like the Etruscan
scroll—the embattled fret—the beak-head—
the nail-head, and upon the capitals the pouch
or semicircular drop-moulding — the small
squares, some alternately deeper than others—
and the flourished, with small beads, usually
on the capitals of pilasters. The latest device,
which became common just before the Saxon
style was abandoned, was a carving round the

may have been erected during the two preceding centuries.
Stukeley in Bucks, and Barfreston in Kent, are his two prominent instances. Avington in Berks presents, according to
the able opinion of my late friend, the accomplished antiquary, S. Lysons, Esq. a genuine specimen of the early Saxon; yet I believe, that such are most rare, and that many
which have been adduced are, in fact, of the first Norman
description, as applied to parish churches. It is most certain,
that Saxon sculpture is much more frequent, and has been
better preserved in crypts, fonts, and door-cases, than the
architecture which it formerly embellished and characterized.
In such, there is but little room to doubt between the true
Saxon ornament, and that which succeeded in the next age.

heads of arches, like trellis placed in broad lozenges, and considerably projecting.*

The classification adopted by King,† according to my judgment, is the most satisfactory. He has given three æras of the undoubted Saxon style : 1. From Egbert, 598 to 872 ; 2. From Alfred to Canute and Harold, 1036 ; 3. To the Norman conquest.   No less than thirty-seven specimens of Saxon ornaments are selected by him, from mouldings upon doorways only, in which there is a certain variation.

Of the first period is Barfreston before-noticed.   2. The nave and choir of Christ Church Cathedral, Oxford ; and Canute's great entrance gate at St. Edmundsbury.   3. Southwell, Notts, and Waltham Abbey, Essex.

He adduces the ruins of Malmsbury Abbey, Wilts, as having retained the most elaborate plan of Saxon ornament, which partakes of

* Consult Carter's *Ancient Architecture in England.* The great ecclesiasticks among the Saxons both studied and practised architecture.   Elfric, abbot of Malmsbury, is said by the historic monk of that place to have been " ædificandi gnarus." (*Wharton's Angl. Sac.* vol. ii. p. 33.)   Aldred, bishop of Worcester, and afterwards archbishop of York, had completed the nave of the conventual church of Gloucester before the Conquest, as it now remains.—(*Florent. Annales Vigorn.* A. D. 1057.)   Bentham, in his *Ely,* (sect. v. p. 33,) adduces this and the former church at Westminster, as instances of the Norman style, adopted or imitated by the last Saxons.

† *Munimenta Antiqua,* vol. iv. p. 240. and pl. v.

Etruscan design, having a guilloche inclosing bas-relievos. The Anglo-Norman ornaments are thus classed: 1. The plain zig-zag, or that slightly projecting and placed in the hollow moulding of the arch. 2. The open lozenge, with or without a cable moulding in the middle. 3. The billet moulding lying in cavettos, or small squares, some alternately deeper than others. 4. The embattled or Etruscan scroll. 5. The spiral column or moulding with a string of beads or pellets. 6. Hatched as if made by the single stroke of an axe. 7. A trellis of broad lozenges considerably projecting. These are combined together upon door-cases, and sometimes with a course of animals' heads, eagles' beaks, &c. The last-mentioned occur as corbels, or as the capitals of small pillars.*

THE SAXON, 900—1050.

The Saxon style is equally recognised by its seeming want of harmony of parts, as by its massive cylindrical columns, or square piers, and semicircular arches. If the several styles of Saxon, Norman, and Pointed are to be discriminated by the round or pointed arch, the semicircular form is peculiar to the two first mentioned. In the earliest instances, those of the mural arcades withinside the church were simply intersected, or interlaced; or were pre-

* See Note [D].

viously, perhaps, introduced to ornament the surface of the external walls. These may be particularised as plain semicircles crossing each other, or as intersecting semicircles, resting upon pillars with a capital, or at least an abacus, by way of impost. The base, mouldings, and capitals, though of exact dimensions and similar forms in the mass, abound in variations in the minuter parts. The arches usually spring from the capitals, without an architrave. In fact, it would be difficult, at this time, to describe any entire building, which can be referred, with certainty, to the Saxon æra, but its characteristic ornaments may be frequently traced.* The nave of St. Frideswide's (now the Cathedral at Oxford) is asserted to have been built by king Ethelred in 1004. Parts of St. Alban's and Durham Cathedral claim to be anterior to the Norman conquest; as does the whole of the east end of Tickencote church, near Stamford, in Lincolnshire.

The capitals of the pillars and the soffits of the arches of St. Peter's Church at Northampton, afford an extraordinary specimen of interior decoration. The chancel of Orford, Suffolk, has a twisted cable wound round the pillar. In the nave of St. Frideswide's (if it be Saxon) there is a certain variation from the Saxon style; especially in the sculpture of

* See Note [E].

the capitals, the double arch between the columns, and the triforia : but the first churches
of Ripon in Yorkshire and of Hexham in
Northumberland, were undoubtedly founded
by St. Wilfred, before the eighth century.
The conventual church at Ely is placed
in the reign of king Edgar (970), which
consisted of a parallelogram (107 f. by 24), a
nave or pace only, with the choir beyond it.
Such was generally the ground plan of all the
Saxon churches. Several learned antiquaries
have insisted upon the priority of the conventual church at Ely, as a decisive example of
the true Saxon. There were ten pillars on
each side of the nave, alternately cylindrical
and octagonal, the latter having a side and an
angle in front. The arches were enriched with
a variety of mouldings.

Prominent instances of enrichment peculiar
to this style, are those of door-cases and windows, as at Barfreston, near Canterbury ; Durham cathedral and palace ; Tutbury, in Staffordshire ; Romsey, Hants ; and Rochester ; not to
mention others. But the doorway of the east
end of the church of Kenilworth, in Warwickshire, exhibits the caput bovis, fret moulding
and pateræ in the spandrils, ornaments more
essentially peculiar to the Roman manner.*

* " The church of St. Martin, near Canterbury, is supposed
to be the oldest in England. Whenever the external coating

Indeed, there is scarcely a county in England in which there will not be found individual churches, still exhibiting Saxon, or at least Anglo-Norman, remains, many of which are engraven. Doorways of the early Norman are not unfrequently discoverable in monastic ruins. Those at Glastonbury, Malmsbury, and Castle Acre priory, Norfolk, Thorpe Salvine, and Fishlake in Yorkshire, are particularly fine. To enumerate more would exceed my limits, for by examining the different capitals of the most complex designs, the variety will be found to be almost infinite, as in St. Frideswide's, now the Cathedral, Oxford.

The rudely-carved scriptural figures, which often occur in bas-reliefs, placed under the arches of door-cases, where the head of the door itself is square, indicate a Roman original, and are mostly referable to an æra immediately preceding the Conquest; but the very curious representation of the deluge, over the great doorway of the cathedral at Lincoln, seems to have been subsequent to it. Similar sculptures appear likewise upon fonts. That at Winchester cathedral, which Dr. Milner discovered to mean the story of St. Nicholas, bishop of Myra, in Lycia, is cited among the most worthy of remark.

is broken away, the original walls of the chancel are seen to be composed entirely of Roman brick."—*Archæolog.* xvii. 27.

The most grotesque combinations of human and monstrous figures were frequently applied to the capitals of low pillars, which support the vaultings of crypts. Such are seen in those of St. Peter in the east at Oxford, and at Canterbury. They are common in the most ancient churches in Normandy. We can scarcely conceive a more rude style of design or execution, than that of some bas-reliefs which are introduced into the semicircular heads of the doorcases of Saxon churches. At Quennington, Gloucestershire, are two, with several figures, and singularly curious.* The general subject of those which are still extant in parochial churches, is Christ, either as sitting, and holding an open book of the New Testament; or standing, and piercing a dragon, intended to represent Satan, prostrate at his feet. The disproportion between the heads and bodies, in these carvings, is always very great.†

The Saxon large churches were divided into three tiers or stories, consisting of the lower arcade, triforia or galleries, and windows. Such was the solidity of the walls and bulkiness of the pillars, that buttresses were neither necessary nor in usage. This assertion may require a certain qualification; as in the nave of the abbey church of St. Alban's, a projecting rib is applied to the centre of the piers, both within-

* See *Archæolog.* vol. x. p. 128.   † See Note [F].

side and without. The prominent external buttress, afterward in use, was not common till the reign of Henry the Third, at its earliest æra.

After the Norman conquest, that style, called by the monks " Opus Romanum," because an imitation of the debased architecture of Italy, was still continued in England. The extent and dimensions of churches were greatly increased, the ornamental carvings on the circular arches and the capitals of pillars and pilasters became more frequent and elaborately finished. Of the more remarkable specimens of what is confounded under the general term of Saxon architecture, the true æra will be found to be immediately subsequent to the Saxons themselves, and to have extended not more than a century and a half below the Norman conquest.* The two churches at Caen in Normandy, built by William and his queen, are the archetypes of many now remaining in England ; but the most magnificent work of

* Ducarel's *Anglo-Norman Antiq.* A satisfactory account of Saxon churches is given in Bentham's *Ely*, sect. v. Another very ingenious investigation of the architecture of the Anglo-Saxons and Normans, by Mr. W. Wilkins, architect, of Cambridge, is seen in the twelfth volume of the *Archæologia*, p. 132. The valuable information it communicates is beautifully illustrated by many engravings, which present a clear view of the varieties adopted by the Normans in ornamenting their arcades.

this kind was the nave of old St. Paul's, London. The vaults were void of tracery, and the towers without pinnacles,* but ornamented with arcades, in tiers, of small intersected arches, on the outside walls.

The Anglo-Saxon æra may be comprised from the reign of Edgar to the Norman conquest, 980—1066. Immediately before that period, Edward the Confessor had, during his life-time, completed Westminster Abbey, in a style then prevalent in Normandy, and with a magnificence far exceeding any others then extant.† No less than eighteen of the larger monasteries, all of them Benedictine, had been founded by the Saxon kings, in their successive

* Of these towers, erected in the Norman æra, some remain as at first ; others have been heightened. They are St. James's Gate, Edmundsbury ; Exeter N. Transept ; Tewkesbury, Southwell, Norwich, Ely, and St. Alban's. Upon some of these were placed spires composed of timber-frame and covered with lead. These cumbrous pyramids were often blown on one side by tempests ; and after threatening a fall for centuries, have been removed. Those of Lincoln were the last which have been taken down, in 1808. St. Paul's was 270 feet high above the tower—burned down in 1561.

† The six principal of these were—St. Germains, Cornwall ; Colchester, Essex ; Tewkesbury, Gloucestershire ; St. Frideswide, Oxford ; St. Alban's, Herts ; Glastonbury, Somersetshire. King selects the western portico of Tewkesbury as the grandest in England, in point of extent and effect. The dimensions of all the English cathedrals and more remarkable churches will be given singly and comparatively, in another part of this work.

reigns; and it is evident, that the churches attached to each, were by far the most embellished part of them, with respect to architecture. There is yet reason to believe, that few of them were spacious. Bentham, in his essay, alleges that the chief and specific difference between the Saxon and first Norman consisted in enlarged dimensions, and a greater variety of ornamented carvings in the door-cases and arcades. If we look for specimens coeval with the Saxons themselves, and which may be attributed to them without controversy, we shall find them only in crypts and baptismal fonts, for many churches were taken down and rebuilt by the Normans, when these were preserved.

The Norman æra may be stated to be from 1066 to 1154, that is, from the Conquest to the death of Stephen. In a general comparison with the other nations of Europe, in that dark age, historians consent, that the Normans were eminent, if not superior, with respect to civilization and the arts. In architectural science, as promoted by their religious zeal, they had made a great proficiency, and many grand structures had been raised to embellish their own province, before they had gained an absolute establishment in England.*

---

* Stowe says (p. 132) that " Hugh Lupus, earle of Chester, sent into Normandie for Anselme, by his counsaile to build an abbey of St. Werburgh in Chester."

Triforia,* or galleries, consisting of an open arcade, which at a subsequent period were placed immediately above the principal arches of the nave, were, in the more ancient examples, introduced in front of the upper windows only, having an arch on either side, and forming a gallery. Two instances occur, where the pillars are brought from the floor to the springing of the roof, at St. Frideswide's, Oxford, and Rumsey Abbey, Hants.

The Norman triforia were, in fact, a repetition of the ground arches, of equal span, circular form, and open; and had, in some instances only, small round pillars attached to each side of the piers. Examples occur in Norwich Cathedral and Waltham Abbey. They are seen in the abbey churches at Caen, built by William the Conqueror and his queen.*

THE ANGLO-NORMAN AND NORMAN.
1050–1150.

Many discordant opinions have been advanced, concerning what really constitutes Norman architecture; and it has been confounded with the Saxon by several able antiquaries, not having sufficiently considered the specific differences. But a still greater confusion occurs when the Pointed Style, first practised in this kingdom in the reign of Henry II. is called Norman. The principal discrimi-

* See Note [G].

nation between the Saxon and the Norman, appears to be that of much larger dimensions in every part ; plain, but more lofty vaulting ; circular pillars of greater diameter ; round arches and capitals, having ornamental carvings much more elaborate and various, adapted to them ; but a total absence of pediments or pinnacles, which are decidedly peculiar to the Pointed or Gothick style. Among the prelates in the early Norman reigns, were found men of consummate skill in architecture ; which, aided by their munificence, was applied to the rebuilding of their cathedral churches, and those of the greater abbeys.

It has been observed, that the Norman architecture had three distinct kinds, in its progress through the first century, after the Conquest :—

1st. Waltham Abbey, Durham. 2nd. Peterborough, Malmsbury. 3rd. Lincoln Western façade ; Choir of Canterbury.

In the largest and earliest specimens, in Normandy, the round pillars are disproportionately high, and the arches narrow, which style may be seen in Tewkesbury Abbey.

The first operative architect upon record,* of our country, is styled William *Anglus*, by Gervase, the historic monk of Canterbury. He was a scholar of William of *Sens (Soissons)*,

---

* In 1175. Styled by *Gervasius de reparatione Dorubern. Eccles. Magister* Gulielmus Senonensis -- *Magister* Gulielmus Anglus, (*Magistri Operum.*)

who had nearly completed the choir of that church, where his talents in invention and practice are conspicuous and admirable. The English William added to the choir the transept and the Trinity chapel. In the churches of Peterborough and Ely, the roofs of the nave are composed of timber frame. William of Sens was the first architect who boldly attempted, with success, to work ribbed and vaulted ceilings, in stone and toph.

A Norman peculiarity is the covering the surface of walls with a projecting ornament, hatched lozengewise; generally in the circular heads of arches, in triforia, as at Rochester and Chichester. This is called by Chaucer* "*hacking in masonrics.*"

No less than fifteen of the twenty-two English cathedrals still retain considerable parts which are undoubtedly of Norman erection, the several dates of which are ascertained. We have the following enumeration of Norman bishops, who were either architects themselves, or under whose auspices architecture flourished: Aldred bishop of Worcester, (1059 —1089,) St. Peter's, Gloucester. Gundulf of Rochester, (1077—1107,) whose works are seen at Rochester, Canterbury, and Peterborough. Mauritius of London, (1086—1108,) built old St. Paul's cathedral. William de Carilelpho, Abbot of St. Vincent's, in Normandy, cathedral

* " House of Fame."

D

of Durham from 1093, completed by Ranulf
Flambard, in 1133. Lanfranc of Canterbury,
(1080—1100.) Roger of Salisbury, (1107—
1140,) the cathedral at Old Sarum. Ernulf of
Rochester, (1115 — 1125,) completed Bishop
Gundulf's work there : they were both monks
of Bec in Normandy. Alexander of Lincoln,
(1123—1147,) rebuilt his cathedral. Henry of
Blois, Bishop of Winchester, (1129—1169,) a
most celebrated architect, built the conventual
churches of St. Cross and Rumsey in Hampshire ; and lastly, Roger archbishop of York,
(1154—1181,) where none of his work remains.
By these architects the Norman manner was
progressively brought to perfection in England ; and it will be easily supposed, that the
improvements made by any of them were
adopted in succession :* and this may be a
satisfactory series.

With equal extent and magnificence many
of the churches belonging to the greater abbeys
were constructed in this æra. Few indeed
have escaped their general demolition at the
reformation.

* It is a circumstance worthy of remark, that so many of
the great Saxon churches should have been consumed by fire.
The monkish writers repeat " igne consumpta"—" totaliter
combusta," and similar phrases. This was the usual pretext
for rebuilding them, in the first Norman reigns. The church
of Canterbury was three times burned before the most ancient part of the present structure. *Gervasii.*

NORMAN. 1100–1150.

The Conqueror's Abbey at Battle, in Sussex, and those founded by Henry I. at Reading and Cirencester, doubtless very sumptuous edifices, have yielded to nearly complete dilapidation. Others exhibit a ruined front, which still excites our admiration. Malmsbury, Wilts; Dunstable, Bedfordshire ; Wenlock, Salop ; St. Botolph's, Colchester ; Waltham, Essex ; are majestic in decay. St. Alban's, Herts ; St. Peter's, Gloucester ; Peterborough and Tewkesbury, preserved as churches, are nearly in a perfect state. Each of these will be visited with veneration, as conspicuous examples.

After this enumeration of the larger cathedrals, of which we have a certain testimony, it is necessary to give a distinguishing idea of what constitutes the peculiarities of the first Norman manner of building. In the façades, or western fronts, are placed a series of arches, of which a few are pierced as windows, and the others are left blank ; a tablet-cornice of the same description was likewise affixed to towers. Of similar instances of these, partly opened, the best example occurs in the cathedral of Norwich ; and withoutside, both there and at Ely, circular mouldings of large diameter are introduced. From the latter part of the eleventh to the middle of the twelfth century, door-ways exhibited all the elaborate ornamental workmanship practised by the Normans. The great thickness of the walls required the door-cases to be very deeply moulded, and invariably surmounted by semicircular arches, of which there were several rows supported by a corresponding succession of columns along the whole depth of the wall. New ornaments were introduced, such as triple and quadruple cheveron work, billet, crenellated and festoon mouldings, round the archivolt, and down the piers. The windows were long and narrow, having cheveron work on the jambs, withinside. Double windows, and then triple, succeeded, the centre one the highest. Those subsequently called "lancet" were increased as far as five or seven.

The principal arcades by which the nave is divided from the aisles, are much varied; they are circular at Gloucester and Tewkesbury; piers composed of different shafts at Durham, and those of a uniform shape, as at Peterborough and Norwich.

The Norman wooden roof was open to the timbers. It has been generally remarked, that there is no building of Norman architecture with the centre aisle covered by the original vaulting; but the chapel in the "White Tower" of London affords, perhaps, a solitary exception. At Peterborough is a flat boarded ceiling, painted in a rude mosaic pattern of stiff leaves divided into lozenges and flowers of the same description. When the groined roofs had obtained more generally, the cross-springers-ribs were entirely composed of the tooth or indented moulding, which had a prevalence in small, no less than in the larger churches. The groined arches of stone were at first used only in undercrofts or crypts, but were applied to the roofs of the nave and transept in cathedrals, particularly in the twelfth and thirteenth centuries, as at Salisbury, with singular effect. " Pointed arches certainly originated in vaultings, and the necessity of having arches of equal heights and different widths; and thus, from its first introduction into roofs, it was gradually diffused over other parts of the same building."

The centre or nave was highest in most of the great churches, and had breadth scarcely less than the span of the pier arches. No instance of a genuine Anglo-Norman building possesses, or was intended to possess, a stone roof; which is indicated by the position of the capitals. Peterborough, Ely, St. Peter's Northampton, Steyning, Romsey, &c. are calculated and constructed for a flat wooden roof only.

The Saxon abbots were always succeeded by Normans. Their chief ambition seems to have been that of entirely superseding the former architecture. As an instance of the degree to which these innovations were extended, Turstin, a monk of Caen, in 1077, became Abbot of Glastonbury, and had begun a church, which his successor, Herlowin, likewise a Norman monk, completely took down in 1097; as not considering it to be sufficiently magnificent :* so general was the prevalence of this " *novum ædificandi genus.*" The cable moulding twisted round pillars, and the zigzag covering them, as at Durham, were characteristic.

The western front of Castle Rising Abbey, in Norfolk, has been cited as the most perfect Norman architecture now extant. Other western fronts have been gothicized, entirely, or in part.†

The first transition from this Anglo-Norman style appears to have taken place towards the close of the reign of Stephen (1135). It discovers itself in the arch, which had hitherto been round, becoming slightly pointed, and the heavy single pillar being formed into a cluster. This decoration had not long been adopted before instances occur, in which we may trace the arch as growing more and more pointed; and the clusters which were at first clumsy and ill-formed, acquiring a greater lightness and justness of proportion. Yet, the facings

---

* *Antiq. Glaston. Gale*, p. 333.

† Of Norman mouldings and their varieties, see an account in the 12th volume of the *Archæologia*, pp. 160–171.

of the arches still retain many of the ornaments peculiar to the earlier æra. This taste
gradually prevailing, led, towards the close of
the twelfth century, to the formation of the
slender pillar supporting the sharply pointed
arch, which, from a certain resemblance, has
been called " the lancet."

In the nave of Llantony Priory, Monmouthshire (1150), the columns have no capitals, and
the arches are extremely acute, which evinces
the imperfect state in which this innovation
was originally adopted. But it soon became
the purest style of simple ornament, applied
exclusively to windows and galleries. The
windows of that age were long, narrow, sharply
pointed, and usually decorated both withinside and without, with small marble shafts,
filleted or banded, conjointly. Where two
only were pierced through the walls, a trefoil
or quatrefoil became the first variation. Five
is the usual number, having the central one
enhanced above the others, and with the interior arcade, as many insulated shafts ; at Salisbury there are seven. Specimens not rarely
occur in their perfect original state. In York
great transept, there is one which is fifty feet
in height, and eight feet wide, the largest in
England ; and a more beautiful and correct
example of the true lancet style graduated,
with the highest in the centre, will nowhere

be seen than in the south transept of Beverley,
or the Chapter-house at Oxford. Of the original simplicity of this manner, the triforium
of St. John's, Chester, is an early proof. This
change to the pointed style pervaded the whole
structure.

As to the first deviation, which followed so
closely upon the lancet as to be nearly contemporary, it is necessary to speak. It is denominated the " trefoil," formed in the heads
of arches by a circle and two half circles. I
have observed no instance more perfect than
in the gallery of Ely, and that of the elder
Lady Chapel in Bristol Cathedral, erected not
later than 1170. The trefoil soon became
much expanded, and the open quatrefoils,
spreading into many halves or lesser portions
of circles, were introduced, which terminated
in bosses or flowers. These were either applied to the walls, more frequently in chapter-
houses, or to door-cases deeply recessed; and
each may be seen to great advantage in Litchfield Cathedral.

When churches were first rebuilt with lancet
arches, the ornamental materials of the former
round-headed, were used in the new modification of form, apparent from the courses of
stonework above them. Almost all the cathedrals of that æra present, at least, one
striking example. But it is not an unsup-

ported conjecture, that the pointed arch appeared, among its earliest instances, in the four well known Round Churches built in imitation of the vestibule of the church of the Holy Sepulchre, at Jerusalem. At Cambridge, 1120; Northampton, 1180; the Temple, 1185; and Maplestead, Essex, of which the true date is not, I believe, ascertained.

When the trefoil arcades and door-cases had superseded the chaste architecture of the twelfth century in its first and plainer form, either circular or lancet, a field for a new and distinct species of ornament expanded itself. The architect and master mason exhibited no inferior skill in carving, or on sculptured heads and bas reliefs, than in the design and execution of the principal edifice.

This assertion may seem to require explanation, as we bear in mind the extreme simplicity of the lancet; but in the same building these specimens were concomitant. At the ends of the transept, and in the presbytery and chapter-house, were series of trefoil arches, with the spandrils carved with leaves and flowers, and sometimes with bas-reliefs. The capitals of the smaller columns were most richly ornamented. Bas-reliefs were even introduced upon the spandrils; and at Ely, in a complete series of the history of a saint, as before observed.

Plain mural surfaces were incrusted over with ornaments very minute and lavishly applied, yet producing an effect of richness, from mere exuberance, chiefly of fruits and flowers. It is not however to be inferred, that such caprices of Gothick invention are often copied exactly from each other, or that they occur frequently. The individual monk or artist indulged his fancy only where he had an opportunity. The sculptured frieze in Edward the Confessor's chapel, in Westminster Abbey, exhibiting the transactions of his life, is of a regular and fixed design; as likewise the capitals of columns at Ely.

Among the *Cotton MSS.* in the British Museum,* is one by Gervasius, a Benedictine monk of Canterbury, relative to the rebuilding of that magnificent cathedral after the fire in 1174. It is of greater curiosity from the extreme rarity of any MS. on architectural science of so early a date as the reign of King John. It includes a very minute account of Lanfranc's original structure, as well as of the restoration made by Gulielmus Sennensis (of Sens in France), or of Gulielmus Anglus, who completed the work, and who is the first architect or master-mason, a native of this country, concerning whom anything satisfactory is

* *MSS. Cotton. Vespas.* B. 2, 191, printed in the *Decem Scriptores*, coll. 1290, folio, 1652.

known. Lanfranc was a Lombard; and as I conjecture, the first mentioned William had learned his art in Italy. The columns and bases at Canterbury have a singular accordance with the contemporary church architecture in that country, particularly with those of Orvietto.

Matthew Paris speaks of William of Coventry* as a very eminent architect in the reigns of Henry the Second, Richard, and John. Of the style prevalent in the reign of Henry the Second, and immediately preceding it, the remains of the chapel of St. Joseph, at Glastonbury, still exhibit a very genuine specimen. The western end of the Priory of Lanercost, in Cumberland, affords a good example of the simple style, in usage towards the close of the twelfth century, which is the undoubted æra of the introduction of the pointed arch into France, to the exclusion of the first circular form of the Normans and Lombards. We were among their earliest imitators. It has been stated, that the first appearance of the pointed arch may be seen in the church of Frindsbury, in Kent, built by Paulinus, the Sacrist, between the years 1125 and 1157.†

---

* Might not this William Anglus be, in fact, William of Coventry, so denominated from the place of his birth?

† Bibl. Topograph. Britann. No. vi.

In the reign of Henry the Third, this beautiful architecture (which may be accurately classed as the TRANSITION style) had gained its perfect completion. Salisbury and Ely cathedrals, and Westminster abbey,* have been generally adduced as the most perfect examples. It may be supposed, that the two last mentioned were constructed upon the same plan, as there is a singular accordance in their chief proportions. Whether this early Gothick originated in Palestine, or was in part previously borrowed from the Moors in Spain, has given rise to conjecture, which is not strongly supported by any evidence; but a more bold deviation from the established style could have been scarcely made. The Gothick or pointed arch (as it has been well observed) took its rise from the variations attendant upon all scientific pursuits. The principal feature of the first style was a combination of the circular with the pointed, an intermixture of ornaments, and a kind of contention between the two styles, which should prevail.† To the

---

* At Westminster there is a series of windows above those of the aisles which are formed of spherical equilateral triangles, and likewise at Litchfield. They were adopted from French examples, but are by no means frequent with us.

† These ornaments were transferred from the Norman round to pointed arches, as seen at Chichester and Peterborough cathedrals in several curious specimens. There is a pointed arch in the tower at Ely, as early as 1180.

enormous round pillar succeeded the slender shaft, insulated, or clustered into a single column, with narrow lancet windows, the highest in the centre, and roofs upon simple cross-springers. The arches were now sharply pointed, the window increased to seven lights instead of one, and with small columns as mullions; and all the pillars, when of disproportionate length, broken into parts by jointed bands or fillets placed at certain distances, as observable in Worcester cathedral, the nave of which is very fine. The " *Gothick or Transition*" style was completely established in England after the commencement of the thirteenth century.

THE LANCET, OR EARLY ENGLISH.
1150–1250.

It will be conceded to the French antiquaries, that this new mode was not exclusively our own, but that it appeared earlier, at least by a century, in the magnificent cathedrals I shall notice as then recently erected in France. If the buildings in the Holy Land suggested ideas of this novel architecture, the French croisaders had the same opportunities of introducing it into France as ours into England, for they were associated in the same expedition.

It has been said, that in the second church of the Holy Sepulchre at Jerusalem, erected by Baldwin the Second, 1118—1131, no pointed arch was seen; but that in the Moorish structures, equally obvious to the Norman conquerors, it is frequent: an evident proof that wherever the Normans obtained a dominion by conquest, they introduced their own national manner in the churches which were entirely constructed by them. Additions to the Empress Helena's original church had been made by Charlemagne in 813, in the style of the Roman basilicæ.

But a manner of constructing churches, or at least parts of them, appears to have more immediately belonged to the æra of the first Crusades, if, as will be allowed, it took its prototype from the circular part including the "Holy Sepulchre." Four perfect examples are still to be seen in England. 1st, The most ancient, that of St. Sepulchre at Cambridge, is attributed to the reign of Henry the First, between the first and second crusades. It has an inner circle of low and large pillars and arches. 2nd, That at Northampton has both its diameters of the same extent, but the arcade has sharply headed arches, and the pillars are less massive. 3rd. The Temple, London, the date of which is 1180, has clustered pillars with capitals, and a mural arcade above them, both pointed, but the heads of the windows are rounded. 4th. At Little Maplestead, in Essex, which has the clustered pillar, and is of the latter part of the thirteenth century. All these churches, though their original design was merely circular, have received subsequent additions of oblong naves, to which they are now vestibules.

The dimensions* of each bear the same proportion between the interior wall, and the circular arcades, and were built by the Knights Templars upon their return from the first and second crusades.

And to this æra we may attribute the prevalence of an improved and reformed manner of building, which was uniformly and consistently executed. Then appeared longitudinal and transverse vaults with diagonal ribs.†

In distinguishing the pure " Lancet style " from any other, it will be evident to the critical observer, that the decorative particles were sparingly introduced, and that regularity of design and a simple uniformity are strictly

---

* Dimensions, Cambridge, 41, 19 f. Northampton, nearly the same. Temple, London, 60, 30 f. Maplestead, 26, 12 f. See plans, views, and descriptions, *Britton's Archit. Antiq.* vol. i. p. 17. It is evident that these corresponded with the church architecture of the time, with respect to their pillars, arches, and ornaments.

† See Note [H].

maintained. A late and most beautiful instance is the nave of St. Mary's Abbey, in York, now dilapidated, 1270—1292.*

T. Warton† has denominated the "absolute Gothic," as being entirely free from any mixture of the Saxon or first Norman style. Westminster, Tintern, Monmouthshire, and Netley Abbey, Hants, are superior examples, which resemble each other so nearly, that it is a fair conjecture that they were all three the work of the same architect. After the total dereliction of what has been aptly termed the Romanesque distinction, as having grown out of an imperfect imitation of Roman models, in the architecture practised by the Normans, arose the " Early English style," which, from credible evidence, made its first appearance in England after the middle of the twelfth century. But the English did not adopt much decoration so early as the Germans and French. " We can imagine that they would abandon with regret, the beautiful simplicity and sobriety of their former style, in which they had so eminently excelled."

Now was first seen geometrical tracery in windows, with mullions of the nail-head and toothed mouldings. Of the same date and description are likewise the elaborate compartments and ribs, which are wrought upon the

---

* *Vetusta Mon. Plates.*   † *Essay on Spenser.*

surface of the vaults, after that the simpler forms were relinquished. The cathedrals of York, Lincoln, and Ely, contain at this time not only the most exquisitely wrought and variously designed specimens of Gothick sculpture, and minuter carving ; but those which remain to us in the greatest perfection. The patterns were composed of geometrical figures, with forms of foliage, all very delicately finished.

But it is beyond controversy, that the first Norman architects, in the lengthened vista of their nave, which was not interrupted by the choir-screen, produced a sublime or imposing effect by their simple grandeur, and amplitude of dimensions. The transition from this noble simplicity to rich embellishment, was in certain instances, from the different æras of the building, sudden and abrupt. In the galilee, or great porch, and the inside of the tower of Ely cathedral, we have perhaps the first instance of a mural arcade, or one placed merely for ornament against a wall, composed of tiers of subordinate arches, which are not interlaced. Of the last description, are many in the earlier Norman churches. They were double cylindrical columns, with bases seated upon a single plinth, wherever they were applied.

A very memorable period in the progressive history of church architecture in England,

were the reigns of Edward the Third and that
of his immediate successor.

In the middle of the fourteenth century, the
first-mentioned monarch had designed, begun,
and completed his collegiate chapel, dedicated
to St. Stephen, within his palace, at Westminster. In skilful construction and excessive richness of internal decoration, it had no
equal in England ; and was the rival of the
Sainte Chapelle at Paris.* As the most gorgeous
specimen of internal decoration, by the application of sculpture, painting, and gilding, this
chapel, when in its perfect state, excited admiration, as an example well worthy of the
best period of curious art.

Paintings upon the walls, which were developed a few years since, at the eastern end,
were the histories of Job and Tobit. There
were then seen portraits, most richly illuminated, of St. George, King Edward the Third,
his Queen, and each of their children. These
have been separately and scientifically described.

Under the auspices of Wykeham, himself
eminently versed in the science, we have the
boldest instance of the second manner or pure
Gothick. Very few Greek or Roman architects
have carried technical ability and a strictly

* See Note [I].

correct calculation of the proportions between strength and burthen, beyond the master masons by whom churches in the fourteenth century were built. The vaults of several of the larger dimensions, are only from nine to ten inches thick ; and the outer walls, though more than fifty feet high, do not exceed two feet in thickness, at their summit. The equally clustered pillar, with a comparatively low and sharp arch, prevailed in the first part of the reign of Edward the Third, over which was placed an open arcade, as originally introduced into the Norman churches, and was adopted, as far as the idea only, from them. Of the beauties which characterise the style of this æra in particular, a complete specimen offers itself in the octangular louvre at Ely, which, and the chapel of our Lady attached to the cathedral, were the sole design of Alan de Walsingham,* and executed by himself between the years 1322 and 1349. It is certain that architecture was understood and encouraged by ecclesiastics in that age, and it is pleasing to rescue the name of a single practical architect, so eminently superior to others of his own time. Whilst those who designed and completed the

* He is styled in an old chronicle of Ely, " vir venerabilis et artificiosus frater."—*Leland's Collectanea.* The mastermason had no higher title than *Latomus* (literally stone-cutter), as it occurs in the same MS. " Hoc anno 1319, obiit H.

great churches on the Continent are recorded scrupulously, respecting their talents and works, our own, not greatly inferior to them, are rarely to be ascertained.

Contemporary with Wykeham, lived Rede, Bishop of Chichester, an adept in the science and practice of architecture; and many others of the prelates and abbots of that day prided themselves in giving certain proof of their architectural skill in rebuilding their churches, or very frequently adding to them and giving to them a pervading symmetry of style.

Much of the fame of the illustrious W. Wykeham, whose establishments have insured the gratitude of posterity, and which is renewed daily in the minds of individuals, was his skill in architecture. The two St. Mary Winton Colleges, and the grand nave of his cathedral, afford a perfect proof.*

Bishop Wayneflete acquired from him, his science and taste, whose great works he imitated in Magdalene College, Oxford, which he

---

Latomus, qui sub Johanne Abbate de Evesham aulam abbathiæ artificiosè composuit."

What is said of Buschetto, the architect of Pisa, is equally true of many a Gothic master-mason.

" ———- prudens Operator, et ipse Magister,
Constituit more soleriter et ingeniose."—*Epitaph.*

* See Note [K].

built, and the plan of Henry the Sixth's College, Cambridge, for which he gave the design.
Beckington, after he became Bishop of Wells,
derived his knowledge from the same source,
and added much to the splendour and convenience of his cathedral.

That we have still the power of viewing so
many ecclesiastical structures in their pristine
state, is an obligation due to the prelates of
the middle centuries, since the conquest,
among whom this triumvirate were eminently
conspicuous.

In a preceding age, Bishop Quivil had given
a complete design for the rebuilding his cathedral at Exeter, which, singularly pure and
beautiful in itself, is more remarkable for the
pursuance of the same plan for fifty years in
succession. So scrupulous was this adherence,
that although many innovations in architecture had taken place during the interval, the
church appears to have arisen perfect at once,
rather than to have slowly grown to its consummate beauty. The stupendous fabric of
York Cathedral has a nave which was erected
in the earlier part of this century. Such a
sameness of manner was effected in known
instances by a total alteration of constituent
parts, in so decided a degree as to produce an
apparently contemporaneous character.

It is a well supported opinion, that in the
second æra of decorated Gothick, the ornaments
of the roof gave a tone and character to the
whole edifice, and, in fact, pervaded the internal plan. About the year 1315, an ornament
was invented, as applied to the mouldings of
windows. It was the placing of small bosses
thickly in the grooves of the mullions, resembling nail-heads. An early and good specimen
is seen in the south aisle of Gloucester Cathedral. The surface of the tower of Hereford
is so covered. Later, in the fourteenth century, was introduced an arch singularly formed
of four segments of circles contrasted, like an
ogee, as commonly called. The cathedrals of
Lincoln, York, and Ely, contain, at this time,
not only the most exquisitely finished and
variously conceived specimens of Gothick sculpture and minuter carving, but those also which
remain to us, most entire. These ornaments
were composed of foliage, flowers, or geometrical forms, very delicately finished: on the
columns and mouldings are embossed ornaments disposed with taste; and upon the
grounds of the various compartments were
paintings of religious or historical subjects,
large and small portraits of eminent person-
ages, with numerous arms, devices, and ornamental scrolls, gilded and coloured with a
splendour which imagination suggested, and

ingenuity brought to perfection.* Externally, the parapets were perforated in triangles inclosing open trefoils, or the round was exchanged for the square quatrefoil. In the groining of the roof, the interlacing was not greatly inferior to the tracery in the heads of windows, with horizontal lines and circular bands on the surface, and richly carved bosses at each juncture. A very common feature of this style is, a small round bud, consisting of three or four leaves which open just sufficiently to show the bud in the centre, placed in a hollow moulding, instead of the toothed ornament, before so common. In such, are likewise placed flowers of four leaves, as well as grotesque heads; the capitals are various, and the crockets are carved with great boldness and beauty, more resembling the natural form than previously. This was the age of most richly ornamented buttresses. The west front of York, and the east of Howland, with the ruined east end of Walsingham, Norfolk, are among the most worthy of selection. Exeter Cathedral and York Minster exhibit a plain

* See the *Account of St. Stephen's Chapel, Westminster, by the Society of Antiquaries.* Founded by Edward the Third, and finished in 1348. Length ninety feet, breadth thirty feet, height fifty feet. The whole of the interior was most richly painted and gilt. Walter Weston was the master-mason.

and decorated roof, both of them of a correct style.

The western doors of York are of the richest execution and deeply splayed, having the flowered moulding with leaves, in the grooves. Other porches are finished by battlements or bands of high open work. In door-cases, we may observe a series of small niches with statues, carried up like a hollow moulding, as in the south entrance into the choir of Lincoln, and another in the cloisters at Norwich.

The windows of this florid style contained as many as nine lights, made by slender mullions having heads, wrought into circles, trefoils, or quatrefoils, feathered or crocketed.

But the Anglo-Norman, having been once relinquished, was never again adopted, either simply or with analogy. Until the close of the reign of the first Edward, the prevalence was decided, and all the previous confusion between the Anglo-Norman and the Pointed styles had ceased, and was universally abandoned about that period. With incredible lightness, the " Early English," or " Lancet" style, exhibited elegance of decoration and beauty of proportions in the reduplication of their arcades and pillars. The art of quarrying large masses of stone was not introduced very early into England ; * and shafts of a single piece, before the

* Cresy's *Arch. of the Middle Ages.*

close of the twelfth century, when they were applied in slender columns, were generally of Purbeck or Petworth black or grey marble, used solely for the purposes of decoration. Of these, were several distinct and insulated shafts, but the whole collected under one capital, at first of the roll moulding only, but afterwards carved, to represent the leaves of the palm-tree, indigenous in Palestine and Arabia. The large middle shaft was surrounded by four or six smaller ones. When applied to the mullions and jambs of windows, they are in two pieces, banded in the middle by a fillet or ring of copper, the hinder part of which is inserted into the stone-work by a staple. From the windows in the transept of York cathedral, known as the five sisters, with those likewise at Worcester, and a single one in Our Lady's chapel at Hereford, we may be inclined to think that the " Lancet style," soon after its introduction, was not surpassed by those in subsequent usage.*

A very favourable view of the manner which distinguishes the first part of this æra (1320), as applied both to roofs and arcades, is seen in the cathedral of Bristol.†   Both the aisles are

* The whole height is thirteen feet seven inches ; the bases nine inches ; and the capitals one foot and three inches in diameter.— *Wild's Worcester Cathedral.*

† " From small pillars in the side walls, corresponding

equal to the nave in height, and have internally roofs of a complex construction, of which none, exactly resemblant, were ever after adopted in England.

But previously to another style of known peculiarities, the longitudinal and transverse roofs were combined and complicated; and the conoid vaultings were studded with knobs of foliage at the interlacing of the ribs; the western front was fringed with pinnacles; and those were again enriched with numerous statues; and the flying buttresses (arcs-boutants), formed of diagonal ribs, inclosing segments of circles, in order to give them lightness, and were rendered ornamental by boldly

with others in the insulated piers, spring arches about half the elevation of those which divide the aisles, having over them a cornice with ornaments of various devices and spandrils perforated in trefoils. Above these is the roof of the aisle, which, rising from each side, is united to ribs springing over points of the insular arches, thus forming two smaller open arches, and thereby increasing the lightness, novelty, and elegance of the design. The groins are extremely slender, and in the centres and angles rest on brackets of human heads."

" Inserted in the lateral walls on the north and south are richly-ornamented recesses, the canopies of which are of so singular a nature, that any exactly similar will not probably be seen in any other cathedral. They have a very remarkable character, each being formed of four segments of circles, having deep crockets and a large finial at every point." — *Buckler's Cathedrals, Bristol.*

crocketed finials.　Of this description are many attached to the French cathedrals, at an earlier period ; but they are among the latest instances, with us, of the " *Decorated* style."

The first professors of the *Decorated*, pointed style, were ambitious not only of excelling each other in point of geometrical skill, but by the invention of an endless variety in designing ornaments which should be applied, more particularly to their arcades and columns, in the spandrils, capitals, and friezes.

This exuberance tended to the complete abolition of the " Lancet," or previous manner, after it had lost its characteristic simplicity ; and in the commencement of the reign of Richard the Second, it appears to have been no longer in usage.

In order to form a criterion of this pure Gothick, let me observe, that the pillars became smaller and more numerous ; that both those and the arches were filled with mouldings peculiarly beautiful in their forms and effect, which were frequently enriched with foliage or other embellishment.　A more complete specimen than the nave of Winchester or Canterbury, cannot be adduced.　The general form of the arches became more open, and those attached to windows and niches were universally adorned with crockets tied at the top in a rich knot of flowers, resembling the blossoms of the

euphorbium.* The windows, especially those
at the east and west, were widely expanded,
and their heads ramified into infinite intersections with quatrefoils or rosettes, which bear
on the points of the arching mullions. The
roof hitherto had not exceeded a certain simplicity of ornament, yet tracery was spread over
the groins of the vault, which rested on brackets or corbels, carved into grotesque heads of
kings and bishops.

The large and lofty central tower (for the
more ancient belfries were usually detached),
and the cloisters richly pannelled, having a
most delicately fretted roof, were added to
many of the cathedrals and conventual churches then existing. Withinside, the canopies of
tabernacle work over saints or sepulchral effigies, the shrines of exquisite finishing, repeat-
ing in miniature the bolder ornaments by which
the building was decorated on a large scale, in
the high altars and skreens of indescribable
richness, continue to fascinate every eye by
their beauty and sublimity. Even on the outside of these magnificent works, as the western
fronts of Wells and Litchfield, and on Bishop
Grandison's skreen so placed at Exeter, there
are embellishments of equal merit. The façade

* The foliage imitated on the finials and capitals is that of
plants which are indigenous in Palestine. When compared
with the euphorbium, the resemblance will be found exact.

of the cathedral of Salisbury, although of the
preceding age, in which the pointed style was
frequently mixed with the round, and the ornaments of either indiscriminately used, is one of
the most ancient, simple, and regular now remaining. The eye dwells with more satisfaction on a broad surface, relieved only, and not
distracted, by ornament. Abbot Whetheham-
stede's skreen at St. Alban's, Prior Goldstone's
skreen at Canterbury, Ralph Lord Neville's
skreen at Durham, and that by Bishop Fox in
Winchester Cathedral, exceed in richness or
correct proportions any specimen I could adduce of the first description, but they are of a
later age.

The shrines and tabernacles applied to burial
chapels or sacella, or to the canopies placed
over altar tombs, were subjects upon which the
most ingenious architects displayed all their
talents—for the sculptors worked only in subordination to their plans. The chapels and
tombs were erected entirely upon architectural
principles, and they afforded a very wide scope
for variety and minuteness of ornament. It
may be remarked, that while the great structures of any century in particular bore a general, and sometimes a near analogy, to their contemporary style of building, scarcely any two of
these sepulchral monuments, although of the
same æra, are exactly similar. Fancy was

indulged to produce the richest effect, uncontrolled by rules, which are indispensably necessary to architecture upon a large scale.

The fashion of canopied tombs prevailed (as in Westminster Abbey) much earlier than the reign of Edward the Third, who erected one at Gloucester for his unfortunate father. It has several tiers of open arcades, piled one on another pyramidally. Our cathedral and conventual churches still retain many very interesting specimens, and many were destroyed at the Reformation, when the edifices which enclosed them, were utterly demolished. For exquisite finishing and various workmanship, those of Bishop Gower and of Archbishop Bowet in St. David's and York Cathedrals are most remarkable for spiral Gothick. For size and massiveness, the series of prelates' tombs at Winchester and Canterbury, are noble examples. A very able and satisfactory investigation of the subject is given in Gough's " *Sepulchral Monuments*," a work that reflects honour on the study of English antiquities.

In this style successful efforts both of sculpture and painting were superadded to those of architecture, by the introduction of carved effigies, in niches or on sepulchral monuments, and of portraits or scriptural subjects, stained upon glass with radiant colours, with which windows of great expanse were most richly embellished. The history of these arts could not be given, in this part of my work, in a satisfactory abridgment. Volumes on these subjects are already before the publick, to which my readers are referred. The industrious Carter has left two volumes of illustrations of "*Ancient Sculpture and Painting in England;*" and sepulchral sculpture has been amply investigated and copied in the works of Gough and Stothard. Of paintings in oil or resinous gums, as a vehicle, upon the surface of walls, the most remarkable are in Westminster Abbey and Exeter Cathedral, as still extant; but a series, more splendid from a profuse application of gold, was that discovered some few years since in St. Stephen's Chapel, then the House of Commons, as I have already remarked.

The history of stained glass in England, would require a distinct work to offer all the information concerning it, which has been collected by myself and others. It may be merely necessary to observe, that it was first connected with architecture in the reign of Henry the Third, and reached its zenith in the fifteenth century; and that we had eminent professors in the reign of Charles the First. That the art was ever lost is a vulgar error; and it has been exquisitely practised, but on a new principle, in the present day.

Philip the Third, in 1285, erected three

crosses on the road between Paris and St.
Denis, the height of each of which was forty
French feet (43.4), with niches containing
statues as large as life, after the funeral of his
father Louis, the canonised King of France.
The crosses in England were imitated from
them in 1296. Those above noticed were
destroyed in the revolution 1790. The Fountain and Stone Cross at Rouen, although built
so lately as 1500, nearly resemble those which
were erected to commemorate Queen Eleanor.*

Of the Abbey Gates, which still remain to
attract the attention of the architectural antiquary, as they are not numerous, a list is sub-

* In the third volume of the *Monumenta Vetusta,* the
crosses at Geddington, Waltham, and near Northampton, are
beautifully engraved in Imperial folio; and more picturesquely in quarto, in *Britton's Arch. Antiq.*

The most elaborately wrought market-cross on the Continent is that at Nurembourg. It is of the same age as that
at Coventry, (so well described by Hollar's etching,) and was
probably its prototype. The destroyed cross at Abington, is
said by Aubrey to have nearly resembled that at Bristol, in
its plan and ornaments. In those later ones the statues were
usually covered with gilding and colours. "For ingenious
invention, elegance of general form and proportion, and
beauty of parts, no exterior of the ornamental kind of the
architecture called Gothick can compete with Queen Eleanor's
crosses. The aspiring shape of the cross, between a pyramid
and obelisk, assists the light elegance of its parts, and gives it
a character of gracefulness. Geddington is now the most
perfect in its remains, and Waltham the most curious in its
details."

joined.* There are several grand specimens peculiar to their several æras, which are admirable, and doubtless many of the dilapidated monasteries could once boast similar appendages. The escocheon of the founder always held a conspicuous place among other architectural embellishments.

* St. Augustine's at Canterbury; St. Augustine's at Bristol; St. Ethelbert's, Norwich; Peterborough; the two at St. Edmundsbury, Suffolk; Battle Abbey, Sussex. More particularly, these later instances in the fifteenth century, as at Malvern, Worcestershire, being nearly entire. But one of larger dimensions and greater beauty remains at Thornham Abbey, Lincolnshire. It is rivalled by another at Kirkham, in Yorkshire, which, previously to its partial dilapidation, was of a still more elaborate and elegant design. The entrance gateway formed under a lofty tower or campanile of Evesham Abbey, in Worcestershire, offers a singular example, and of much greater magnitude than any of the above mentioned. It was a last effort of Gothick, at the beginning of the sixteenth century. The entrance gates of Magdalene College, Oxford, and of St. John's and Trinity Colleges at Cambridge, exhibit a remarkable style of architecture.

NOTES AND EXTRACTS ILLUSTRATIVE
OF THE FIRST DISCOURSE.

[A] page 16.—I believe that I am the first traveller who published this conjecture, in 1800. During a short stay at Pisa, upon a first view of the Baptistery, I was led to form this notion, which I will acknowledge to have required a more minute investigation. Mr. Smirke followed me soon afterwards, and published a paper in the *Archæologia*, vol. xv. p. 363, addressed to our common and most respected friend S. Lysons, Director, in which my first idea is confirmed. His proofs, with the arguments he has deduced from them, were controverted by the late Sir H. Englefield, (vol. xv. p. 373,) with that correct knowledge of the subject which he certainly possessed.

Within these few years past, two gentlemen to whose decision I bow with respect, have assured me, after a sedulous examination, that the Gothick ornaments, both of the windows of the Campo Santo, and externally, in the Baptistery, are adscititious, and not coeval with those original structures.

[B] page 19.—To the names of Gray, Bentham, and T. Warton, as classicks in the science of Gothick architecture, may be added that of Dr. Milner, of Winchester, who, whatever be the acceptance of his new theory of its origin, must be allowed to have been intimately conversant with the general subject. It is remarked by T. Warton, when comparing the Grecian with the Gothick, that "truth and propriety gratify the judgment, but they do not affect the imagination."—*Notes on the Minor Poems of Milton*, p. 91.

It was T. Warton's intention, had he lived longer, to have published the *History of Gothick Architecture*, for which no man was more eminently qualified, with, perhaps, the exception of Mr. Gray. He announced that plan in 1781, in the third volume of the History of English Poetry. *Diss. Gest. Rom.* p. xxii. The intended work was to consist of "Observations, critical and historical, on castles, churches, monasteries, and other monuments of antiquity, in various parts of England ; to which will be prefixed the history of architecture in England."—*Vol.* I. *Diss.* 2, *note.*

James Essex, architect, of Cambridge, purposed to have written the History of Gothick Architecture; but he did not find leisure or encouragement sufficient to more than the commencement of a work, for which his practice had in a great degree qualified him. He published an Essay on " *Round Churches*" *in England.—A collection of Essays on Gothick Architecture,* was published by Taylor. 8vo. 1801. These were among the first efforts to introduce a knowledge and love of our national architecture, and pointed the way to the new opinions and the numerous and extensive investigations, which have been since given to the public.

[C] page 20. — This fancy is older than Warburton. Stukeley, in his Itinerary, describing the cloisters at Gloucester, remarks, " that the idea of Gothic is taken from a walk between trees, whose branching heads are curiously imitated by the roof."—*Iter* iv. p. 69.

Spence, in his *Anecdotes of Pope,* (8vo. p. 12.) relates a conversation to prove that he suggested the original idea to Warburton. Both the theory and practice have been recommended in a quarto volume, with many plates, by the late Sir James Hall, which depend on surmises and reasonings on them, much more ingenious than satisfactory. He assumes as a fact, that the first Christian churches, founded in England, were solely composed of wicker work; that such were the prototypes of those which were built with stone ; and that they furnished the original examples of every ornamental form or particle, which was afterwards introduced. With deference to the ingenious author, such a position would be substantiated with difficulty.

[D] page 23. — The Norman columns are various, both in point of form and ornament, but are of equal thickness from the base to the capital. The earliest known are rude cylindrical upon a high plinth, to which succeeded polygonal ones, and others formed by a combination of slender half columns round a thick pillar. Those of the second period are ornamented on the surface with a variety of mouldings, and sometimes channeled either perpendicularly or spirally.

[E] page 24. — It is said to be a proof of genuine Saxon architecture, if the mouldings upon the face are likewise continued upon the soffit of the arch, as in the remains of the conventual church at Ely. The OPUS ROMANUM, or *Romanesque*, is indubitably the original of the Saxon round or semicircular arch. There are not wanting in this age of architectural controversy, individual critics who deny this test, and the Saxon pretensions of Barfreston, Waltham, &c.

[F] page 27. — The Saxons had, in fact, no style of their own, but introduced the debased Roman, as then practised in France, and chiefly during the tenth century. Edward the Confessor brought the improvements in that style from Normandy ; and the most that we have now remaining, is coeval with him. William of Malmsbury distinctly marks the variation of style brought here after the Saxon æra, by the ecclesiastical architects, who were introduced and patronised by the Norman bishops, " *novo edificandi genere.*" By certain German writers, it is contended that the Saxons, upon their invasion, brought with them their own debased Roman.

[G] page 31.—Triforium *(Glossary)*. " Imo, in ipso muro, in modum claustri per muri vel parietis interiora, eo perductum, ut transitum præbeat locum ambire sive perlustrai i et circuire, ex alto, volentibus." From the original Saxon ꝼuꝑh-ꝼaꝛe, thoroughfare. Triforium, according to Du Cange, is a surrounding border. — *Decem Scriptores edit. Gervasii Hist. Dorubernensis ecclesiæ.* " Super quem murum, via erat quæ triforium appellatur, et fenestræ superiores," in Lanfranc's building at Canterbury. In the earliest instances, this kind of passage was made only before the upper windows; and the space afterwards so occupied, was left solid. The triforia were large in proportion to the work above and below them, and applied as galleries in the substance of the walls. The first known are said to have been those in the vestibule of the Holy Sepulchre at Jerusalem, built by Constantine Monomachus in 1018. The circular or basilic termination of choirs originated in France. It was adopted by Norman architects at Peterborough, Norwich, Gloucester, Canterbury, Tewksbury, and Litchfield. The choir was more anciently in too short a proportion to the nave; the space between the transepts was subsequently added.

[H] page 47.—It is remarkable at Waltham Abbey, that the arcade of six massive cylindrical pillars have a correspondent number placed immediately above them, which are entirely open, and having no division or ornament placed against their sides, as in other instances; but at Chepstow in Monmouthshire there are, in the nave, three stories or tiers of round arches. It was the same priory of Strighoel, built soon after the Norman Conquest.

[I] page 50.—La Sainte Chapelle at Paris, was built by St. Louis, begun in 1248, and finished in 1274, from the designs of Pierre de Montreuil, one of the earliest and most celebrated of the French architects, in 1275. The interior was so exquisitely carved and painted under the inspection of Raoul, the famous goldsmith, that it had, previously to the erection of St. Stephen's Chapel by our Edward the Third, no rival in Europe, in point of splendid embellishment. Both these chapels have received a different destination— one for the archives of France—the other as attached to the House of Commons. *St. Stephen's Chapel by the Antiquarian Society. Plates.*

[K] page 52.—" In the year 1384, the munificent founder completed the building of New College, the north side of which, containing the chapel and hall, was an edifice which for extent and grandeur exceeded any then known, in either University. The elevation has all that dignity which results from proportion and harmony of parts. The internal proportions of the chapel, (antechapel, eighty feet by thirty-six; choir, one hundred feet by thirty-two, and sixty-five feet high before the lowering of the roof,) are symmetrical and correct, even so as to emulate those of a Grecian temple; and the lightness of the arcade dividing the antechapel, could have originated only in the genius of the immortal Wykeham. I speak of them as they were left by him; and of the subsequent alterations, those in 1630 and 1684 had spared the architecture. From the decay of the roof in 1789, it was found necessary to renew it totally, and Mr. James Wyat was intrusted by the Society with the remodelling of their venerable structure.

" To disparage by petty criticism, a work which few survey without admiration, would be an invidious attempt. It is with diffidence and respect for the eminent talents of Mr. Wyat, that I venture remarks, dictated solely by a love of truth.

" It will be previously inquired, whether it were Mr. Wyat's intention to restore this chapel to a perfect correspondence with the style of architecture by which Wykeham's age is definitely marked? or was he at liberty to introduce the ornaments of subsequent architecture, by his judicious adaptation of which a beautiful whole might be composed? With no great hazard of probability, we will suppose that these improvements had been gradually made during the lapse of the last centuries; yet it can scarcely be allowed, that Wykeham's plan has been followed with accuracy.

" For the restoration of the altarpiece, as a part of his design, Mr. Wyat has great credit; and we will not scrutinize too closely whether the scriptural histories, in marble bas-reliefs above the altar, could have been made by any sculptor of any country then in existence.

" Considering that the very numerous canopies and pedestals were not to be restored to their original destination of containing images, would it not have produced a better effect if the series had been composed of fewer and larger niches ? There is now no bold mass of ornament ; and the largest, which is the organ-case, is violated by a conceit, which a *very fastidious* spectator might call a peep-hole. The whole is so coloured, as to convey an idea that it is constructed with stone ; and candour must allow, that upon every principle, a stone organ-case is more novel than well adapted. In the restoration of a Gothick chapel, we expect to be gratified by ornaments, taken from known authority, and applied, as we may suppose that they might have been by the original architect ; nor are we content with mere efforts of fancy.

" It is the opinion of a considerable critic (*Gilpin*), that the Gothick roof loses its beauty, in every degree, in which it is rendered more flat ; an effect sufficiently obvious upon a comparison of the great centre arch and the heads of the windows, with the expanse of the new vaulting, with which they have an imperfect accordance.

" In the canopies of the stalls, we are brought forward to the luxuriant Gothick of Henry the Seventh ; and the application of the grotesquely-carved subsellia to the present reading desks, is a new idea with no adherence to costume.

" Viewing the present chapel, not as a restoration, but an imitation of styles, subsequent to that of the founder, where will the archetype of the organ-case be found ? The execution of the whole is exquisite : and it might have been supposed that Mr. Wyat would have recurred, at least to the tomb of W. Wykeham, in Winchester Cathedral, built by the Bishop himself, for the purest of all authorities in the minuter Gothick or shrine work. In that church is an unrivalled series of sepulchral sacella, including the whole of the fifteenth century, from Wykeham to Fox. In the first-mentioned tomb, all is simple and harmonious—the progressive richness of the two others, and the exuberant littleness, yet heavy in effect, which distinguishes the last, appear to have been imitated, by Wyat, without much discrimination. If, indeed, the question be, whether in this instance, he has imagined or collected what is most beautiful in the style called Gothick, the suffrage in his favour will be universal: but if it be referred to the single point of just combination, those will be found, who will not scruple to avow their dissent upon known principles and characteristics of the Gothick manner, familiarized to them by many examples.

" Yet whatever dispositions for censure may be indulged at the moment, no mind, especially a poetical mind, can quit this beautiful and highly-decorated scene, without sentiments of the fullest gratification."—*Observations on English Architecture*, 8vo. 1806, p. 116.

Of those parts of the Cathedral at Winchester, which are attributed to Wykeham upon just authority, the rebuilding of the nave is the principal.

DISCOURSE II.

ON THE VARIOUS MODES OF ECCLESIASTICAL ARCHI-
TECTURE IN ITALY, SICILY, FRANCE, GERMANY,
THE NETHERLANDS, SPAIN, AND PORTUGAL, TO
THE CLOSE OF THE FOURTEENTH CENTURY.

IN ITALY.

WHEN the architecture of Greece and Rome
had lapsed into oblivion and decay, and its
former splendour was faintly demonstrated by
its ruined temples, the establishment of Christianity induced a necessity for sacred edifices.
The churches built by Constantine and his
immediate successors were all of them formed
upon the plan of the Roman basilicæ.*　During
his reign, and under his auspices, in the fourth
century, arose the magnificent church of Santa

---

* *Gibbon* (vol. iii. p. 292, 8vo.) quotes from the ecclesiastical history of Eusebius an account of these early churches,
with their splendid architecture and ornaments.　With respect to ecclesiastical architecture in Italy and France, from
the age of Constantine to that of Charlemagne, the most per-

Sophia at Constantinople, the admiration of the Christian world at that earlier period, as that erected upon its ruins by Justinian remains to the present day. To Constantine likewise are attributed the nearly equally spacious and splendid churches (basilicæ) of the Holy Apostles at Constantinople and of St. John at Ephesus, both of which, although reconstructed upon the model of the Santa Sophia, are now to be discovered only by their ruins. He is likewise said to have founded the church of St. Paul, without the walls, at Rome, which was rebuilt or perfected by his successors—by Theodosius in 386, and by Honorius in 395. Each of these grand structures could boast an interior composed of marble columns of excessive height and beauty, transferred to them, being the richest spoils of ancient cities. In two of the instances above-mentioned, they

spicuous account is that given in the Essay by *Whittington*, a work deservedly valued by all who wish for sound information on the subject of Gothick architecture, and to which it is more expedient to refer the reader, than to extract largely from it. I have already adverted to these facts in the introduction to the *first Discourse*, p. 3.

The first church of Santa Sophia, in its whole interior, was covered with paintings and mosaics in gilding and colours, with masonry not unworthy of the best state of the arts, after they had begun to decline. What remains in the second church built by Theodosius, unmutilated by the Turks, when they had adapted it to their own worship, is a splendid proof of original excellence.

still are seen, and present to us, identically, many wonderful specimens.

This slight notice of the earliest Christian basilicæ may introduce the æra and style of the great church of San Marco at Venice. Of the origin of that singular structure, we learn that two nameless architects, from Lombardy and Constantinople, were employed in great works by the Republic or the Doges (1046—1072), and that the latter gave the design; which will account for the prevalence of the lower Greek manner of roofs, with cupolas and semi-cupolas, as peculiarly characteristic of this instance. This example stands alone; and the change of style which took place in the succeeding century precluded imitation. These Greek architects were employed in Italy to apply the fragments of classical edifices to buildings of their own irregular designs.

The Duomo or Cathedral of Pisa appears to have been nearly contemporary; its foundations at least having been laid as early as 1069. After its completion, arose the Baptistery in 1153; the Campanile* (leaning tower) in 1180; and the cloister of the Campo Santo in 1275.

* See *Discourse* I. p. 17. The exact declination of the Campanile is twelve feet eleven inches, English. It is an absurd fancy that the leaning tower was built so, intentionally, only to show how far a tower might gravitate before it fell.

The

Of the first-named, the plan describes a Roman cross: the nave has double aisles, styled collectively " cinque navate ;" the transept and choir have also double ones; the termination is circular, and a dome rises from the transept. The absis or chevet of this cathedral was the prototype of those subsequently applied in Italy, and was certainly copied from the Roman basilicæ. The columns in the interior are very numerous. Clusters of small arcades, so supported, are placed before the walls both of the façade and transepts, are alike numerous and conspicuous on the outside, and thus discriminate a style, of which this church in particular has been considered as the prototype, in Italy.* These architects of the early Pisan school were Boschetto, Bonanni, and William the German (Tedesco), Nicola da Pisa, his son Giovanni, and their descendants Andrea and Tommaso, to the fourteenth century. The

The largest bell weighs ten thousand pounds, and the total height is two hundred and seventy-eight feet. There are two hundred and seven columns, in all, attached to the exterior walls, which are circular, the capitals of which are all of them whimsically different. — From a late survey by E. Cresy, Architect.

The Campanile, or Bell Tower of St. Jean, at Caen, is round, built with marble, having seven ranges of columns, the total height being ninety feet, with a declination of thirteen from the base:—97.6—14.1, English.

* See Note [A] page 113.

marble much more frequently used, was not dug in Italy. Greece offered to the plunderers a much more abundant quarry ; and the genius of the architects was most admired in the adaptation of Grecian fragments to the churches which they were employed to build. The ships which were sent into the Archipelago by the Genoese and Pisan merchants, were usually laden upon their return with the spoils of classic architecture, when the dilapidated temples near the coast were left an easy prey to these mercantile adventurers. To controvert this opinion, in part only, it must be allowed that there were very considerable remains of Roman architecture in Pisa.

Towards the close of the eleventh century, we may fix the true æra of ecclesiastical architecture in Italy, which is known to possess a distinct and individual character, varying equally from the ancients and the style afterwards generally denominated as Gothick, which ultimately prevailed in other countries of Europe. Almost at the same period were constructed in Pisa, the Duomo, the Battisterio, and the Tower: at Venice, Florence, Sienna, Padua, Modena, Pavia, Piacenza, Orvietto, Bologna, Milan, and lastly the Vatican and the sanctuary of Loretto. Each of the large and magnificent structures opened an ample field to artists for the display of their talents in architecture, sculpture, and the arts of design in general. Upon the subject of the original foundation of these buildings, severally considered, very satisfactory notices are afforded by *Cicognara*, in his interesting work.*

But the Lombard, or heavy Norman, had then obtained in Italy, and can be scarcely discriminated from the same *Opus Romanum* in the more northern parts of Europe. It is observed by the late well-informed and industrious investigator, Mr. Kerrich of Cambridge, " That it maintained its usage there, in all its different styles and ages, there can be no doubt. The cathedrals of Piacenza, Parma, Cremona, and Pavia, are all of them of what we call Romanesque, or of the Transition style of architecture, and do not differ more from some churches in England, than our churches do from one another." † The church of St. Francis at Assizi, seventy miles from Rome, built in 1240, is precisely similar to that of the same æra in England, at Tintern Abbey, where the vaulting is with few ribs, the windows highly pointed, and the tracery simple. In the churches of S. Maria Novella and Santa Croce at Florence (1279—1350), are windows formed with Gothick arches. " The

* *Histoire de plus célèbres Architectes, &c.*—Paris, 2 tom. 8vo. 1830. par Quatremère de Quincy.

† *Archæologia*, vol. xv. p. 299.

pointed arch alone does not constitute Gothick architecture, although it may be said tò be peculiar to it. Its light pillars, long thin shafts, elegant foliages and vaultings—its tracery, and numerous other graceful and nameless forms of beauty, are originally essential to it, and full as necessary to its general character."* Giovanni da Pisa, the son of Nicola, was employed to build the small church of Maria della Spina, near the bridge over the Arno at Pisa. It is of the lightest Gothick, and so highly ornamented, and wrought to such perfection, that it was, according to Vasari, *tenuta miraculosa*. In later times, the term Gothick has been restrained to the lighter style only in architectural descriptions in every language of Europe.†

The knowledge of construction gradually declined in Italy from the death of the old Lombardic or German architects, and finally expired with Arnolfo Lippi, who began the church of S. Maria del Fiore, according to Gothick rules : this circumstance prevented the completion of the cupola for upwards of a century; and the arduous task was reserved for Brunelleschi, the celebrated inventor of a style of architecture introduced by him into Italy, during the fourteenth century. It has been said,

* MSS. Kerrich, Brit. Mus.   † See Note [B] page 114.

that by his means his countrymen were first
induced to abandon the Gothick style; and
that he brought back to the minds of the Italians the love of Grecian, or, at least, of the
best Roman architecture. At that period, the
subject ceases to belong to the present inquiry,
and has been introduced merely for its historical analogy.*

IN FRANCE.

The style of architecture of the earliest usage
in France, and peculiar to that country, must
be in a degree considered as the true prototype
of our own, as we have borrowed nothing from
the schools of Italy,—yet with decided varieties
and deviations; we may therefore be called
either imitators or rivals. That regular progress which, in English architecture, appears to
form a gradation, is seldom found in France.
Here it may be traced from the simple arches
of Salisbury to the gorgeous turrets of Henry
the Seventh's chapel. In a general and com-
prehensive view, we must yield the superiority
to France, for loftiness both of conception and
practice, with a single abatement, that the rich
vaultings of our later Gothick far excel any
thing of a similar description on the Continent;
and with respect to certain parts of the edifice,

* See Note [C] page 114.

the cloister and chapter-house have a space and elegance, of which no comparative examples are there seen. A greater simplicity prevails in the capitals of clustered columns, in the early French style. In this respect, a comparison of the nave of Salisbury* with that of Amiens will decide this fact, although they will not be found to be strictly analogous. The excellence of the English Gothick school is seen more conspicuously in certain parts and details. In the best specimens of the French school, we are struck with the admirable effect of comprehension, in the architect, both of unity of design and consequent beauty. The elevation of the most celebrated churches rises firmly from the basement, and is composed of very bold and commanding masses. Of their great dimensions and space, it may be competent to observe, that the western front of York could be placed beneath the roofs of the choirs of Beauvais or Amiens. Nor is the whole effect produced by magnitude alone. The façade, which presents broad and imposing members in its porches, buttresses, and towers; and the perforated tracery in the divisions and openings, scarcely ever practised with us, demands our praise of its admirable beauty. These are

* See an accurate comparison of their relative parts in *Whittington's Essay*, p. 199.

slight and general observations, and lead us to
a more historical detail concerning the progress
and perfection of the art.

The manner of building peculiarly Norman
had prevailed in the north of France ante-
cedently to the Conquest of England. We
have evidence, that the church of St. Denis
by the Abbot Sugerius, Nôtre Dame at Paris,
Chartres, and Rheims, were in a state of completion before that period, which fact the still
remaining parts of each sufficiently confirm.*

Among the most genuine instances of architecture in Normandy,† which may still be inspected, are the two great conventual churches
of St. Stephen and the Holy Trinity at Caen,
erected by William the Conqueror and his
queen, during their lives. And as it is the undoubted prototype of our own, it may be more
to the purpose of this Discourse to confine remarks to Norman examples in a great measure;
although it is certain that the same principles
prevailed in every other province in France,
which however were adopted with a certain
discrimination. For the Roman ornaments
were more frequently imitated, and the want of
correct taste and barbarous massiveness were
almost peculiar to a Norman structure. Comparison has established this fact. The twelfth

* See Note [D] page 115.   † See Note [E] page 115.

century, indeed, produced three several revolutions in the architecture of France.* At first, all was Lombard; which then became intermixed with, or was in fact superseded by, the sharply-pointed arch; and at its close, this was expanded, and, in several instances, ornamented to a degree of perfection not even attempted in England before another century had elapsed. The highly decorated and florid style originated and reached perfection in Germany and France many years before we possessed any similar demonstration of the change. In those countries, the golden age of this style continued from the middle of the thirteenth to the latter end of the fourteenth century (1250—1390).

The circular style had reached its zenith between the close of the eleventh century and the beginning of the next ensuing. The round and pointed are then seen frequently intermixed, particularly in the windows, which are, in fact, the distinguishing marks of an æra. Clustered columns are annulated, or tied toge-

---

* " A severe simplicity characterises Lisieux; Coutances (1056) is distinguished by its elegance, abounding in decoration; Seez (1080), at the same time that it unites the excellence of both, can rival neither in that which is peculiarly its own."—Cotman. The French antiquaries have considered the crypt and chevet of St. Denis as of the earliest date now remaining. St. Germain des Prez and Nôtre Dame at Paris succeeded to them. Clugny was rebuilt in 1093.

ther in the middle, as at Bayeux, St. Stephen's, Caen, and Westminster Abbey, Salisbury, and the Temple Church.

It is worthy remark, that in the Cathedrals of Nôtre Dame at Paris (1175), and Canterbury (1174), the round Norman pillar, finished by an irregular Corinthian capital,* are most frequent. Such had previously appeared (1140) in the conventual church of Clugni, the dimensions of which far exceeded those of any other monastery, the total length being not less than six hundred feet. They are likewise in the ruined chapel of Castel Vetrano in Sicily.

The exuberance of Gothick fancy was displayed in rude sculpture during the earliest Norman æra, and applied itself principally to the capitals of pillars, in naves, crypts, and chapter-houses. The subjects are multifarious: leaves, flowers, and vegetable representations in almost every possible combination of them; satirical postures of the human and animal form, but rarely as in nature; monsters combating with, or destroying each other; Our Saviour thrusting a spear into the mouth of a serpent, or weighing souls, with Satan, as a monster, pushing down the opposite scale with a sword. These designs were anterior to, or

* See Note [F] page 116.

contemporary with the most ancient in England, and the very fertile parents of similar invention, although less capricious or luxuriant.*

I will now advert to those instances more particularly, which, by a certain selection, may point out the progress and change of architecture in Normandy, chronologically stated.† The earliest and leading peculiarities, and which were brought by Norman architects into England, were subterraneous chapels called crypts, supported by many short columns with carved capitals, always under the choir; the basilic, or semicircular terminations of the choir, styled by French writers chevet; two tiers of round arches in the nave, springing alternately from square piers and round pillars, and nearly

---

* In the Chapter-house of St. Georges de Bocherville is a double capital sculptured with subjects of real curiosity : it is a band of musicians, each with an instrument then in usage, and forming a concert. They afford an authentic evidence of the history of music as practised by the Normans in the thirteenth century, and are satisfactorily elucidated by *Mr. Douce*. *Turner*, vol. ii. p. 13.

The pillars of the church of St. Pierre in Caen have all the capitals sculptured in bas-relief, of which the Abbé de la Rue, in his " *Essais Historiques sur la Ville de Caen*," has given a satisfactory explication. They represent subjects taken wholly from poetical romances. The double columns and capitals in the choir of Canterbury, built by William of Sens, resemble those in the cathedral of the last-mentioned city.

† See Note [G] page 115.

equally divided. Of these, the upper one opened into a gallery for walking, or triforium,
sometimes over the vaulting of the aisles, or
confined to a passage within the thickness of
the walls. The windows were single, narrow
externally, but placed under an open arcade
within, having the central one considerably the
highest. These details occur in the Abbey of
St. Stephen at Caen, built by the Conqueror.
Jumieges, contemporary, and equally curious,
was desecrated and destroyed in 1793; and
Bec has been entirely taken down: Fécamp
has escaped the storm.

The above-mentioned are of the first æra;
but the same gradation from the most simple
to the most complicated, which may be traced
in England, does not occur in France. There
were several distinct schools, of various charac-
ters. The change was instantaneous.

It were beyond the compass of these remarks
to enumerate the peculiarities or excellence of
such magnificent structures as the Cathedrals
of Rheims, Beauvais, Chartres, Amiens, &c. and
to enter into any detail concerning them.*
The reader may pursue such investigations
with great satisfaction in several scientific publications which have lately appeared both in
France and England.

* See the opposite page.

Confining these descriptions to Normandy, the two great churches at Rouen command our attention, and will best serve to communicate an accurate idea of French Gothick when it had reached its ultimate perfection, or, perhaps, exuberance.

It would be a difficult attempt to present to the mind of an English artist or amateur, who had never visited the Continent, an accurate idea of two such buildings as the Cathedral and Church of St. Ouen, at Rouen ; for although we have delineations of both, in parts, nearly as perfect as can fall within the compass

---

* CATHEDRAL CHURCHES, DATES, AND ARCHITECTS, BEFORE THE CLOSE OF THE THIRTEENTH CENTURY.

CHURCHES.	DATES.	ARCHITECTS.
Chartres . .	1029	Fulbert.
Charité sur Loire .	1056	Gerard.
Clugni . . .	1070	Hugues.
Nôtre Dame, Paris .	1161	Maurice de Sully. Finished by Jean de Ravy, 1257, and Pierre de Montereau, 1270.
Bec . .	1212	Ingelramme. Finished by Waltier de Meulan, 1216.
Rheims Cathedral .	1215	Hugues Libergier. Completed by Robert de Coucy.
Cathedral of Rouen	1216	Ingelramme. Finished by W. de Meulan.
Sainte Chapelle, Paris	1245	Pierre de Montereau.
Lyons . .	1270	Robert de Lusarches.
Nôtre Dame, Mantes	1280	Eudes de Montrieul.
St. Germain des Prez, Paris, Chapel of Our Lady	1288	Finished. Foundations laid in 1227. Pierre de Montereau.

of the art, such can never communicate the effect of an actual inspection.* Nor will it fare better with verbal description, if it be extended beyond the mere statement of facts, as to the effect they produce upon the imagination, or the proofs they supply to comparative criticism. Omitting any account of an earlier edifice, the Cathedral, as it is now seen, was completed between the years, progressively, from the beginning of the fourteenth to the end of the next century.

The points of entire distinction between the cathedrals of France and England, and which present themselves on the first view, are in the grand façade, or western front; and, in some instances, in the transepts; the portal, or great door of entrance; the chevet, having a round or octangular end, with an hemispherical roof; the extreme height of the vaultings of the nave; the vast expanse of the circular, or rose-windows; and the numerous chapels by

---

* *Description, &c. de Nôtre Dame de Rouen — Description, &c. de l'Eglise de St. Ouen; par M. Gilbert,* 8vo. 1816.

Plates in Pugin's Norman Architecture, 4to. 1828.

Three Views by C. Wild, folio, 1825—being part of a series of twelve etchings of the interior and exterior of French Cathedrals, which, for accurate perspective and picturesque effect, are as yet unequalled. Twelve of the English have been likewise completed.

Jolimont, Cathedrales Françaises, fol. 1826–30. — *Lithographes, en Livraisons.*

which the choir and side aisles are surrounded.

We can scarcely imagine an architectural effect of greater sublimity than that of the façade
of the Cathedral of Rouen, or sufficiently admire the profusion and excellence of the carved
ornaments of which it is composed. A stately
expanded mass occupies two hundred and fifty
feet at the foundation, and rises to a pyramidal
roof of one hundred and seventy, flanked by
two towers, which are each of the height of
two hundred and thirty feet, in which respect
only they are similar. These are, indeed, majestic proportions.* The grand entrance may
serve, in this description, as an example of many
others in France, in point of style, although it
is by several exceeded in the effect, as produced by more elegant proportions. It requires
a minute investigation, but I shall only attempt to give a general idea, for the purpose
of national comparison.

The grand porch occupies the central division. It is placed between two large pillars of
a pyramidal form, with finials of open work,
having a lofty pediment; so wrought, with a
delicacy and variety beyond the scope of detail.
Niches richly canopied occupy the whole space,
adapted, as may be required, to the several parts,

* See Note [H] page 117.

and literally peopled with carved figures, from the size of life to diminutive forms.

The architects of the middle centuries (1250 to 1450), in order to avoid the inconvenience of immense folding-doors, and yet to give the entrance a proportion suitable to the size of the building itself, made the inner opening of the gates such as convenience required; but the exterior merely to produce an effect. The opening, which widens in an oblique, splayed direction, from the inner gate to the outer face of the wall, is usually ornamented with columns, statues with their bases and capitals, and foliage-work most curiously embossed, and thus is made to form a covered porch, having at once the effect of grandeur, richness, and solidity. Of the western fronts of our English cathedrals, two only, those of Peterborough and Wells, have any analogy to many in France with respect to their composition or architectural ornaments; but the great portals, with receding arches, are not seen here in any instance of consequence. The portals of Rouen, Rheims, and Strasbourg, present to us pre-eminent examples.

In the tympanum, over the head of the door-case, was frequently placed a large group of sculpture in bas-relief. This of Rouen designates the tree of Jesse, or the genealogy of the Virgin Mary, by almost innumerable figures.

Two grand component members of this magnificent edifice are the towers, of great dimension and height. The intervening space between
them is decorated in a higher style than in
other parts, by a parapet and an acutely-formed
pediment, composed of a succession of small
open arcades, the arches of which are found
terminating with trefoiled or trilobed heads.
This fret-work conceals the high-pitched roof,
placed between four large and lofty turrets,
with pinnacles, likewise of open work, all of
which, admitting the thorough light, produce
the most airy effect. The northern tower is
the more ancient, but it owes its present elevation to a singularly high pavilion roof, such
as were prevalent in France early in the
sixteenth century. The southern is of a totally
different construction, as an octangular tower,
with very large open windows, rises from it,
and is finished by a rich perforated balustrade.
It was entirely completed by the second Cardinal George D'Amboise, in 1542. Each of
these towers has an elevation of two hundred
and forty feet, and the central, with its spire,
now in rebuilding, of four hundred and thirty
feet English.

Time has treated the decorative parts of this
beautiful façade as it usually does a beautiful
woman; yet the former charms are not wholly
obliterated. The decay of years has worn off

the polish, but the grace remains. Notwithstanding that mutilation prevails, the degree of original excellence cannot be mistaken.

As a general observation, it may be remarked that the towers, with or without spires, in other provinces of France, are very rarely uniform or complete : those at Rheims are certainly a beautiful exception to this statement. Upon entering the interior, the great length will excite more admiration than the breadth or height.* To the English visiter, the circular termination of the choir presents a new and imposing effect; whilst the three round or rose windows,† with their radiations of richly-coloured glass, excite an intense and lasting surprise. The last-mentioned are fifty feet in diameter, and may be considered as superior to those in the church of St. Ouen, and the design of the geometrical tracery still more elaborate.

---

* This circumstance is elucidated by a comparison made between Rouen and York Cathedrals. Nave of Rouen, f. 269 by 27.4 inches, and f. 91 high ; of York, f. 250 by 103, and f. 91. 6 high. The difference of length is only f. 19 ; of the width, f. 75.10 ; whilst the height is nearly the same in both. But great interior length diminishes the width to the eye, and the impression of space is less at Rheims than in the Nôtre Dame.

† In the French descriptions of their cathedrals, we have the terms " Oeil des ailes," " Rosa vitrea ;" and of a chapel in St. Germain des Prez, " Fenestris egregiis et magnâ gloriatur Rosâ." Forty feet is not an unusual span. — *Topog. Gallic.* p. 1, 93.

Of the last-mentioned edifice,* unparalleled in architectural ornament, a similar and slight notice may tend to a clearer comparison of the system with which Cathedrals were constructed in England, and upon the Continent, in the fourteenth century.

The façades of Rheims, Amiens, and St. Denis, are more pyramidal than those in England; the triangular gable-ends are profusely covered with statues, and the space between the towers is narrower. In comparing the ground-plans of the two churches of Nôtre Dame at Rouen and Paris, a memorable distinction occurs. The last-mentioned has two double aisles, the exterior of which are subdivided into numerous chapels, and the outline of the wall is plain; whilst the semicircular end of the other is clustered with small oratories of a round or octangular form, which last plan is the more prevalent. Flying buttresses are finished by very tall and richly crocketed pinnacles. At Amiens, the space between the semicircular and diagonal ribs is

* The foundation of the present church of St. Ouen is attributed to the Abbot Marcdargent, in 1318; and its completion to Alexander de Berneval, a celebrated architect, who died in 1440.

The spire of the Cathedral has been twice set on fire, in 1117, and in 1804. Since the last restoration in wood, and of a discrepant design, the new spire, now completed, has been made entirely of cast iron, upon the model of Salisbury. — *Gilbert, Description,* &c.

occupied by window-frames of stone placed closely together, which are elliptic, with quatrefoil heads.

The western façade of the church of St. Ouen, in its lateral towers, has been left incomplete : their intended plan is octagonal. Over the portal is a gallery with a perforated balustrade, and the space immediately above it is occupied by a rose window, the compartments of which are unequalled in point of delicacy. A parapet of open trefoils runs round the aisles and nave of the church, and the central tower, octangular in the upper part of it, is almost wholly composed of tall open windows and arches of tracery, terminated, like the south tower of the Cathedral, with a crown of fleurs-de-lis. This armorial figure is peculiar to France, and is often introduced into its ornamental architecture. One of the most beautiful porches is that which opens to the south transept. The roof has several pendents *(culs de lampe)*, the octagon sides of which are wrought into canopied niches, containing small statues. It is surrounded by pendent trefoil arches, springing from carved bosses, and forming an open festoon of the freest tracery. Every artifice of construction, and open work of infinite variety, are exhibited here. Over the door-way is a large bas-relief from the history of the Virgin Mary, which will gratify the most curious inspection. The interior view from the great western door will excite an instant surprise by the boldness of its architecture, the scarcely credible work of human hands. "A profusely decorative style spreads itself over the vaulting in various angular compartments, with bosses, heads, and wreaths at the joinings, and in such an abundance and lightness, as to have the appearance of embroidery in stone."*

From the extreme length of this nave,† the height of the vaulting,‡ as well as the breadth, appear to be much diminished in optical effect, yet there is an exquisite uniformity in all its parts. Of the dividing arcade, the component members are columns elegantly clustered with small flowered capitals, and pointed arches. Above them are the triforia, continued through every part; the second tier of windows is brought down immediately behind them, and a thorough light is so universally admitted, that we lose the idea of a solid wall. These columns, about mid-way, have a very large canopy and base for statues, which were destroyed by the insurgents in 1793; but the effect of them, even though so far denuded, is very picturesque, particularly in their profiles. At Milan, such are placed at the springing of the arches, instead of capitals.

* See Note [I] page 118.
† F. 264. 4, by 36. 10.   ‡ F. 100.

One of the greatest advantages which this
style of church architecture supplied, was the
space which could admit of the worship of a
multitude, and an abundant supply of enriched
or pure light: a provision contrary to the plan
and system of the ancient Grecian temples.
Light, so modified, was a chief consideration
in giving the windows so near an approxima-
tion, scarcely consistent with the safety of the
walls.*

I have perhaps digressed too far in thus indulging a pleasing reminiscence, having inspected
both these sumptuous buildings in 1826, with
some attention. An acquaintance with their
principles and effect may give us clearer views
and a better knowledge in examining the cathedrals of our own country, and discriminating,
by a true comparison, what we have originated,
adopted, or improved upon.

Towards the end of the thirteenth century
two of the best specimens of Gothick were
built from the designs of Pierre de Montereau,
of the Sainte Chapelle, and Our Lady's Chapel
in St. Germain des Prez, at Paris.

The church of St. Maclou, at Rouen, may be
cited as an unique example of the French filligrain style of embossed work, which was at its
zenith at the close of the fifteenth century.
They chiefly consisted of the imitation of fruits

* *Fenêtres presque continuées.*

and flowers. When I saw them in 1826, they were nearly in a state of decomposition on the outside, and within, sadly clogged with washes of white-lime. Such carvings in the German large churches, are not inferior in point of high finishing and delicacy.

In France, during the course of the fifteenth and sixteenth centuries, the ornaments were more and more attenuated ; their Gothick filla-gree became a web and woof composed of stone. The bosses of the key-stones spread around the groins in large circles and roses, perforated and filleted with a singular effect. Bas-reliefs of sacred subjects are seen on the outside of the low skreen, placed behind the altar. But the most elaborate and beau-tiful open carved work excites admiration in the noel or circular staircases. Extraordinary specimens remain at Rouen, Strasbourg, and D'Alby.*

Surprise produced by the sublimity of the vaulting, or the intricacies of decorative art, in which the French churches exceed ours, will not compensate to the eye of taste for the heterogeneous and frequent introduction of modern altars, stuck against large pillars,

* The grand façade of the Cathedral of Orleans was built from the designs of M. Gabriel, so late as 1723. It was the last, but very interesting effort of expiring Gothick, in France. —*Jolimont, Description.* .

totally destroying all the relative proportions;
poorly painted pictures; and figures in bro-
cade dresses as large as life. Such is the
sacrifice made to the superstitions of the common people!

In England, we enter the naves of York
or Salisbury, of a commanding and unencum-
bered space. Architecture reigns in sublime
and simple grandeur. There is no distraction
caused by subordinate or mean objects: taste,
judgment, and science are satisfied; and the
heart of man is elevated to a pure veneration
in the house of God.

"PRESENTIOREM CONSPICIMUS DEUM."

IN GERMANY AND THE LOW COUNTRIES.

The proposed analogy would not be complete, if these cathedrals were passed by without a short investigation. In the earlier ages,
as in other countries, the debased Roman
style prevailed in all the German churches.
In the second style, the semicircular arch is
still retained, but the towers and pinnacles are
pyramidal, the windows pointed, and the roofs
very highly pitched. Another style succeeded
during the middle centuries, when were erected the grandest works of architecture which
Germany possesses,* and which are anterior to

* See Note [K] page 119.

those in England, if not in France, for which the late German writers contend plausibly, if not with complete success. In the eleventh century, the cathedrals of Spire, Worms, and Müntz, were built, and are still admirable for their solidity and magnificence.

A German professor *(Wieseking)* advances a very high claim to the invention of the Gothick in that country, or, at least, that it was there employed earlier than in others. He asserts that St. Bernard, bishop of Hildesheim, was the inventor of the ancient German style, according to which the cathedral of Naumberg was commenced at the close of the tenth century; then followed, in 1009, the cathedral of Minden; and in 1064, that of Hildesheim was completed. Soon after 1100, it was introduced into Spain by San Domingo della Catrada, in the churches of Leon and Lugo. In the same century, Bishop Fulbert adopted it in France in the cathedral of Chartres. The German architect Lapo, Master Nicholas of Pisa, with his son Giovanni, brought it into Italy, mixed with the Lower Greek, soon afterwards; and it was employed alone at Urbino, Arezzo, Assizi, and Bologna. William of Sens, in 1175, first used it in England at Canterbury; and it is worthy of remark, that a few, exactly similar, are seen in Sens Cathedral.

Of the succeeding æra are those of Cologne and Strasbourg, Friedbourg and Oppenheim, which last is much dilapidated. A whole century, from 1377 to 1478, passed, during the uninterrupted building of the cathedral at Ulm, not exceeded by any church in Germany in its stupendous height, profuse ornament upon a large and small scale, and sublime interior effect.*

The porticoes and the rose windows nearly resemble those already described in France: one of the last-mentioned, at Strasbourg, exceeds in diameter any other known instance.

But the construction and amazing height of the spires are peculiar, and are solely of German origin and adaptation. The sculptured ornaments are finished with extreme delicacy, and almost universally confined to the representation of trees and fruits, flowers and leaves, fancifully combined in garlands and wreaths. The open trefoil occurs externally, but niches and statues more rarely; they are chiefly of kings or bishops, of gigantic proportions, so as to be viewed from the ground.

The towers, with their single spires, of Strasbourg, Vienna, and Antwerp, are the most celebrated. We have an account of those intended

* Commenced in 1377, and finished, with the exception of the tower, in 1478. Length, 416 f.; width, 166; and 141 f. high, inclusive of the thickness of the vaulting.—*Moller.*

at Cologne, which would have rivalled them.
Strasbourg has a total elevation of five hundred and seventy-four feet from the ground.
A square, solid tower has, first, an elevation of
three hundred and thirty-four feet; then suc-
ceeds an octagon, flanked by four external octagon staircases, which are perforated throughout, and strengthened with cramps of iron ;
and lastly, a solid pyramid most richly crocketed at the angles, and finished by a kind of
open lantern : the whole structure is exactly
twice as high as the highest pinnacle of the
two towers of the western façade at York.

The most curious spire in Germany for its
lace-work in stone filling the interstices between each rib or panel, is that of Fridburg
in the Brisgaw : it is likewise of extraordinary
height, four hundred and fifteen feet with the
spire.

At Malines is the most regular and beautiful
tower, built in 1452, three hundred and forty
feet high without the spire, which would have
been one third more.

In most instances, the roofs or gables are so
very highly pitched as to occupy half the structure, not concealed by parapets, as in France.
They are covered with glazed tiles of many different colours, placed in mosaic figures. Nothing can exceed the peculiar but unharmoniz-
ing effect of this fanciful combination. Such

are the leading features of the greater German churches, particularly that of Vienna.

The tower of Strasbourg with its spire was the stupendous design of Erwin de Steinbach, who superintended its execution for twenty-eight years; his son continued it; and it was brought to a wonderful conclusion by John Hültz, a native of Cologne.* By progressive stages, it occupied no less time than the interval between 1277 and 1439, a lapse of one hundred and sixty-two years.

IN THE NETHERLANDS.

The spire of Antwerp exhibits a similar plan, and rises to an almost equal degree of elevation, four hundred feet. Had the total completion of the façade at Cologne taken place, or that of Mechlin been completed according to the plan engraved by Hollar, Strasbourg would have been rivalled in sublimity and rich workmanship.†

The deficiency of a corresponding spire is equally apparent at Antwerp as at Strasbourg, which last mentioned is exactly twice as high as the highest pinnacle of the towers of the

---

* Begun in 1439. It is full 530 f. English in height, and consequently thirty feet higher than the top of St. Peter's at Rome.

† See Note [L] page 120.

western façade at York. As early as the year 1248, the German architects began to build the cathedral of Cologne upon its present plan, and in 1276 the porch of the minster at Strasbourg, under the direction of Irwin von Steinbach : two structures which, though unfinished, will be the admiration of all ages, from the boldness of their design, the beauty and elegance of their parts, and the excellence of their execution.*

In Austria, the spire of the church of St. Stephen, at Vienna, is advanced to nearly as high a point (four hundred and thirty-two feet *German*). There is a great difference in its plan. It is not connected with the façade, but rises from the foundation, solid, but sloping gradually to its apex. Excepting that the upper division is thickly pannelled and canopied, and the spire itself studded with crockets, it is comparatively heavy, having no thorough light.

The roof of St. Stephen's, which is so highly pitched as to occupy the sight nearly as much

---

* *Moller.* " Cologne cathedral is the unrivalled glory of this class of buildings, the most splendid, and perhaps the earliest exhibition of the beauties of this style." *Essay*, p. 67, published anonymously, written by Professor Wheley of Cambridge. The lover of Gothick architecture will find ample satisfaction in the correct plans, descriptions, and engravings of several of the Flemish and German cathedrals lately published.

as the lower division of the whole fabric, has a singular, and by no means a pleasing mode of ornament. Glazed tiles, of many colours, are formed into squares and lozenges, and various mosaic patterns, and have a very inharmonious effect under a bright sun. On the contrary, in France, although the roofs are scarcely less elevated, they are carefully concealed by very lofty parapets of open work, in crocketed pinnacles.

In Flanders, at Malines and Ypres, the cathedral architecture has more of the regular simplicity of the English. The tower of the former, finished in 1452, is three hundred and forty-eight feet high, without the intended spire, which would have been one-third more. Ypres has a tower and transept in the style of York or Lincoln. In Holland, the towers are square, then an octagon having very high and sharply-pointed pediments; and sometimes very large pinnacles, which are, but in a small degree, lower than the central spire. The windows are made of disproportionate tallness, as at Gouda, in order to receive the exquisitely rich stained glass, of which the far-famed manufacture was established in that city.

The octangular hemispherical tower by which another is finished, attached to the cathedral at Utrecht, has furnished Sir Christopher Wren with his idea of the Campanile at Christ-Church,

Oxford.* But the Maisons de Ville, or town-houses, in many of the cities in Flanders, engrossed, in a peculiar degree and extent, a style of grand and most richly-ornamented architecture, superior even to that conspicuous in their churches of the higher order. Many might be enumerated, but the instances best known are those at Brussels, Ghent, Lovain, and Sedan. In France, there is one eminent rival —the Palais de Justice at Rouen, which is of a style somewhat dissimilar. A leading peculiarity in Flanders is seen in the extremely lofty towers, which rise from the centre of the front, and sometimes are conducted to a height of nearly four hundred feet : these are all of the fifteenth century, and in the manner first introduced and patronized under Philip, Duke of Burgundy. The external surface of the whole building is literally incrusted with minute filligrain in stone.

IN SPAIN AND PORTUGAL.

When the Arabs, by their extensive conquests of the richest countries, had acquired immense wealth under the Califs and their successors; they adopted and cultivated the study

* *Etchings of ancient Cathedrals, Hotels de Ville, &c. in France, Germany, Flanders, Holland, and Italy, by J. Coney,* imperial folio and quarto, 1830.

of the most splendid architecture, both in point of the stateliness of exterior dimensions, and the exuberant ornament of the apartments. They caused the learning of the Greeks to be transfused into their own language, and excelled in mathematics and all the dependent sciences ; and the perfection to which they attained in architecture was solely accomplished by these means, the earliest instances having their date in the eighth century. All representations of human or animal forms having been interdicted by the Mohammedan law, other ornaments were substituted, such as coloured glazed tiles and mosaics, and also that species of decoration called from their usual application of it " Arabesques," which is certainly of Egyptian origin. " Although the Arab or Moorish style may not present an appearance of strength and security, yet it gratifies the eye by picturesque decorations, and it is worthy remark that all its parts are perfectly symmetrical, and never degenerate into heaviness and incoherence."

But in Egypt, at Cairo, Fez in Morocco, Ispahan, and Damascus, and more especially in Hindoostan, there are still to be seen numerous specimens both of the ancient remains and modern structures, in mosques, mausolea, and palaces.

The only pure specimens of ancient architecture, as practised by the Arabs, which are familiar to us, are those in Spain, and a few in Sicily; and from these, proofs may be collected of the usage of pointed arches long anterior to the introduction of them, as a decisive criterion, in the first Transition style from the heavy round arch of the debased Roman, peculiar to the Saxons and Normans in all the great churches which they built in this kingdom.*

In the church architecture of Spain and Portugal, the Moorish and the Norman-Gothick appear as distinctly applied in various structures of different æras. Sometimes they are mixed in the same.

The affinity which may be discovered between the Gothick style and that which characterises all the Moorish, or more properly the Arabic buildings, seems to prove that, after the irruption of that people into Spain, it prevailed to a certain degree, even posterior to the dominion of the Saracens, in that country. There were, in fact, no similar examples to be found among the ruins of Greek or Roman architecture, which were then remaining all over Europe; and that manner and those proportions which so far resemble such as were adopted

---

* " The Moorish architecture of Spain, from which some writers have endeavoured to derive the Gothick, is certainly not Gothick, and is connected with that style only by slight and superficial resemblances."—*Essay*, *Anon.* (Wheley.)

by the constructors of Al-Hamra, Al-Canzar,
and the mosque at Cordova, the cathedral of
Monte Reale at Palermo, and of similar edifices, were only taught by the Arabs or other
Eastern nations, where these prototypes abound.
The Califes erected stupendous temples both
in Spain and Sicily, and likewise in the south of
France, before the Saracens were expelled from
thence by Charles Martel.*

The cathedrals at Toledo and Segovia have
been much celebrated. It has been observed
by Swinburne,† that the style of one race of
Saracens, the Moors, who possessed the southern part of that kingdom, was totally different from the Gothick. The characteristic of
their architecture is a horseshoe, or more than
a semicircular arch, at first suggested by the
crescent, the emblem of Mohammed, which
prevails in all their works, from the mosque
of Cordova, built in 800, to the palace of Al-
Hamra, in Grenada, begun about the thirteenth, and receiving additions till the end of
the fifteenth century. The ancient mosque of
Cordova does not exhibit the slightest resemblance to the Gothick, but there are a few
pointed arches in the Al-Hamra.‡ A splendour of ornament, in the most perfect style

---

* *Cicognara*, 1. ii. p. 230.   † *Travels in Spain.*

‡ *Murphy's Arab. Antiq. in Spain*, imperial folio, a most
splendid work in point of embellishment.

of the East, was seen within these walls, which is not yet totally obliterated. It abounded in mosaics and tiles for floors and wainscoting, of porcelain richly enamelled with gold and azure, " mosaics of gold, white, purple, blue, and green, intermixed, in gorgeous display of beauty."

In the cathedral of Cordova, which is of a square ground-plan, a subdivision internally is made by many aisles, divided by eight hundred and fifty columns, nine feet from the base to the capital, originally Corinthian, of a diameter of one foot and a half only, and resting without a base or plinth.

There is a cathedral, nearly of the Gothick character, at Burgos, as having been built by Gothick architects, John and Simon of Cologne, after 1442.

In Portugal, at Leira, there are several specimens of Norman design: at the monastery of Alcobaça, the whole is narrow, having a nave with an arcade of thirteen Gothick pillars, like those of the fourteenth century.

Murphy, in his scientific account of the ˙Batalha, has discovered that David Hackett, an Irishman, was employed by John the First, king of Portugal, in the next century; an anecdote honourable to the English school. The plan of this cathedral, with the mausoleum, is in the Gothick of that time; the ornamental parts only are upon the Moorish model.

The monastery of Alco-Baza in Portugal was founded in 1170, and nearly resembles the Norman style, excepting that the arches are pointed. The eastern end is circular, and the style in conformity to the Norman, with a great similarity in the sculptured ornaments.*

The façade of the church of Batalha has a deeply splayed doorway of retiring arches. There are many arcs-boutans, or flying buttresses, against the walls of the nave, having richly-crocketed semicircles on the lower side.†

As a corollary to the foregoing observations, let me observe, that by so great a contrast as that which is usually seen between the height and breadth in most of the cathedrals on the Continent, and so frequent a perforation of the walls, the magical effect of the perspective is produced. But the architects had a difficulty to counteract, and an indispensable arrangement to consult. The narrow roofs of the nave and aisles might be protracted to any given length; which, if the church had not been divided by internal arcades, could not have been stretched from wall to wall with any degree of practicability. The numerous ceremonies of the Catholic religion, of which processions composed so great a part, required

* *Murphy's Tour in Portugal.* † *Murphy's Batalha,* folio.

temples of the most extended length, which was capable of being tripled by the parallel division of the whole space into three parts. The disproportion above stated will be found, in the French and German churches, more frequently, because unmixed with the circular or first style, upon a due comparison with those of England.

The lovers of Greek architecture will indeed contend, that our first surprise is produced by a total absence of regular proportions, which we gradually lose upon a strict examination. The contrary is the effect of a classical structure, of which St. Peter's is readily adduced as the most memorable instance. It is principally the want of breadth which makes the length appear excessive, and which seems to elevate the roof to so extreme a height, in the more stupendous of the foreign edifices.

This comparison does not exemplify a more pure or correct taste in any of the nations which offer it, to the disparagement of the rest. If, in architecture, taste consist in a just relation of parts, in forming a whole, which accords with the idea we give to the Orders; and the choice and imitation in ornament be collected from the rich or simple beauties of nature; it is certain that the Gothick architects, of whatever country, have exhibited much ingenuity and skill in every instance, but taste, correctly speaking, in few of them only. It should at the same time be kept in mind, that it has no analogy with classical architecture, nor can it be fairly judged of upon the same principles ; nevertheless, there is a character of originality, which, in its general and complete effect, surprises till we become enchanted with its influence.

NOTES AND EXTRACTS ILLUSTRATIVE

OF THE SECOND DISCOURSE.

[A] page 76. — The antiquarian reader will consult *Theatrum Basilicæ Pisanæ, Josephi Martini*, fol. Romæ, 1705 ; and the work by Flaminio del Borgo. See likewise *Durand Paralele des Edifices*. In Gunn's *Inquiry into the Origin and influence of Gothick Architecture*, 8vo. 1819, we have a succinct and satisfactory view of the early Italian architecture. " Among the architects of the eleventh and twelfth centuries Boschetto ranks first, for the cathedral at Pisa, begun in 1063, and completed in 1092 : Dioti Salvi (or Allievi) who constructed the Baptistery 1152, Nicola da Pisa, and his son Giovanni, (who long presided over the schools, and who were probably the masters of Cimabue, Raimondo, and Bonanni,) and the two friends and fellow-students, Di Lapo and Arnolfo, were all Italians, and, excepting the last, who was a Florentine, most probably Pisans. The twelfth century was also a remarkable æra for buildings and masonry, both for secular and religious purposes. The towers, which are a striking feature in the older cities in Italy, were constructed, some for ornament, others for defence — of which that of the Asinelli at Bologna, (1109,) and De' Frari at Venice, (1234,) are among the more conspicuous."

" The first masters in whose works remarkable proficiency appears, were, next to those of Pisa, two of the school of Sienna, three of Florence. Among the Siennese was Lorenzo Maitani, the architect of the Cathedral of Orvietto, a work which assigns to him the first place among the artists of the thirteenth and fourteenth centuries. He not only planned, but for forty years (1290—1330) superintended the progress of that astonishing structure. The early builders

I

(*magistri lapidum*, as they were called,) were commonly skilled in all the sister arts, and he directed the execution of the sculptures, bronzes, and mosaics, with which they were then embellished. It were to little purpose to enumerate his contemporaries and fellow-citizens." pp. 59, 60.

[B] page 79.—It should be remarked, that the interior of the Cathedral of Milan, which is of the close of the fourteenth century, is of the same Gothick style which prevailed in France and Germany during that æra: the architect was called Zamodia Tedesco, the German. May not the distinctive appellation " *Tedesco* " have been given to Zamodia, as the first architect from Germany who introduced their national Gothick into Italy? The Italian architects of that æra were denominated from the place of their birth, as Nicola and Giovanni da Pisa. It is not certain that Lapo or Jacopo, who has been so styled, was, in fact, a German architect: he built the cathedral at Arezzo in 1240.

"We have nothing which might authorise a strict comparison with the Cathedral at Milan, as to the immensity of the work, or the astonishing and endless labour which has been expended upon it. Without ascending the roof, no idea can be formed of the vast profusion of elegantly-carved ornaments, the Gothick work, or the astonishing number of statues and alto-relievos which are found there, some very small, others of a gigantic size — generally speaking, good. They possess, of course, different degrees of merit, as having been made in different ages. There is a singular application of them, which is seen, I believe, nowhere else — they stand upon the very summit of pinnacles and finials. The Louvre, in the centre of the church, is very large, and of grand effect, but is disfigured by a wooden spire. The flying arches are literally feathered with crockets."—*MSS. Kerrich, Brit.Mus.*

[C] page 80.—A general view of that peculiar modification of the Gothick style, which prevailed in Italy before the period limited to 1437, may be more usefully presented in a tabular form.

*Dates, Dimensions, and Architects of Cathedrals, &c.
in Italy, Sicily, and Calabria.*

NORMAN AND GOTHICK.

NAMES.	DATE.	ARCHITECT, &C.
Genoa . . .	1125	Founded by Martino Doria.
Messina . . .	1180 }	Founded by Ruggiero Count
Palermo, MonteReale	1185 }	of Sicily, in 1100.
Benevento . .	1198	Bishop Ruggiero, his nephew.
Padua . . .	1231	Nicola da Pisa.
Arezzo . . {	1240 to 1260	} Lapo or Jacopo, a German.
Spoleto.		
Orvietto . . .	1290	Lorenzo Maitani.
Naples . . .	1260	Giovanni da Pisa.
Sienna . . .	1338	Lapo da Sienna.
Milan . . .	1387	Zamodia.

The churches in Sicily, which were erected either by Count Ruggiero or his successors, who formed the Norman dynasty, have not been, as yet, examined with scientific minuteness. None, for its great curiosity, deserves more than the Cathedral of Palermo.

[D] page 82.—It appears that, after the age of Charlemagne, in 835, Rumualde, an architect, constructed the Cathedral of Rheims ; Azon built that of Sees in Normandy, in 1060; in 1222, Robert of Lusarche began that of Amiens, which was finished after his death by his scholars, Thomas de Cormont and his son Renault. (*Le Noir.*) St. Denis, built by Eudes and Mathieu de Vendosme, and the façade by Suger, contains, in the crypt, the most ancient instance of sculptured capitals and ornamented building in France; and in the whole structure are seen complete specimens of the three æras of its architecture.

[E] page 82.—*Architectural Antiquities of Normandy*, by J. Sell Cotman, accompanied with historical and descriptive notices by Dawson Turner, F.A.S., two volumes, imperial folio, 1822.

A Tour in Normandy, for the purpose of investigating the Architectural Antiquities of the Duchy, by D. Turner, two volumes, octavo, 1820.

Pugin and Le Keux's *Engraved Specimens of the Architectural Antiquities of Normandy*, quarto, one volume, 1827.

Description Historique et Critique et Vües de Monumens Religieux et Civiles les plus remarquables du Département du Calvados (Caen), par T. de Jolimont, fol. 1825.

Ducarel's *Anglo-Norman Antiquities*, fol. 1767, translated, with copious Notes, by M. Léchaudé, Caen, 1823.

Whittington's *Historical Survey of Ecclesiastical Edifices in France*, octavo, second edition, 1811.

Boisserie, *Histoire et Description de la Cathédrale de Cologne, avec de Recherches sur Architecture des Anciennes Cathedrales*, imperial folio, with a volume of plates. 1827.

[F] page 84.—They are likewise to be observed at St. Georges de Boucherville, and St. Hildebert de Gournay. Sometimes two isolated columns rise from one base, and are crowned by one capital. At the church of Than, near Caen, the terminating arches of the nave are larger than the intermediate ones; at Jumieges, they alternately spring from round pillars, and from square piers with semi-cylindrical columns affixed to each of their sides; and at Pavilly they are supported by clustered columns, with unadorned capitals and enormous hexagonal bases.

[G] page 85.—*Cicognara* has observed (l. ii. p. 228) that the "oltra montani," or architects in the countries north of Italy, during the later centuries, had the ambition to enlarge, improve, and embellish the style of their ecclesiastical architecture; for they had persuaded themselves that the greatest possible beauty in an edifice consisted in the labour, difficulty, and expense of erecting it, and by loading it with ornaments of the most capricious description. They are best described in his own language, as the variety of discriminative terms may be curious to the intelligent reader: — "Alti loggiati, strani capitelli, di archi acuti che intercano arcati circulari ; di colonne longissime, isili, annodate, ritorte, spirali, aggrupate ; ponendo intorno alle maggiore porte dei tempj lunghe sfuggite di colonetti capillari, a guisa di prospettivi ; dando alle fenestre una configurazione di fissure furtive, più che aperture capaci al' introduzione libera e larga della luce — così constituerono quel ordine," which prevailed from 1350 to 1500, in the greater French and German churches.

" In Italy, Gothick architecture appears to have been introduced at a very early period, and to have acquired a degree of richness which the Gothick buildings of this country did not assume till many years afterward." Examples adduced are, a window in the Cathedral of Messina in 1120, and the Baptistery at Pisa, 1152—*Archæologia*, vol. xv. p. 363.

[H] page 89.—*Dimensions in English feet.*
CATHEDRAL, ROUEN.—Total length, f. 442 by 89. 11 inches. Nave, f. 210 by 27. Transept, f. 177. 8 by 27. Choir, f. 110 by 35. 6 inches. Louvre, f. 164. 8 high. General height, f. 91. Aisles, f. 45. 6 high. *External heights :* W. towers, f. 230. Façade, f. 180 wide, and f. 230 high. Spire, 380.

CHURCH OF ST. OUEN.—Total length, f. 451. 4 inches by f. 89, including the aisles. Vaulting, f. 100 high. Nave, f. 264. 4 by 36.10. Transept, f. 140.10 by 36.10. Choir, f. 110. 6 to the chevet, and f. 76. 6 beyond it. Pillars of the nave, eleven on either side, f. 15. 6 apart. Those of the louvre and central tower are f. 10. 10 in diameter. There are one hundred and twenty-five windows, and three roses. The octagon tower is f. 240 high.

We may acquire a more immediate knowledge of these proportions, by comparing them with others in our own large churches.

Church of St. Ouen, nave, f. 36. 10 wide ; f. 108 high. *Westminster Abbey,* f. 38, and 101. Louvre, under the central tower, f. 164. 8 high. At *York,* f. 180. Choir of *Gloucester,* f. 34. 6 wide ; f. 86 high. Of *York,* f. 43, and f. 101. 6 high. *King's College Chapel, Cambridge,* f. 290 by 45, and f. 78 high. *Henry VIIth's Chapel, Westminster,* f. 103. 4 by f. 35.9, and 60.4 high.

Proportion of the excess of the height beyond the width, in several choirs and chapels.

Westminster Abbey, f. 62. 8.	Gloucester, Choir, f. 51. 6.
Hen. VIIth's Chapel, f. 40. 7.	King's Coll. Chapel, f. 33.
York . . f. 58. 6.	
Rouen Cathedral, f. 45.	St. Ouen, f. 72.

Comparison is the only true scale by which an architectural judgment can be formed.

In the church of St. Ouen is a slab with two portraits in brass, of an old and a young man, in lay habits, each of which points to a plan upon a tablet in one hand, and with a compass in the other. Inscription:—ALEXANDRE DE BERNEVAL Maistre de Œuvres des Maçonerie de ceste eglise M CCCC XI.

[I] page 95.—*Actual measurement of the component parts of several chief Cathedrals in France, taken in French feet, and adapted to the English.*

NÔTRE DAME, PARIS.—Western towers, f. 221 high. Within the walls, f. 492. 6 long. Nave, f. 243. 9 by 42. 3. Two double aisles with galleries over them, of equal dimensions. Choir, f. 157. 1 by 37. 11. Vaulting, f.112. 8 high. South rose window, f. 45. 6 in diameter.

RHEIMS CATHEDRAL. — Façade, f. 140. Towers, f. 253 high. Length, f. 438. 8 by 93, including aisles. Vaulting, f. 116 high. Nave, f. 37. 11 wide. Transept, f. 150. Aisles, f. 22. Triforium or gallery, f. 10 high.

CHARTRES CATHEDRAL.—Old spire, f. 342 ; new, 378 (the highest double spires in France). Length, f. 376 by 103. Vaulting, f. 106 high. Nave, f. 222 by 46. Transept, f. 195 by 40. Pillars, f. 8. 6 in diameter, with statues of the Apostles f. 8 high. Choir, f. 114 by 46.

BAYEUX CATHEDRAL.—Length 296 by 76, and 76 high. Nave, f. 140 by 48. Aisles, f. 17 wide. Transept, f. 113.

Choir, f. 118 by 36.   Central Tower, f. 224 high : the
western, f. 230 each.

The finest French cathedral, in point of dimensions, is that
of Amiens.

[K] page 98.—An Essay on the origin and progress of
Gothick architecture, traced in and deducted from the ancient
edifices of Germany, from the eighth to the sixteenth century,
by *Dr. G. Möller*, architect, &c. (excellently translated, 8vo.
1824.) The original work was published at Darmstadt in
1819—1822, in fourteen numbers, imperial folio, containing
eighty-four plates, all of which are of Cathedral Churches in
Germany. In 1830 was published at Cambridge what the
very well informed author (Professor Wheley) calls merely
a subsidiary "*Essay on German Churches, with Remarks on
the Origin of Gothick Architecture*," 8vo. It is, indeed,
replete with novel and most satisfactory intelligence upon
those subjects. He observes, that " the adoption of the
pointed arch in vaulted roofs arose from the requirements of
vaulting, and from the necessity of having arches of equal
heights with different widths ; and it appears that the succession of contrivances to which these circumstances gave birth,
is found more completely developed, and probably more ancient in German edifices than in our own."

" Some of the modes of building which had been only
hypothetical suppositions, when applied to English churches,
were found to have existed as common architectural prac-
tices in Germany."—*Essay, (Wheley,)* p. 3.

Moller attributes to the architecture of Germany two distinct styles—first, that of the southern provinces, which were
more immediately under the Roman power, and was borrowed
from them by a rude imitation ; second, that which originated
in the twelfth and thirteenth centuries, the leading peculiarity
of which was the pitched roof of extreme height, instead of
the flat gables, which rendered lofty internal pointed arches
under the triforia essentially necessary ; pinnacles, filled up
with the form of ornamented windows, surmounted by gables,

and finished by pyramids. " The main forms, as well as the whole system of their ornaments, are in perfect harmony in these churches, and rest upon the pointed gable, the pyramid, and the pointed arch. A similar harmony of form reigns in all the best German churches, from the thirteenth to the fourteenth century." With respect to ornamental carving, a prevalence will be observed of leaves, variously composed and in garlands, above any geometrical form. Such are frequently very finely finished, and offer very bold profiles. The small canopies over the statues are shaped like little towers, which admitted of greater embellishment in the progress of the art." The German antiquaries and artists have published, or are engaged in several magnificent works, of the greatest expense and curiosity.

Moller has published *Monumens de l'Architecture Allemande*, with descriptions in German, 15 livraisons, folio, with numerous etched plates, (nine plates elephant size,) illustrative of the Cathedral of Cologne in detail.

Plans and Elevations of the Church of St. Elizabeth, at Marburg, folio. *Large ditto of the Cathedral of Oppenheim.*

Boisserie's Cathedral of Cologne, and the Architecture of the Upper Rhine, a magnificent work, with a volume of plates, elephant folio.

[L] page 102.—"The Abbey of Altenburg, at a little distance from Cologne, now a manufactory, had a church of the same admirable style, and which still exists : this is said to have been built by the same person who was the architect of Cologne ; and as it was finished, we are enabled, from the exquisite lightness and grace of its interior, to form some conception of the splendid and majestic vision which would have been embodied by the completion of the original plan of Cologne." — *Essay, Wheley,* p. 67. Many, and those among the finest specimens, it is much to be deplored, both in France and Germany, have been converted to profane purposes. Some of the most highly-finished churches in Rouen are now workshops and *messageries.*

A GLOSSARY

OF THE FRENCH TERMS OF ARCHITECTURE USED BY
THE MASTER-MASONS OF THAT NATION, AND BY THE
AUTHORS ON THAT SUBJECT.

Croisée — croisées fenêtres, the transept of a church — the large windows of a church.

Roses placées à ses deux extremités, the circular or marigold windows, generally three, in a church ; one at the west end, and one at either end of the transept.

Jubé, a lofty gallery or pulpit at the entrance of the choir, from whence the precentor regulated the choir at high mass.

La nef, navis ecclesiæ, the mid-space of a church, from the west end to the transept, or to the choir.

L'axe de la nef, the central line of the roof of the nave.

Les maitresses voutes de l'église, qui comprennent la nef, la croisée, et la chœur, the principal roofs, those of the nave, the transept, and the choir.

La voute, a roof formed by stones which support each other — in Gothick architecture, by ribs of stone, springing from a centre.

Le rez de chaussée, the ground or basement, as high as the water-table.

Des piliers qui sont accompagnés de culs de lampe, et les petits dais destinés à recevoir des statues, a kind of pendentives which are placed below the intersections of Gothick roofs : — canopies and pediments of niches which contain statues.

Faisceaux de colonnes, the small pillars round the central one ; reeded pillars ; clustered pillars.

Portails, the great entrance of churches, occupying much of the façade. An ornamented porch.

Tenans en fer, a piece of iron bound round a square, upright beam, and fastened by a loop.

Les arcs-boutants et contreforts, upright or flying buttresses; abutments to support the clere-story.

Les pyramides et l'amortissement, finials which rise from a square or polygonal turret.

Les croterés de la balustrade, small pillars or pediments for statues placed on the summit.

Les frontons, the highest triangular part of the façade, including the nave.

Les mineaux des fenêtres, the mullions and transomes of a window.

Les montures des piedroits, the mouldings or grooves of the jambs or head of a doorcase or window, into which are inserted canopies and figures of small size, and which follow the course of the arch.

Les murs contrebutés, the walls of a church abutted by flying arches between the windows.

Les piliers boutants des quatre angles de la croisée qui reçoivent à la fois la retombée de trois arcs-boutants, plain buttresses which are the basis of flying arches.

Galeries bordées de ballustrades à jour, galleries on the roof, guarded by ballustrades of open work.

Un luxe d'artétes rosaces et des culs de lamps ou pendentifs, toujours croissans jusques à la renaissance, the richness and variety of the bosses, roses, and pendants in the roofs, which were still increased till the revival of the Roman architecture.

Grosses poutres avec figures à l'extremité, large beams with little figures at their extremities, carved out of timber.

Bas-côtés, lower side-aisles.

Escaliers tournant en vis, noel or winding staircases. *Vis* is the small circular pillar which ascends from the bottom to the top, the steps like a screw.

Les retombées réposent, &c. that part of an arch which has its bearings without a centre.

Arcades sur bassées, low arches which rest upon the ground.

Pignons à jour, les tous enrichis de statues, perforated or thorough-light pediments, surmounted by statues.

Fenêtres prises dans le comble, construites en ogive, windows resting on the walls and taken out of the roof, finished in a pointed form, with finials, &c.

Chardons, the points of iron palisades, wrought like fleurs-de-lis.

Montans, the moulding or projecting member which finishes the cornice of a building.

Pourtour de la nef, the internal extent of the nave in all its parts.

Toit en pavillon, a roof, the timber frame of which is raised like a tent or a pavilion.

Statues adossées à chaque pilier, statues affixed and placed with pedestals and canopies against pillars.

Bas-reliefs gravées en creux, bas reliefs with under-cutting.

Pierre de liais, freestone from Caen ; liais.

Les boisseries, exquisite carving in alto and bas-relief in wood.

Couronnement Gothique d'un porte, the pediment of Gothick moulding placed on the face of a wall, above a doorcase.

Gargouilles, masquerons à figure chimérique, waterspouts of a capricious form in the parapets of churches. At Rouen were two human figures, called Adam and Eve, with closed mouths, the water passing as in nature. Gargouille means literally an open throat : the figure is generally that of a flying dragon.

Clochetons—clochetons à jour délicatement travaillés, turrets thorough-lighted, with open lace-work in stone.

Clochard, a campanile or bell-tower, always detached from the main body of a building ; sometimes constructed with timber-frame, covered with lead or slate tiles.

Menuiserie, carved in wood, or moulded with iron or plaster.

Un toit pointú. This very sharply-pointed roof was used generally for church-towers : others similar, but of greater span, when applied to the towers of castles or palaces, are called pavilions, either oblong or circular, from their obvious resemblance to a tent.

Massifs, an upright buttress or pedestal, supporting a statue or figure.

Nervures, additional ribs or veins diverging from the top of the vaulting pillar.

Conoids, spandril, a pyramid with many sides, with a curvilinear slope; an inverted curvilinear pyramid. The concavo-convex vaulting.

Voussures, separate hollows of a vaulting.

Chrochet. Crocket, a hook, or curled lock, like hair.

Pendentives, au milieu duquel est placée une image, pendants, having a canopy and figure carved in the sides.

Lunette, a vaulted bay window made in the sides or flank of an arched roof, or a cupola, in order to admit light. *Louvre,* the same, common in halls for the emission of smoke.

Fenêtres lucarnes, windows projecting from the roof, nearly as high as the ridge, and which rest upon the side walls, and are richly ornamented in front.

Grenier ou dormier fenêtre. Grenier windows are made in the high roof, to light the granary—Dormier, for the dormitory. The above are peculiar to the large mansions erected about the reign of Francis the First.

Perpendre, a large stone balanced by equalling the thickness of a wall.

Quarelles, the square space included within the arcade or division.

Hovels avec gabletz, niches composed of canopies and pediments.

L'œil des aisles, the large circular windows in the nave and transept, filled with rich stained glass, set in mosaic patterns without figures.

La retour d'équerre, right angle.

Une galerie intérieure prise dans épaisseur de murs de face, an interior wall, taken out of the thickness of the wall, from the face of it.

Chambranle, an ornamented groove made in the splay of a door-case.

Le fond de l'apside, the end of the absis and choir. This

kind of termination prevailed in the thirteenth century : it has a Roman origin, and has been copied in all Norman buildings.

Contre-retables en menuiserie, carved wainscot behind the altar—reredoss, usually of rich cabinet-work in wood, but in other instances of bas-relief in stone.

Petits dais travaillés à jour, a small canopy over a niche wrought in open work.

Les contours de la voussure, des arceaux, the outline of the vault or retiring surface of a doorcase.

Le trumeau de la porte, a pillar placed from the base to the centre of a large door-case, sometimes sculptured with a niche containing the figure of a Madona.

Cadre ogive, a frame in the shape of a pointed arch. The term *ogive* has been applied by French writers to describe the pointed in distinction to the semicircular arch.

Les arcs rampants, flying arches which spring from buttresses to support a wall.

La charpente de grand comble, the timber-frame of the chief roof.

Doubles bas-côtés formant des larges peristyles, side aisles divided by a peristyle, as at Nôtre Dame, which makes them appear to be double.

Grosses colonnes isolées et engagés dans les murs, great pillars insulated, or which are detached from the walls.

Travée, the space between two beams, or between one and the wall.

Amortissement : it includes all the ornaments or statues placed upon the summit of a church. *Fastigium.*

Arcs ogives et les nervures croissées diagonalment, pointed arches with ribs, which cross each other diagonally. " Longitudinal and transverse bands were first used in roofs. The rib ran along the top of the vault."

Evidées à jour, wrought or voided open work ; perforated parapets.

Chapelle de Vierge situé au chevet de l'eglise, the chapel of the Virgin, always placed beyond the choir.

Comble en charpente en la forme de pavillon, a roof, the timber-frame of which forms a pavilion.

Une porche en saillie, a porch which projects far beyond a building.

Le linteau du chambranle de la porte, the lintel, or piece of wood or stone placed to support the masonry above the door-way.

Sculptures et d'entrelacs, carvings and scrolls interlaced over grooves and mouldings.

Obélisques à jour, finials perforated or thorough-lighted with carved work.

Naissances de voutes ou arrachemens en pierre, the part above the impost, from which the arch springs to the centre : —*servent à contrebuter la poussée des voutes,* to abut against the splaying or lateral pressure of the wall.

Le fastige du toit du chœur, the ridge of the roof of the choir.

Trumeau qui sépare la porte en deux, the upright which divides the space of the great doorway.

Grands arcs en pierre, en plein ceinture, principal arches of stone, with circular heads.

Cadre ogive, grand cadran de la porte, the great pointed moulding which encloses the door-case.

Traves de la nef, cross-beams.

Le maitre autel, the high altar placed in the chevet of the choir.

Les voutes qui par leurs divisions en angles, rentrans et saillants, decorées de figures et de rinceaux d'ornemens, vaults with intersections of salient and retiring angles, decorated with carvings.

Ceps de vignes découpés à jour qui suivent les contours des arcs ogives ainsi que des entrelacs et des rinceaux, branches of vines which follow the outline of the pointed arches, as well as scrolls and other foliage with stems.

Tympan au-dessus de la porte, the space under the arch, above the doorway.

L'avant corps de la porte, the projected building of the porch.

Piliers ornés sur chaque face de colonnes engagés, pillars ornamented on each face of the principal columns.

Grosses tourells surmontées de cones, large turrets surmounted with spires.

Branches d'ogives dans les voutes, nouvelles arcades en ogives, sections of vaults made by ribs, in the form of pointed arches.

Ressaut, a projecting moulding or fillet in the splay of a Gothick arch.

Fueilleur, the groove into which doors or windows are shut.

Arcs doubleux, a double arcade on either side the nave, exactly formed, one above the other, as at Nôtre Dame at Paris.

Surmontées de clochetons et de pyramides, small towers with low spires.

Rond-point du chœur, chevet, the eastern termination of the choir, round or polygonal.

Grand comble de l'église est couvert en ardoises, blue slate, applied as the covering of roofs instead of lead.

La toiture de la croisée, the roofing of the transept.

Escaliers en limaçon, en vis, a winding staircase; a noel, as in belfries; *beffroi*.

Arc ogive ornée d'un découpure à jour, a salient angle forming two faces, which passes under a vault from two opposite angles; a cross-springer; or merely a ribbed arch pointed, with open work enclosed within it.

L'extrados de la voute, external facings of the ribs of a vault.

Cartouches, a tablet of stone of a capricious form, with carvings or inscriptions.

Façade surmontée d'un pignon, principal front surmounted by a triangular face, nearest the roof, and highly ornamented.

Des trefles découpés à jour, trefoils wrought in open work, and frequently other leaves.

Contreforts surmontés de clochetons et de pyramides, flying buttresses surmounted at the base with turrets and finials.

Extrados orné des jolies découpures, external facing of the arch, ornamented with open work.

Couronne ducal travaillée à jour, ducal crown, or balustrade of a tower, composed of open work, as those at Rouen.

Beffroi, belfredus, borrowed from the English term belfry.

Nervures croissées, cross-springers or ribs supporting vaults.

Centre de rond-point, the centre of the chevet or termination of the choir.

Bas côtés, side aisles under the triforium or gallery.

Dans œuvre, withinside the building.

Pendentifs ou encorbellemens, pendants or corbel-stones, so placed as to project one over the other.

Portes pratiquées sur des profonds voussures ogives, doors in the thickness or substance of a pointed arched door-case or vault.

Deux jambages de la porte, the two jambs or sides of the above-mentioned.

En arrière corps, part of a building placed behind another.

Charpente, the roof of timber-frame.

DISCOURSE III.

FLORID GOTHICK. 1400—1520.

CHURCH architecture in England, when it had reached the zenith of excellence, very soon passed beyond it. Simplicity, with its harmonious effect, was now superseded by an accumulation of minute ornament, which invention and skill were employed to supply, and caprice frequently usurped the place of beautiful construction. This has been designated the FLORID, with as clear a definition as by any other subsequently made.

I have already noticed, that in the course of the twelfth and thirteenth centuries such alterations of the Saxon and Anglo-Norman styles, by which it had been reconciled to the Gothick model, were frequently made by those ecclesiastics whose opulence and taste led them to practise or patronize the science of architecture. We have abundant memoirs of bishops and abbots who cultivated with assiduity and success the elements of geometry and the principles of decoration, when to be applied to structures of which they had furnished the plans, or at least had suggested the main design.*

The allowed utility of certain discriminative terms has led to many, which have been offered, but with doubtful acceptation. By some authors, too, many divisions have been specified which have incumbered the purpose of distinctness. " Where, as in not unfrequent instances, a style of general analogy has been mixed with one that is antecedent to it ; or where one manner of construction or ornament has, as it were, slid into another, to mark or fix the precise gradation or transition has often proved a perplexing rather than a satisfactory task. In fact, a single church should not absolutely decide the chronology ; but the age would be more truly inferred from many churches, resembling each other." The earlier has been designated as the " Plantagenet," and the later as the " Tudor " architecture, as being applicable respectively to those reigns.

Of the Anglo-Norman and Early English or Lancet-arch style, I have already treated. The next in succession has been denominated, from the admission of more ornament, the " Decorative," or " Florid," which has been defined to differ from the Early English principally upon that account. From a characteristic, to which

* See Note [A] page 163.

there scarcely occurs an exception, the succeeding style has been termed the " Perpendicular," as having all its lines and forms drawn
upwards or enhanced from either the circular
or horizontal ;* and it differs mainly in having
certain perpendicular members, mullions, pannels, &c. which, in the last mentioned, are only
so in part.

The fifteenth century, beginning with the
reign of the fourth, and extending nearly to
the close of that of the seventh Henry (1400—
1509), will be found to include the total progress of that particular manner of building,
called, for the sake of distinction, the " Florid
Gothick." It has been lately advanced, if not
proved, that we borrowed much from the lower
style of German Gothick, and more particularly
from that which was then prevalent in Burgundy. In the subsequent age, even that style
was abandoned for the inventions of Holbein,
and John of Padua, in England, imperfectly
adopted from those of Brunelleschi and Palladio, the great reformers of architecture in Italy.

* See *Rickman's* useful and very judicious *Attempt to
discriminate the styles of English Architecture*, 8vo.

Cottingham, in his Introduction to his *Account of King
Henry the Seventh's Chapel at Westminster*, divides the subject
of Gothick architecture into three grand periods. His definitions are clearly and distinctly given, and they present a view
of the transitions which succeeded each other, and their dates,
with a sound knowledge of his profession.

The leading peculiarity of this later manner of building is chiefly to be perceived in the vaultings of roofs connected with windows, and the construction and ornaments of cloisters and towers.*

In the roofs,† the intricacy of figures described by the intersecting of cross-springers, or diagonal ribs, and the exact adaptation of the complex groins of the vault to the heads of the windows, which are more pointed than in the preceding age, together with the scarcely credible height and thinness of the side walls, fill the eye of the astonished spectator with an instantaneous alarm for his own safety.

———— Jam lapsura cadenti
Imminet assimilis.   ÆN. l. vi. 503.

---

* Comparative mensuration.

	LENGTH.	BREADTH.
King's College Chapel .	340	78 feet.
Windsor .	218	65
Henry VIIth's . .	120	64

For the complete external renovation of this last-mentioned structure, the sum of 42,028l. was defrayed by Parliament between the years 1807 and 1822. The whole was most ably and satisfactorily executed by the late T. Gayfere, the master-mason, who has published an ample account both of the elevation and interior, in imperial folio, comprising a complete series of architectural delineations.

† Hearne informs us, that Adam de Sodbury, abbot of Glastonbury in 1330, after having vaulted the roof of the nave with stone, " adorned it with beautiful paintings." The same was done as late as 1500, at Winchester and Chichester, by the bishops Fox and Sherborne, and had, indeed, an ancient origin.

A fertile source of decoration, peculiar to the Florid Gothick, is pierced pannelling, richly traced with graceful foliage, and indiscriminately introduced into every part of the original design. Although it exhibits the virtues and power of the chisel, and the patient skill of the artist, it unquestionably diffuses a gaudiness over the whole, which greatly tends to diminish the imposing, yet sober effect, which was peculiar to the Gothick in its meridian splendour.

After having varied and exhausted the forms of leaves, knots, and bosses with rosettes, or pendentives surrounded with pannels or small niches containing statues,* the artists frequently introduced images of angels with musical instruments in full choir, over the high altar.†

Tracery, particularly when spread over roofs, was expanded into a beautiful system of harmonious intricacy. Yet a recurrence of these minute parts fatigues the eye, and prevents a comprehension of the whole design at a first view.

A true knowledge of construction is the basis of architectural fame; and superfluity betrays

---

* Where the tall shafts that mount in massy pride,
  Their mingling branches shoot from side to side;
  Where elfin sculptors with fantastic clue
  O'er the long roof their wild embroidery drew.

T. WARTON.

† In the choir at Gloucester. See Appendix, p. 183.

no less a deficiency in real science, than the obvious weakness of constituent parts, proportionably to each other. The four-centred arch is the distinguishing feature of the Florid Gothick, for there is scarcely a building of that period in which it does not predominate, and which has not a groined roof with a ridged band. These edifices are magnificent as a whole, and are extremely delicate in detail, and, consequently, are more frequently admired as the perfection of the Gothick style by the generality of observers.

In the windows we remark an expanse beyond all proportion when singly placed; or otherwise, that they are crowded into a very inadequate space. Circular windows were in usage with the Saxons. The architrave of that at Barfreston is filled with chimæras, masks, and grotesque figures; and the divisions are made by pillars, the capitals of which are formed by human heads. But the Catherine-wheel window was certainly borrowed in the fourteenth century, from our neighbours on the Continent, but distantly imitated. Its more usual and ancient English name is the Marigold. In most of the great east and west windows of this age, a circle or rosette, beautifully variegated, is introduced into the upper compartment. Few cathedrals in France are without them. They are rarely seen in

England, in a detached form, but only occasionally introduced, as at Canterbury, York, Chichester, Lichfield, Westminster, Lincoln.

The perforated parapet and pierced battlement were first introduced towards the close of the same century, and subsequently gained both variety of forms and greater lightness, by being made open to the air. The elevation is infinitely improved by them.

The chief pinnacles of the Beauchamp chapel at Warwick have flat terminations: upon these, large crests, usually beasts, carved in stone, and holding vanes or banners of metal, were originally placed. The same, likewise, were at first on Windsor chapel. These ornaments have been removed from both.

About this period it became more usual to place carved escocheons of armorial bearings, held against the breast of half the human figure winged as angels, and affixed as corbels, under the springing of an open arch or groining.

I omit, in this part of the general disquisition, to describe many important accessories to large ecclesiastical buildings, which, in later centuries, were most remarkable for dimensions and beauty. Of such, I have given a critical examination in the general appendix of illustrations.

Cloisters, which were originally, with few exceptions, unornamented enclosures for the purposes of exercise or religious offices, were then found to admit of the full embellishment of the shrines or chapels existing in other parts of the church. This new application of the ornamental particles was assisted in a very striking degree by perspective, and the almost infinite reduplication of a small vault, springing from four semicircular groins at the angles, which rest upon pilasters. For this kind of fretted roof upon a diminutive scale, the term " fan-work " has been used—an idea suggested perhaps by a certain resemblance to the shape of an old-fashioned feather fan, as spreading from the base.

In beauty and variety of carvings, no cloisters in England exceeded that attached to St. Stephen's chapel, Westminster, when in its perfect state, and that which is still so at Gloucester. In general, from the opportunities which occurred to me of making the observation, this kind of building on the Continent is extremely inferior. Almost every convent has its cloisters; and those annexed to the great churches are probably the best; but they are chiefly plain unornamented enclosures, for the purposes of exercise and devotion. The most extensive I saw, those at Pisa, while the contiguous buildings are in a style of the highest Lombard-Gothick, are in a great measure void of architectural embellishment; which defi-

ciency is supplied by the works of Cimabue, or
of Giotto and his scholars. Less frequently,
indeed, the walls are covered with fresco paintings, of which the more celebrated instances
are, that at Florence, in the monastery of the
Annunciation, where is the Madonna del Sacco,
by Andrea del Sarto; and that of the Carthu-
sians at Paris, where Le Sueur has so admirably
described the life and death of St. Bruno.* In
the fifteenth century, the windows of cloisters
in England and France were generally filled
with scriptural stories, in series, in stained
glass, and the walls sometimes painted in
fresco. The Dance of Macabre (Holbein's
Dance of Death) was painted on the walls of
the cloisters of the Innocents at Paris, and in
those of Old St. Paul's cathedral, London, which
were double, one placed above the other.

In the first æra of Norman architecture,
towers of very large dimensions and great
height were placed either in the centre or at
the west end of the cathedral and conventual
churches. Many of these, which now lose the
appearance of their real height from their extreme solidity, as at Winchester, St. Alban's,
and Tewkesbury, were, as before remarked,
finished by tall spires of wood covered with

* These are now in the Louvre gallery, having been transferred from pannel to canvass with admirable intelligence and
skill.

lead.   Old St. Paul's, Lincoln, Tewkesbury, and Malmsbury, had, each of them, a leaden spire of amazing sublimity; and in monkish annals are found accounts of many others, which have been destroyed by tempests.   Salis- bury, as it was almost the earliest, was the most successful attempt to construct them with stone.   The towers,* which are known to have been erected in the fifteenth century, (with the single exception of that at Lincoln,) espe- cially towards the close of it, have certainly gained little in point of aërial elevation, but are much more beautifully constructed; as they are usually panneled with arcades and half-mullions, like those which compose a win- dow, from the base to the summit.   Nothing can exceed the boldness of the parapets and pinnacles, which consist of open embattled work in numerous instances; the most remarkable of which are seen in the western counties of England.†

It is a singular fact, that during the com- motions between the houses of York and Lan- caster, and their adherents, so prejudicial to the progress of the arts of civilization, archi- tecture in England flourished in a great de- gree.   The superior ecclesiastics were con- fined to their cloisters, as few of them had

* See Note [B] page 163.   † See Note [C] page 164.

taken an active part in the dispute; and some of the fairest structures which remain,* arose in consequence of wealth accumulated by instigating the noble and affluent to contribute to the general emulation of splendid churches, built under their own inspection. One of the most beautiful sepulchral chapels is that erected by the executors of Richard Beauchamp, earl of Warwick, in the reign of Henry VI. which adjoins the parish-church at Warwick: lately restored without taste.

The choir at Gloucester, which has no equal, was completed during that turbulent period, by abbot Sebroke, with the arcade which supports the tower.

The meek Henry VI. better suited by his education and habits to have been a priest than a potentate, encouraged this prevailing taste by his own example. King's College chapel at Cambridge was begun only under his

---

* A cavil has been raised against my former assertion, in the *Observations on Architecture*, " that the reign of Henry VI. was particularly marked by the actual erection of some most beautiful ecclesiastical buildings,"—the usual consequence of half information and flippancy. What will the author say of the nave of Canterbury, Bishop Beckington's works in the cathedral of Wells, Prior Silkstede's at Winchester, the Divinity School and All Souls' College at Oxford, Redcliffe church, Bristol, and the singularly fine towers of Gloucester, Thornbury, Taunton, and St. Stephen's, Bristol; — not to quote others in the north of England?

auspices and at his expense, and although he
was prevented from carrying on his munificent
intentions by his personal distresses and vio-
lent death, when these celebrated walls had
arisen scarcely twenty feet from their foundation, it is evident that the original plan, given
under the direction of Nicholas Cloos (afterwards Bishop of Ely), was partially adhered
to by Edward IV., Richard III., and by
Henry VII., whose will was performed by his
executors, in the first part of the reign of his
son.

King's College chapel was the wonder of its
own, as it has been of every succeeding age.
A minute detail of its history, if collected from
genuine documents, will tend to throw a light
on the state of architecture, as the grandest
example, now perfect, of the " Florid Gothick,"
and on the manner in which so vast a work was
conducted to its gradual completion.   Hitherto,
we have had more general praise of its beauty
and excellence than satisfactory accounts of its
origin and progress, even in those disastrous
times.

One of the first acts of the ill-fated Henry
VI., after he had taken the government into
his own hands, was the foundation of two
magnificent colleges at Cambridge and Eton.
His chief counsellor, with whom these plans

were consulted, was William of Waynflete, and who lived to be himself the founder of Magdalene College, Oxford.

In the twenty-second and following year of his reign, and the same of his age, the king charged his duchy of Lancaster with a payment of 2000*l.* a-year, towards the erection of his two colleges at Cambridge and Eton ; and he confirmed this donation in his will, (dated March 24, 1447,) to be continued for twenty years.*

Eton was designed "to be replenished with goodly windowes and vaultes, laying apart superfluities of too great curious workes of entaile and busy mouldinge." Little attention was paid to this simple injunction by the architects of Henry VII. The monarchs of the house of York appear to have patronised the great work at Cambridge, in which but a slow progress had been previously made. Yet the sums given by them, were either so sparingly or irregularly paid, that the roof, external ornaments, turrets, pinnacles, vaulting, the small oratories and glazing, remained to be finished by Henry VII., and this celebrated structure was completed by his executors, soon after his decease.

* See Henry the Sixth's will, first printed in *Royal and Noble Wills*, 4to. p. 191.

A more commanding elevation than that of this Chapel will not be found in any other part of the English dominions. Being a mass, the height of which is sufficient to relieve its great length, it instantly communicates an idea of Gothick grandeur, almost without parallel.

The chief cause of our admiration upon the first entrance into this chapel, is the unity of design: from which it appears to be smaller than in reality, or that upon frequent examination it would do, a circumstance invariably happening to those who visit St. Peter's. The grand whole instantly fills the eye without any abatement or interruption. When we find leisure for the detail, we may admire the infinite parts which compose the roof, and the exquisitely finished arms and cognizances of the house of Lancaster; and regret that being so large, they should be stuck against the finely-wrought pilasters like monumental tablets in a parish church. The stained glass heightens the effect of the stonework, and gives it a tint which can never be produced by any wash of lime, with whatever substance it may be compounded, when the light passes through diminutive squares of raw white glass.

King Henry VI., as it is evident from the injunction he makes, in the instance of both his colleges, against superfluous masonry, never intended a roof so splendidly elaborate as that designed and perfected under the auspices of his successors. His objection was not to the difficulty or impracticability of the work, for several of great, though not of equal extent, had been erected prior to and during his reign, but to the enormous expense it would require.

Considering therefore the roof of King's College chapel as the utmost effort of constructive skill, and the paragon of architectural beauty, it may not be irrelevant to recapitulate briefly the works of that nature of sufficient celebrity which had been finished in England.*

The more ancient roofs in those cathedrals where the Norman style prevails, were composed of wood in rafters only: but in the progress of architecture, those were concealed by pannels, and painted in a kind of mosaic of several colours.† The surface was even made flat by these means, as in the transept of Peterborough. The naves, both of that cathedral and of Ely, afford instances of the ancient timber roof.

Of the vaulting with stone the more frequent examples are in the reign of Henry III. It was formed by groined arches, springing from corbels in the side walls, between the windows, and, when first invented, was composed of plain ribs of stone, called cross springers, with

* See Note [D] page 164.   † See Note [E] page 165.

a key-stone in the centre of them, and the interstices were filled up with some lighter materials.   There was always a space of several feet
intervening between the vaulting and the roof.
As the principle of their construction became
more scientifically understood and practised,
about the reign of Edward III., by the more
frequent and complicated intersection of the
ribs, more ornament was introduced, and delicately carved orbs and rosettes were applied,
where not necessary to any architectural purpose.   The arch of the vault was pointed, and
that highly embellished part of it did not, at
first, extend many feet on either side the common centre.

This circumstance is remarkable in the choir
at Lincoln, Our Lady's chapel at Ely, and many
others erected during the fourteenth century.
In the choir at Gloucester this elaborate work
is spread over the whole roof, in an equal profusion.   To reach a higher degree of excellence, probably because a greater difficulty, the
architects of the latter æra invented an arch,
from four centres, flattened, and with groins
hemispherically wrought.   That peculiar species of architecture and carving called fan-
work (from its resemblance to a feather fan),
which, on account of its extreme cost and delicacy, had been confined hitherto to cloisters
and sepulchral chapels, was now applied to

whole roofs ; and with an equal defiance of cost and labour, made to supersede all the excellence of construction and finishing, that had previously been attainable. It is an allowable conjecture, that this new method was either known to few of the master-masons, or was too expensive for frequent adoption, upon a large scale.

Certain it is, that the vaults of Windsor, the choir of Winton, King's College, and Henry the Seventh's chapels were commenced and completed within twenty years ; and that no farther attempts of consequence were subsequently made.

The tradition, that Sir Christopher Wren declared " that the construction of King's College chapel was beyond his comprehension, but that if any person would describe to him where the first stone should be placed, he would then be enabled to effect it," is not altogether deserving of credit. Mr. Walpole took it from the notes of G. Vertué, who might have been told it, among other wonders, by the verger who showed the chapel.

The point of difficulty will be solved, in a great measure, if, instead of contemplating the roof, as a whole or entire work, we consider the space only which is contained within four buttresses, as independent and complete in itself ; and the connexion between each compartment concealed, for the purpose of producing a very surprising effect of elongation. One proof that the vault consists of many such individual parts, is the agreement with master masons for each "severey," or partition, to be engaged for as a distinct undertaking, and to be paid for in proportion. Allowing this fact, the length ceases to be wonderful, excepting on account of the labour and expense.*

The hemispherical carved courses of the groins, as I have been assured by a very able master-mason, might have been worked on the ground, and with the key-stones, though of a ton weight each, raised to that height, by means of an ancient instrument now called a *Lewis*, of the powers of which a curious account appears in the Archæologia.† My informant has frequently elevated stones of nearly twice that weight, by the same means, in the magnificent restorations made in Arundel Castle, by the late Duke of Norfolk. The idea that the carving was excavated from a solid arch, as the easier mode, is not worth attention; nor would it have been very practicable,

Where ancient art her dædal fancies played
In the quaint mazes of the crisped roof.

T. WARTON.

---

* See Note [F] page 165.   † Vol. x. page 223.

The high honour of being the designer of this superb fabric has been, perhaps, too hastily attributed to a Fleming, named Cloos, or to his son Nicholas, as the sole architect. The last mentioned having died in 1453, it is not possible that he had any share in the amended plan which was adopted by Henry the Seventh. Great as the merit is, which is due to the unknown designer, the execution deserves a still higher degree of praise : and the names of John Woolrich, Henry Semark, and John Wastell, may be handed down to posterity as the most skilful master-masons of their age and nation.

The remark may probably have more novelty than justness, but I am of opinion, that the admiration which the inspection of the vault of King's College chapel universally excites, is directed to an inadequate object, if it be other than of the complex beauty and the labour which the formation of such a roof must have required and exhausted. A traveller who views the pyramids, knowing previously that their construction was practicable, will rather wonder at an expense in which the powers of calculation would be lost.

The skreen which divides the choir from the antechapel is of rich sculpture in wood, and was probably the work of some of those foreign artists, who received so great encouragement from Henry VIII. Holbein carved a whole-length small figure of him in wood; and I have seen another in alto relievo, of the same material. This delicate art was introduced into England by Pietro Toriggiano and his followers, and a school was established here, which existed, till Grinling Gibbons eclipsed all former fame.

A leading peculiarity in the French and German cathedrals is, that the nave and choir are almost always surrounded by separate oratories or small chapels. This mode of constructing the larger churches occurred but seldom in those of our own country, in the earlier periods. But in the prevalence of the Florid style, an imitation of that distribution of the ground plan was adopted, and more conspicuous instances are not found, than in the twelve oratories or small chapels of King's College, and the eight which surround Henry the Seventh's, Westminster Abbey.

Humphrey Duke of Gloucester was the munificent patron of learning and learned men. He began the Divinity School at Oxford, and the Public Library above it, in 1427: the fretted and pendentive roof was completed in 1480. It is of a flat arch, and is much too low for its length. Bosses of the groined roof are wrought into filligrain work, extending over the intersections, which are visible through it.

When Edward IV. had gained peaceable possession of the crown, he rebuilt the royal chapel at Windsor, probably from a design of Beauchamp Bishop of Sarum, whom he appointed surveyor of his works. But the glory of this style and age was the sepulchral chapel erected by Henry VII. at Westminster. The exterior of the choir at Winchester was the admired work of his minister, Bishop Fox.* Alcocke, Bishop of Ely, where he had built an elegant chapel, and had given proof of his skill in architecture in several colleges at Cambridge, was appointed surveyor of the works by that monarch, and associated with Sir Reginald Bray. These eminent men were equally versed in the theory and practice of architecture, which their joint performance, the conventual church of Malverne in Worcestershire, sufficiently evinces.

In the far-famed edifice at Westminster, the expiring Gothick seems to have been exhausted by every effort. The pendentive roof, never before attempted on so large a scale, is indeed

* The exquisite little sepulchral chapel, built by that sovereign on the bridge of Wakefield in Yorkshire to the memory of his father, who fell in that disastrous battle, well deserves particular notice for its façade of singular richness and beauty. The chapel of Charles de Bourbon Archbishop of Lyons, erected in that cathedral in 1478, is the most beautiful and the latest work of that kind in France.

a prodigy of art; yet, upon inspecting it, we are surprised rather than gratified. That "magic hardiness,"* of which Mr. Walpole speaks as characteristic of the last style of Gothick, has in this instance gained its utmost bounds. There is an infinity of roses, knots of flowers, bosses, and pendents, with diminutive armorial cognizances, clustered without propriety upon every single member of architecture, and we are at length fatigued by the very repetition which was intended to delight us.

In this point of view, this chapel of Henry the Seventh much exceeds King's College, which had not been completed when this was begun. It affords by far the most exuberant specimen of the pendentive roof, with pannels diverging in rays, varied into many graceful figures. There are eight clere-story windows above the aisles, which, as at King's College and Windsor, are low, and depressed by the flying buttresses. The side walls are exuberantly covered with sunk pannels with feathered mouldings. In a profusion of niches are statues, angels with escocheons, and the royal heraldic devices, Tudor-roses, and fleurs-de-lis, under crowns.

* The term " hardiesse" and " arditezza," so frequently adopted by French and Italian architects when describing the extreme loftiness of Gothick structures, is so translated by *Walpole in his Anecdotes of Painting*, vol. i. p. 202. last edit.

This last manner has often deviated into absolute confusion, by which taste and selection are equally precluded ; whence results a littleness, whilst the eye is diverted from any particular object of repose.

Whilst so much admiration is excited by vaults wrought in stone, it will not be withheld from many still remaining, which are composed entirely of timber-frame. They occur, indeed, most frequently in the great halls of castles and palaces. Those at Westminster, Christ-Church, Oxford, and Hampton Court, are scarcely inferior in beauty and constructive skill to the stone vaults already mentioned. Pendents, or pendentives, were first executed in timber-frame before they were attempted in stone, as in Crosby Hall. The choir of the cathedral of St. David's is a most curious example.

The fashion of timber-frame roofs originated about the reign of Edward III., as applied to great halls. They are common about 1400, in churches in which the stone vaulting, prior to that date, appears to have been more common. The first Norman castles had arches of stone in the interior of their keeps and halls, as had all those built by Edward I. in North Wales.

Remarks so slight as the foregoing, have occurred incidentally in the course of the present investigation, with respect to the component parts of Gothick buildings.

Of the ecclesiastical architecture in Scotland, the venerable remains of which will amply gratify antiquarian research, even the following cursory notice must not be omitted. David I. king of Scotland, was the founder of the magnificent abbeys of Melrose and Kelso, in the twelfth century. Their style accords in general with that prevalent in England at the same period. In the same reign, both Dryburgh and Jedburgh were built. These are all of them in Roxburghshire, a border county, and were built in emulation of Tynemouth Abbey and the cathedral of Lindisfarne in Northumberland. Other interesting remains are seen at Linclouden College, at Dumblaine, Aberdeen, Elgin, and Glasgow.

But the just boast of Scotland are the chapels of Roslin * and Holyrood. For richness, quantity, and variety of ornamental carvings, both withinside and without, the first-mentioned cannot be exceeded. Of arches, there are no less than thirteen different forms. The whole plan is absolutely without a parallel, and conformable with no other specimen of the fifteenth century, in which it was erected by Sir William St. Clair. Holyrood chapel is anterior, having been finished by King James, second of that name, in 1440. It is a beautiful specimen, and has a remarkable peculiarity in the forms.

* *Britton's Architectural Antiquities*, vol. iii. p. 47, 4to.

Flying buttresses, more rich in ornament than any in England, are applied in either instance.

Contemporary with these specimens of " Florid Gothick " is the abbey church at Bath, partaking in a very small degree of that description of ornament.* It was the last building of equal magnitude, entirely Gothick, and remains in the same form as when finished in 1532. Oliver King, Bishop of Bath and Wells, who died thirty years before that time, may be considered as the founder, and as having furnished the plan.

In an age when ecclesiastical fabrics of the first degree were constructed with a vast profusion of wealth and labour, we are the more pleased to contemplate this work of a prelate who preferred the admirable simplicity of the earlier school of Gothick, to the overcharged decoration which other architects of his own time were so ambitious to display.

As far as the knowledge of the powers of construction, the Gothick architects maintain a superiority over the moderns. The most able geometrician of that day, the great Sir Christopher Wren, is reported to have confessed, (but upon uncertain authority,) from frequent surveys of the roof of King's College

---

* The two latest specimens of unbastardised Gothick are said to be, Archbishop Warham's tomb at Canterbury, 1522; and Bishop Langland's chapel in Lincoln Cathedral, 1547.

chapel, that it exceeded his utmost efforts in construction ; and upon inspecting the churches of Salisbury and Westminster previously to repairs, he declared that the architects of a darker age were equally versed in those principles. M. Sufflot, the most scientific architect France ever produced, and an indefatigable investigator of the fine cathedrals which abound in that country, was clearly of this opinion. From such researches he collected many useful hints for his exquisite cupola of St. Genevieve at Paris.

Had caprice alone directed these architects, they would not in so many instances have merited this praise, namely, that the boldness and lightness of their works have been always accompanied by a correspondent solidity, the effect of scientific construction, which their perfect duration amply proves.*

We must in candour acknowledge that these efforts of skill defy any imitation by the moderns with success, excepting in very rare instances.†

The plans are irretrievably lost, for I cannot allow that they never existed, as some have asserted. In France, and more especially in Germany and the Low Countries, there were accurate details of ecclesiastical architecture in MSS. collected from conventual archives, which

* See Note [G] page 165.   † See Note [H] page 166.

have been either printed by their antiquaries, or were carefully preserved, before the Revolution. In England, at the suppression of monasteries, their MSS. were destroyed, with a very limited exception only; and it is a fair conjecture, that many were written on subjects of geometry, mechanics, and architecture, elucidated by drawings.* When the zealous but tasteless reformers of the Romish church seized upon all MSS. in the conventual libraries, they generally destroyed them without selection. But illuminated books rarely escaped destruction; and as those which treated on architecture, or any of the other sciences, were usually so elucidated, they were involved in one common annihilation: we cannot, therefore, wonder that such most interesting documents will be now sought after without a probability of success. The stupendous examples of the practice of these sciences will surely vindicate the ancient artists of this kingdom from that partial acquaintance with the theory, which has been imputed to them.

It will be surprising to a casual observer, that a church of similar style and equal dimensions should be found in the opposite extremities of England, and so analogous in its whole plan, as to appear to be a repetition or copy. The provincial architects can hardly

* See Note [I] page 167.

be supposed to have followed a divulged system, when the intercourse with each other,
or with any school, was almost impracticable.
The fact is, that the master-masons were chiefly foreigners, incorporated by royal authority.
When the foundation of an abbey was medi-
tated, these artisans removed themselves in
great numbers to any spot in any part of the
kingdom.   In the earlier ages, at least, they
are not to be considered as the inventors,
but as the executers of the plans which were
proposed to them by ecclesiastics, the only
men of science at that time.   The free-masons
were blessed by the Pope, and were first encouraged in England by Henry III. where they
were constantly employed till the close of
Gothick architecture.

When the rebuilding of their cathedrals,
either totally or in part, had been determined
upon by the great ecclesiastics of the thirteenth
century, they had become conversant previously with the powers, and had designed the forms,
of the new style.   The artificers had become
masters of its geometrical principles, were associated in a fraternity under the denomination
of free-masons, and removed themselves from
one English province to another, wherever
these new churches were to be built.   Their
constitution and internal government were
strictly regular; and from the peculiar privi-

leges which they obtained upon their first institution, they were enabled to conceal their
art and modes of practice from the rest of the
world. We may thus account for the general
coincidence and character maintained throughout each æra of the Pointed style.

It has been remarked by a French critic in
Gothick architecture, that to compose a church
where every perfection of which that style is
capable should be combined, he would select
the portal and western front of Rheims, the
nave of Amiens, the choir of Beauvais, and one
of the spires of Chartres.*

Upon a similar idea, in England, I would
propose the elevated site of Durham or Lincoln; the western façade of Lincoln, Peterborough, York, or Wells; the octagon louvre
or presbytery of Ely; Our Lady's chapel of
Ely, Gloucester, or Peterborough; the nave
and transept of York and Westminster; the
towers of Lincoln, York, Canterbury, or Gloucester; cloisters of Norwich and Gloucester.
Yet this opinion will apply strictly to the excellence of these several parts, exclusively considered, and not to any definite idea that their
union would exhibit a perfect model of composition.

A positive preference or decision in favour
of any single specimen which I have adduced,

* See Note [K] page 167.

I am unable to make; each of them being so
decidedly in the manner and æra to which they
belong, and possessing an excellence peculiar
to itself.

Our reformers demolished nearly as many
fine specimens of Gothick as they left entire.
We have ample proof in monastic ruins, as well
as in those churches which were spared and
applied as cathedrals, or given to parishes, that
the greater abbeys were possessed of consecrated buildings no less magnificent than those
of the episcopal sees, which comparative statements may place in a clearer point of view.

A perfect analysis would be made with difficulty, and exceptions should be very numerous,
to invalidate a rule which generally prevails. It
is yet an obvious inquiry, whether the usage of
particular styles may be invariably confined to
distinct æras; and whether in every instance
they mark the date with absolute precision?

It has occurred to me, that, whilst in cathedral and large conventual churches a new style
succeeded, in similar buildings, with so general
an imitation as to be certainly appropriated to
æras; in parochial churches, such a gradation
was not always attended to. There abound
documents to prove the true date of the erection of parish churches to be at least a century
after the architecture of it had fallen into disuse. The provincial-masons were content to

copy only what existed in their neighbour-
hood, or which lay within their knowledge and
acquirement.

Whether the foregoing observations be satisfactory, or otherwise, certain it is, that the
Gothick churches, whatever be the peculiar
manner of their æra, present their beauties to
every eye. We cannot contemplate them without discovering a majestic air well worthy of
their destination, with a knowledge of what is
profound in the science and practice of building, and a boldness of construction, of which
classic antiquity furnishes no examples. The
Romans gave to their large vaults six or eight
feet of thickness; a Gothic vault, of similar
dimensions, would not have one. There is a
heaviness to be perceived in all our modern
vaults, whilst those of our cathedrals have an
air which strikes the most unpractised eye.
This lightness is produced by there being no
intermediate and projecting body between the
pillars and the vault, by which the connexion
is cut off, as by the entablature in the Grecian
architecture. The Gothick vault appears to
commence at the base of the pillars which support it, especially when the pillars are clustered
in a sheaf, which, being carried up perpendicularly to the height, bending forward to
form the arcades, even to their centres, ascends
to the roof itself; and stone there seems to

possess a flexibility equal to the most ductile metals. In the fine churches of Peterborough and Ely, this harmonious effect does not exist, as it is broken by raftered or flat painted roofs, of gaudy colours.

To the credit of the present age, the Gothick style has been much more accurately understood than it was in the last. Bentham, and Essex of Cambridge, were the first who exhibited any thing like precision or true taste in the restorations which they superintended or made.

The numerous publications of the Society of Antiquaries have laid open the sources of information on that subject, and proposed genuine models for the direction of those architects who are not misled by capricious attempts at novelty or improvement. The cathedral at Lichfield was the first specimen of restoration by the late James Wyat, who, by incorporating Our Lady's chapel with the choir, has extended it to a disproportionate length, by which means the " artificial infinite," which is considered by Burke as a source of the " sublime," wanting both gradation and variety, is, in a great degree, lost in the same extent of plain surface. At Salisbury, although he has merited the praise of Mr. Gilpin,* for the propriety and

---

* *Western Tour. Dissertation on the modern Style of altering ancient Cathedrals, by Milner, 4to. 1798.*

simplicity of his alterations, he has done the
same. He has likewise rebuilt the nave of
Hereford cathedral, since its complete dilapidation. The restorations of York minster
were made by Carr and Halfpenny; and since
the conflagration of the choir (the work of an
insane fanatic in 1828), it has been renewed internally, upon the exact model of the original
choir, superintended by R. Smirke.

Those who contend so much for the picturesque, seem willing to sacrifice the characteristic of a great church, which was not originally planned as one vast room, but to consist of dependent and subordinate parts, con-
ducting us from one to the other, in succession.

Nothing can exceed the neatness with which
St. George's chapel has been repaired by the
munificence of King George III. Originally
one of the most beautiful structures of the æra
to which it belongs, it has gained every advantage that taste, aided by expense, could give it.

To Sir Reginald Bray, already mentioned,
the nave may owe its original design, although
he died before its completion in 1508.* The
roof is perhaps too much expanded for the
height, and its proportion to the imposts, which
are small and light; but the aisles are exquisite — they have all the magic perspective of
the cloisters at Gloucester, even improved by

* See Note [L] page 168.

loftiness. A good effect is given to the elevation by the transept, with its hexagonal termination, equally dividing it in the centre.

Contemporary with Sir Reginald Bray, and enjoying the same favour under Henry VII. lived Richard Fox, Bishop of Winton, who, adding to a fund established by Cardinal Beaufort, determined to give a new exterior structure to the choir of Winchester cathedral. It is one of the most elaborate and beautiful in England, particularly in the flying buttresses and the sculpture, which, from the nature of the stone, is in fine preservation.

The lover of ecclesiastical Gothick, during the middle centuries after the Conquest, will dwell with admiration and delight on the recollection of the stupendous elevation and interior of York, Lincoln, and Canterbury, in their several parts. In the seemingly magical construction of the louvre at Ely, and the imposing richness of the western front of Peterborough, he will contemplate the concentrated efforts of that style. Yet, taking the abstract idea, as of a general effect, produced by the Florid style of architecture, he will consider Windsor as the " beauty of holiness ;" and of sublimity, with the exception only of King's College chapel, in Cambridge, (which is not strictly analogous,) will seek no more admirable specimen than the choir of Gloucester.

NOTES AND EXTRACTS ILLUSTRATIVE
OF THE THIRD DISCOURSE.

[A] page 130.—" Like every other human art, which on attaining the summit of perfection tends gradually towards its decline, so did Gothick architecture now begin to retrograde from the purity, the elegance, and grandeur, which distinguished it during the whole period of the second style.

" Towards the end of the fourteenth century, innumerable innovations were made, both with regard to form and decoration, which broke the rectitude of its lines, and interfered with the harmony of the general design. In the fifteenth, it more perceptibly degenerated into fantastic refinement and false taste, by departing from the nobleness of elevation (the arches, which would be equilateral, gradually assumed an obtuse form, until they almost lost their pointed character); and by acquiring, towards the end of the period, a superabundant mass of unmeaning ornament, which totally corrupted the style, and brought it into disrepute."

[B] page 138.—The height of most cathedrals is equal to the breadth of the body and side-aisles. Spires and towers are usually as high as the nave is long ; or perhaps more accurately, the transept. The cross or transept extended half the length of the whole fabric; and the aisles just half the breadth and height of the nave added together.— *See Pref. to Willis's Mitred Abbeys*, p. 8.

It is a distribution of parts which will hold generally—that the width of the nave is that of the aisles, measured in the plan to the extremity of the buttresses externally; and that the breadth and height of the whole building are equal. The internal height of the nave doubles that of the aisles.

M 2

[C] page 138.—Prominent examples in the western counties are, the tower of Gloucester cathedral; St. Stephen's, Bristol; Thornbury, Gloucestershire; Taunton, Huish, and St. Mary Wells, Somersetshire. In Lincolnshire, and the north of England, very lofty spires rise from towers of great height. Of the last mentioned, there are, indeed, numerous examples, with which every lover of this style is conversant, and contemplates them with admiration.

" Molem propinquam nubibus arduis."—Hor. *Od.*

The pinnacles and open balustrade of the towers exhibit an infinite variety. At Doncaster, Yorkshire, like feathers or fleurs-de-lis. The pinnacles of the tower of Wrexham are octagons, — and that of Gresford, both in Flintshire, shows a singular application of statues, externally placed, as standing upon an open parapet. At St. Stephen's, Bristol, and other towers in the vicinity, a wing of open latticed-work is protruded from each angle.

[D] page 143. — It may introduce a curious comparison of the actual expenditure of money in the fifteenth century and that in the nineteenth, in the erection of great buildings of the ecclesiastical character, by adducing the following examples, as far as they may extend. But the excessive advance in the price of both materials and labour, must be taken into the account.

Beauchamp chapel, Warwick, computus for seventeen years, from 1443, 1806*l*. 3*s*. 8*d*.

King's College chapel, Cambridge, from 1441 to 1515, 22,469*l*. 2*s*. 7*d*. finished in 1516.

Windsor chapel, from 1478 to 1482, 6572*l*.; but much more was afterwards added to this sum. Roof, 1506 to 1508, 700*l*.

Henry the Seventh's chapel, Westminster, according to an account mentioned, but not specified, by Holinshed, 14,000*l*. in all. Indenture between the executors of King Henry VII. and J. Wastell and Henry Semark, dated 1513, " roof to be made according to a plot thereof, made and signed," 1200*l.* in these times nearer 12,000*l.*

[E] page 143.—The mode of painting the original timber-frame-roofs is first authenticated by Gervasius, in his description of the second cathedral of Canterbury, 1175. " Cœlum inferius egregiè depictum," and " cœlum egregiâ picturâ decoratum."

[F] page 146.—Among the very curious MSS. bequeathed to the British Museum by the late Mr. Kerrich, librarian of Cambridge, are the papers of T. Essex, architect, who was distinguished for his knowledge and practice of Gothick architecture, particularly at Ely. He made a most minute and practical survey of King's College chapel, and had collected many original documents, with a view to publish an authentic history and a scientific investigation of the principles upon which it was constructed. He printed in 1756, a " *Proposal to give fifteen plates, explaining the various designs and proportion of parts, with a plan of the College, as designed by the Founder, and observations on the original Contracts.*" The architectural student will regret that his intention failed of due encouragement.

It appears from a contract, made in 1512, that the masons were summoned by T. Larke, Archdeacon of Norwich, the Comptroller, and that the following items occur. " Memorand. For the great stone roof, 1200*l.* ; for three towers, 100*l.* each ; for the roofs of the two porches, 50*l.* each ; for sixty-eight images, 72*l.* ; pro imagine Regis stantis ad magnam portam, 1*l.* 6*s.* 8*d.* The roof was constructed with much timber frame, none of which is seen from below." A bell tower was intended, but not built. See a plan of it, upon two large leaves, in the *Cotton MSS. Brit. Mus.* Engraved in Lysons' *Magna Britannia.*

[G] page 154.—" The Gothick architects varied the proportions of their columns from four to one hundred and twenty diameters, and contrasted the ornaments and the parts with equal licence; and though a column so slender, employed to support a vaulted roof of stone, may offend the eye of a person who suspects it to be inadequate to its purpose, therefore associates ideas of weakness and danger with it; yet to those who know it to be sufficient it will appear extremely light and beautiful, as is proved by the columns in the cathedral of Salisbury, which are of this proportion, and which have been admired for centuries. The contrivers of this refined and fantastic Gothick seem to have aimed at producing grandeur and solemnity, together with lightness of effect; and incompatible as these qualities may seem by attending to effect only, and considering the means of producing it as wholly subordinate and in their own power, they succeeded to a degree which the Grecian architects, who worked by rule, never approached."—*Knight's Inquiry*, p. 172.

[H] page 154.—The rawness of new stone is totally unfavourable to Gothick buildings of the ecclesiastical kind. So long accustomed to contemplate churches when of harmonizing tints,

——" in their old russet coats
The same they wore some hundred years ago,"

HEADLEY.

we annex an idea of inferior dimensions and unappropriate trimness to edifices of a most ancient semblance indeed, but only a few years old. This observation may apply to numerous modern imitations of the Gothick style, designed and executed by the village mason at the command of the churchwarden.

The great architects have generally failed. Palladio gave plans, neither Grecian nor Gothick, for the front of the church of St. Petronius at Bologna, a very ancient Lombard structure. Inigo Jones placed a Corinthian portico before Old St. Paul's: he built the chapel at Lincoln's Inn, and called it Gothick. Sir Christopher Wren's towers at Westminster, and Christ Church, Oxford, are not happy productions. The chief deficiency in modern imitative Gothick is in point of scale, and is imposed upon our contemporary architects by the circumstances of the age. In our criticism upon these modern edifices, it may be just to remember, that churches were not then built by parliamentary grants, but that from the superstition or piety of individuals, the necessary funds issued from a more prolific source ; and that many who could not give money, contributed large portions of gratuitous labour. Yet, in not a few of the churches lately erected by Act of Parliament upon a Gothick model, we are too often compelled to see " Gothick in masquerade."

[I] page 155.—" There is a basso-relievo in the cathedral at Worcester, by which is represented an architect presenting his plan, marked on a tablet, to the superior of a monastery. It is of high antiquity, and affords a certain proof that ecclesiastical buildings were not erected without plans, elevations, and what are called working drawings."—*Carter's Architecture of England*, p. 54.

[K] page 157.—Architecture is said to have been introduced into France by Charlemagne in the ninth century. A school of architecture was then established in France ; and it is asserted that they were not indebted to foreigners for the magnificent works which abound in that country. Rumalde, the architect of Louis le Debonnaire, the son and successor of Charlemagne, built the cathedral of Rheims in 875. Ason built that of Seez in Normandy in 1050. Hilduard, a Benedictine monk, in 1170, planned the church of St. Peter at Chartres. Hugh Libergier, who died in 1263, was the architect of the celebrated church of St. Nicaise at Rheims. His contemporary, Stephen de Lusarche, began the cathedral of Amiens, which was completed by Robert de Lusarche in 1222. The Abbot Suggerius had previously finished the church of St. Denis in 1140, which was considered as a model of perfection. The Nôtre Dame at Paris was built in the reign of Robert the Pious, but probably not the edifice now seen.

The churches of Verdun, Laon, Lizieux, and St. Remi at Rheims, are all of the thirteenth century. The architect Montreau attended Louis IX. into the Holy Land; and upon his return to France designed several churches, in which he introduced the ornaments and the style of those he had seen at Jerusalem. The Sainte Chapelle at Paris, and the Abbey of Poissey, are monuments of his skill. Associated with him was Joscelin de Courvault. At Rouen are two superb specimens of Gothick architecture, which have been noticed more at large in a former Discourse.—*Dargenville, Vies des Archit. Le Noir, Musée des Mon. Franç.*

It is creditable to the architects of our nation, that several of the finest cathedrals in France were built by the English, during their possession of the northern provinces. In the Netherlands are some fine churches. Antwerp is 500 feet long by 330, and the spires 360 feet high. Malines has a very regular and beautiful tower, built in 1452. It is 348 feet high without the spire, which would have been one-third higher.

Ypres, regular, and more in the English style, with a tower and transept resembling York or Lincoln. The abbey church at St. Omers, called St. Bertin, is of vast dimensions and fine architecture. At Ghent the tower is light and elegant, particularly in its upper tier. The western front of the cathedral at Brussels nearly resembles that of Wells, but is inferior in point of ornament. I have not learned the name of any celebrated Flemish architect. A professor of Gothick architecture flourished in France as late as the commencement of the sixteenth century. Jean Texier began, in 1506, one of the spires of the cathedral at Chartres 378 feet high, which he completed in 1514. In England, the architects, generally, had relinquished spires, and were at that period engaged in the beautiful towers of Gloucester and Canterbury. Lincoln and York had preceded them.

[L] page 161.—" John Hylmer and William Vertue, freemasons, undertook the vault of the roof of the choir for 700*l.*

in 1506, and to complete it before Christmas 1508." *Ashmole's Hist. Garter*, p. 136. The executors of King Henry the Seventh contracted with John Wastell and Henry Semark, for 1200*l.* to complete the roof of King's College chapel, in Cambridge. *MS. Indent.* These contracts were drawn up with great strictness, and considerable penalties were annexed to the breach of them. In the Duke of York's agreement for the building of the chapel at Fotheringay, Horwood, the freemason, stipulates, " to yeild up hys body to prison at my lord's wyll, and all hys moveable goods," in case of non-performance, and that " he shall neyther sett mor nor fewer freemasons, roghsetters ne leys thereupon, but such as shall be ordeigned ;" and that the Duke shall find all materials, " ropes, bolts, scaffolds, gynnes, &c. and all other werke that longyth to such a body, nave, isles, &c." *Dugdale.*

ARCHITECTURAL TERMS

AS OCCURRING IN ANCIENT DOCUMENTS, AND USED BY
THE MASTER-MASONS IN THEIR CONTRACTS WITH THE
SUPERVISORS OF GREAT BUILDINGS, WITH EXPLANA-
TORY OBSERVATIONS.

THIS is a Glossary of selected terms only, such as can be
proved by the authority of genuine documents to have been
the language of the early architects, from the thirteenth to
the fifteenth century. In a MS. published by HEARNE, it
is called " the universal language of masonnes." I omit
many which have been investigated and published, reserving
the liberty of offering such objections as may occur to certain
definitions, by proposing others which appear to be more
consonant.

The present series will consist of terms found in documentary evidence, and which are confirmed, as to their implication, as occurring in contemporary poems. Those which
are more modern will form no part of this inquiry.

From CHAUCER.

Chaucer, and others of our early poets, are extremely minute as to their architectural descriptions, and apply the
terms, usual in 'their own age, to edifices of poetical imagery.
But he seems to have been well aware of this difficulty.

" It were, in sothe, almost a daies werke,
And the tearmes also ben so derke."

Shrine-works are thus described in his " First Boke of
Fame."

" In which ther were mo ymages
Of gold standing in sondrie stages;
In mo riche tabernacles;
And with pierre (*precious stones*) moe pinnacles,
And moe curious pourtraptures
And quent mannere figures," &c.

Castles.

" All was of stone of berple *(agate or carnelian)*
Bothe the castle and the towere,
And eke the halle and every bowere, *(chamber)*
Without pieces or joinings;
But many subtill compassings,
As babcuries and pinnacles,
Imageries and tabernacles,
And quoint manere figures." *(grotesque carvings.)*

" Of these pates flourishinges,
Ne of compaces ne of kerbinges,
Ne how the hacking in masonries;
As corbelles and imageries."

Third Book of Fame.

Which includes the several members of ornamental masonry, and formed the perfection of decorated Gothick, both as to design and workmanship.

" And of a suit were all the toures,
Subtilly carben, after floures,
With many a small turrett high."

The Dreme.

LIDGATE, in his account of Troy, is not less minutely descriptive.

" Every towere bretered *(embattled)* was so clene
Of chose stone, that were far asundre;
The workmen have with fell and sterne bisages
Of riche entaple *(carvings)*
Wrought out of stone, and never like to fail,
And on each turrett were raised up figures
Of savage beastes."

" And Portekollis strong, at every gate,
And many a gargoyle, and many a hideous head."

Gargoyle, a water-spout, formed of the open mouth of some monster—simply a dragon.

Tabernacles, called *habenries* by Chaucer. *Hovels,* niches for images to stand in.

Gabletz, gobbets, squared blocks of stone — " *ex qua-drato lapide.*" *Rymer,* vol. vii. p. 1191.

Alures, open walks on the walls. *Warton's Hist. Poetry.*

Reredoss, the back part of an altar.

Coillons, hewn stones; corner-stones. *Speke's Glossary.*

Corbelles, trusses, or projecting stones, on which images are placed, richly carved.

Croquets, crockets, locks of hair imitated in the angles of pinnacles. *Speke's Glossary.*

Querelles, the square space included within the arcade or division.

Fretté-vowted, vaults broken into numerous intersections by longitudinal and transverse bands.

Mitre-headed turrets. Henry the Seventh's chapel.

Perpent or *perpender stones,* " Lapis frontatus, qui utrin-que lævigatus parietis crassitudinem exæquat." — *Skinner.* Neck-moulding, crocketed in canopies, forming the upper part.

Bosses, at the intersection of the ribs of roofs, elaborately sculptured, with leaves, bousquets, rebus, armorial bearings, and small histories, in bas-relief.

Groined roof, Salisbury the best early instance. The rib-mouldings consist of rounds and hollows, which have the toothed ornament within them, and often leaves.

Respounds, parallel corresponding walls or demi-pillars at the end of a building or arcade.

Weather and crown mouldings, applied to drip-stones; canopies over arches, windows, and doors.

String-course, a circular tablet which is conducted round the whole face of a building, within or without; and some-times composed of the Norman hatched moulding, called likewise the cable-moulding.

Sediles (sedilia), stone-seats on the left of the altar, sel-dom exceeding three in number, for the officiating priests, with the *lavachrum,* or *piscina,* usually attached, under the same arcade, called likewise " *a stoup,*" with a hole to take off the water used in washing the sacred vessels. The seats, which may be turned up, are called *misereres*, and were so contrived, that the monk could only sit on the edge of them, and if he fell asleep would be precipitated into the midst of the choir.

Ribs and *cross-springers*, mouldings conjoined, and spreading and intersected, longitudinally over the whole roofs.

Flying groins, which compose a vaulting springing from corbels, supporting a pillar and its capital.

Crockets and *creepers*, leaves running up the outward angles of pinnacles, spires, canopies, &c.

Trefoils, *quatrefoils*, *roses*, and *rosettes*, have sometimes reduplications, called *feathering*, or *foliation*, or *fleurs-de-lis*, at the points.

Sunk squares, pannels with quatre or trefoils, enclosing a rose of eight leaves; a *rosette* has more, and the exterior lines form a square.

Battlements, *crenelles*, or *parapet*, sometimes open within a triangle, inclosing a serpentine fillet ; or with trefoils without a point ; but more commonly with mullions only.

Quadrants, the square formed by a cloister. *Pannel:* each walk or ambulatory was so termed — as East or North Pannel. It is applied likewise to the octangular division of a spire.

Window of so many dayes, lights or partitions which are made by mullions.

Over-story, or *clere-story*, erected upon the dividing arcade of the nave, to contain a row of windows.

Panneling, most frequent in the fifteenth century. It covered the face of the wall with perpendicular tablets headed with arches of open foils, and divided by a horizontal fillet of two or three lights, inclosed in a square. So predominant was this manner, that it pervaded the walls externally and internally, so that the doors and windows are pierced pannels only, flowered, cinquefoiled or feathered, *i. e.* having the external lines repeated. Frequently spread over the whole surface of the building.

Clochard, Bell-tower, anciently an insulated dwelling.

Franca-petra, free-stone brought from Caen in Normandy, and used in the finer kinds of masonry.

Vise (as a screw), *Noel,* or winding staircases. *Vise* is the small circular pillar ascending from the bottom to the top.

Vaulting-shaft, which rises from the floor to the centre of the roof. Longitudinal and transverse bands first used in roofs, and connected with the rib which runs along the top of the vault.

Coigne, a corner-stone of a castle tower, and when projecting as a machicolation or hanging tower, termed by SHAKSPEARE, " *coign* of vantage."

Sperware embattailment throughout, perforated parapet.

Bottrusse. Every botrusse finished with a finial. *Perpeyn* walls of *free-stone clene-wrought.* These terms occur in the contract for Fotheringay College.

Knottys. " Ycorven with crocketts on corneres, endilong with knottys graven clere."—*P. Plowman.*

From W. WYRCESTRE's survey of BRISTOL, 1480:

Loover—louvre, from " *ouvert*," an opening in the roof.— *Du Chesne.*

Bowtells—boltellæ, a perpendicular moulding when surrounding the shaft of a pillar.

Felet or *fillett,* a narrow, flat, or horizontal moulding.

Resaunt or *resault,* single and double, and now called an ogee.

Casement with levys, a moulding, deeply hollowed, of carved foils, rosettes, or crockets.

Costera, one whole side of a building. " *Costera versus borialem*," the inside of the north wall.

Broche sive spera, a spire placed upon a tower.

Gentise great and small—Gentil entaile—busy entaile, elaborate carving in open-work.

Resaunt-lorymer, an ogee with an edge so deeply carved as to form a drip-stone, or " *larmiere*," to conduct water.

Earth table—base tablets—" a course without," the first horizontal moulding above the ground.

A felde—field, the flat interior part of the casement or sunk pannel.

A set-off, a plain or ornamented drip-stone over windows, often small, and supported by grotesque heads.

Labels are square-headed, and almost peculiar to buildings of the Tudor style.

Severee. A severy is the space or division made by two arches, springing from two side-walls, in which are windows, and open space in the other two. They are connected like vertebræ, and would stand independently of each other. This mode of construction originated in the fifteenth century. *Civerée, William of Worcester.*

Champ-ashlar — champre — chamfered, grooved or hollowed out.

Formarets, the ribs of vaulting.

Hood-mold, or string-course.

Mehereme, mærennium, framework of timber.

Entaile, carving or embossing.

> " A worke of riche entayle and curious molde."
> SPENSER.

Hyling, the roof of any building.

Parget, a smoothed wall. *Pargitor, parietor, cæmentarius.*

Poyntel, a floor set into squares or lozenge forms, generally composed of brick, and common in halls or cloisters. " Ypaved with poyntill eche point after other."—*P. Plowman.*

Orbs, circular carvings which project at the intersection of roofs. *Bosses — bosquets,* orbs composed of wreathed leaves and flowers.

Purfled-work, the feathering attached to pediments and finials.

Moynels, mullions, perpendicular shafts, as dividing the open space of windows.

Hip-knobs, ornamental facings on ridges, placed on the gable-ends, rising above the external roof, in the Tudor age.

*Terms of masonry which occur in the contract between Rich-
ard Duke of York and W. Horwood, free-mason, dated
13 Hen. VI. 1435, for building the College of Fotheringhay.*

Bench-table stones, pillars and *champerers,* " that the arches and pendants shall rest upon." *Sperware* embattlement
throughout, — " and both the ends embattled and resting
against the stepul." *Bottrusse,* every botrusse finished with
a finial. Two *perpeyn* walls, joining, of free-stone " clen-
wrought." *Clere-story, table-stones,* and *crestes,* strong and
mighty *arches. Vise* or circular staircase—" and in the seyde
stepul there shall be a *vice turning.*"

Clere-storial windows: *turret canted off,* octagon or polygonal.

In this contract we find an application of the terms above-
mentioned.

HISTORICAL AND CRITICAL ACCOUNT

OF

Gloucester Cathedral.*

IT has been considered to be more accordant with the present plan, to retain in an appendix the following observations upon Gloucester Cathedral, printed in 1806. Since that period, several more enlarged descriptions have been given to the public. The first and most important of them, written by the late Sir H. Englefield, was splendidly edited by the Society of Antiquaries. This has been followed by other descriptive and critical essays by Storer, Buckler, and Britton, all illustrated by engravings, of which the merited praise of superiority must be given to the last mentioned.

" As the object of this essay is to confirm opinion by example, I trust it may be excused, if I attempt, as an elucidation of general remarks, the architectural history of the cathedral of Gloucester, which, during a residence in that city, was investigated by me almost daily, and was the school in which I first imbibed any intelligence of ecclesiastical architecture which I may have acquired.

" The area in which this sumptuous edifice is placed, is singularly spacious and neat. This great advantage it possesses in common with Salisbury, and a few other cathedrals. How much several of our most magnificent fabrics lose, by being so closely surrounded by common domestic buildings may be seen at Canterbury and Winchester ; and what is taken from the dignity of elevation, when they are placed in a parochial churchyard, as at Chichester."†

* Reprinted from *Observations on English Architecture, by J. Dallaway,* 8vo. pp. 62, 1806, with subsequent additions to 1832.

† The nave was elevated by a clere story, when the present roof was erected by Abbot Thokey, between 1307 and 1329 ; but which was reduced

N

" At periods very remote from each other, this church has been made to have an appearance, on the outside, conformable to a prevailing style of pure Gothick." Of the original exterior elevation, although the essential walls may be said to remain, there is little besides. In every century during the middle ages since the Conquest, some new or greatly altered feature has presented itself. " A few years only before the suppression of the Benedictine abbey, the tower was completed, under the direction of Robert Tulley, (one of the monks, and afterwards Bishop of St. David's,*) to whom that charge had been devised by Abbot Sebroke,

to the present regular form by Abbot Morwent, between 1420 and 1437, by the rebuilding of the façade or western front. Similar alterations were effected in the south transept by Abbot Thokey above mentioned. But the magnificent appendage of the lofty choir was completed during successive Abbots, who presided in the fourteenth century. Our Lady's chapel subsequently rebuilt, and of great internal beauty, adds nothing to the general effect.

* Robert Tulley was consecrated Bishop of St. David's, 1469; ob. 1482. Over the dividing arch of the nave and choir is written in the Gothick character.

" Hoc quod digestum specularis opusque politum
Tullii ex onere Sebroke abbate jubente."

He was patronized by Waynflete. Thomas Sebroke, who was elected Abbot in 1453, died in 1457; and it is a fair conjecture that Tulley was appointed by him to superintend the execution of a plan he had given for the tower. The same R. Tulley laid the foundation-stone of Magdalen College, Oxford, in 1473. A. Wood.

A great confusion has occurred, when Abbots and Prelates are considered as the architects or designers of the structures which have arisen under their patronage. Tulley was comptroller only " ex onere." According to a tradition contained in a vernacular rhyme, the name of the master mason was John Gower, whose superior merit is conspicuous in another instance in this county.

" John Gowere,
Who built Campden church and Gloster towre."

In the south transept is a very singular monument, which is attributed to him. It is a projection from the wall, in the form of a mason's square, supported by the figure of a man. See *Carter's Ancient Sculpture and Painting*.

who died in 1457. The ornamental members and perforated pinnacles are of the most delicate tabernacle work, very full, but preserving an air of chasteness and simplicity.*

" Its peculiar perfection, which immediately strikes the eye, is an exact symmetry of component parts, and the judicious distribution of ornaments. The shaft of the tower is equally divided into two stories, correctly repeated in every particle ; and the open parapet and pinnacles so richly clustered, are an example of Gothick, in its most improved state.

" The extremely beautiful effect of large masses of architecture by moonlight, may be considered as a kind of optical deception, and nearly the same as that produced by statuary when strongly illuminated. Thus seen, the tower of this cathedral acquires a degree of lightness, so superior to that which it shows under the meridian sun, that it no longer appears to be of human construction.

" As to the parts nearer the ground, under the same circumstance, I avow my preference of the Grecian style ; for a portico and colonnade, casting a broad shade from multiplied columns, and catching alternately a striking light from their circular form, become distinct ; and a grand whole results from parts so discriminated. The Gothick, on the contrary, when merely solid and impervious, owes all its effect to its mass and height.†

---

* The height to the summit of the pinnacles is 224 feet; width internally 23 by 21 feet six inches. The great bell which it incloses ranks with many of the largest in point of weight (7000 tons).

A strange mistake has been repeated with respect to the inscription :

" 𝕸𝖊 𝖋𝖊𝖈𝖎𝖙 𝖋𝖎𝖊𝖗𝖎 𝖒𝖔𝖓'𝖈𝖍𝖆𝖙𝖚𝖘 𝖓𝖔𝖒𝖎𝖓𝖊 𝕻𝖊𝖙𝖗𝖎."

Moncutus, and the explanation made of it, are perfectly absurd. No such word as monchatus occurs in any glossary of the Monkish or low Latin; but an inscription preserved by A. Wood, formerly in Gloucester Hall, Oxford, belonging to this monastery, adopts the same term :

" Mors medicina necis, via vitæ, pax populatûs.

  Sit spes prompta precis, lex curæ, laus *monachatûs*."

Dugdale's Monast. vol. iv. p. 405. new edition.

† I could not adduce a more apposite instance to prove the superiority of the Gothick style for towers and spires, over that introduced in London by

" The statues of tutelary saints and benefactors, which were dispersed in various parts of the external view, have suffered much, even in their pedestals and canopies, by the mutilation of fanatics. It is to be regretted, that some of the English cathedrals which have escaped it, in a certain degree, should have been built with friable stone, of which that of Lichfield is a lamentable specimen. For a collection of statues in a perfect state, the western fronts of the cathedrals of Wells, Peterborough, and Lincoln, are the most worthy notice.

" At Sienna, the exterior of the great church is covered with marble, which retains the minutest ornament, in a complete state. Those who have not visited the Continent, can scarcely imagine how much we have lost in our best instances, by the destruction of effigies and carvings, whilst the above-mentioned remain as entire as when first erected.

" The vacant niche lessens the luxuriance of the rich Gothick in a degree proportioned to a defaced entablature of the Corinthian order.

" Few churches in England exhibit a more complete school of Gothick, in its gradations from the time of the Conquest, than the cathedral of Gloucester." Subsequent observations have induced me not to retract, but to modify this assertion. There is certainly no prominent example of the second Norman, or Pointed style, as at Salisbury or Worcester. In fact, any decisive alteration did not take place until that peculiar manner of insulated columns, under one capital, was relinquished. There is yet one memorable specimen of the Early Pointed architecture, which has some peculiarities rarely to be met with, which are noticed by Sir H. Englefield, in a building at the end of the north transept, called, upon no authority, the Monk's treasury. I have observed, that the great architects of the Norman æra were as industrious as they were skilful, and that, in the course of one century and a half after the Conquest, there were few of the larger

Sir Christopher Wren, than those of the western front of St. Paul's, and that of Gloucester. Incredible as it will appear from inspection, there is only the difference of a single foot in the height of each.

churches which were not totally rebuilt. Many parts have, in successive centuries, been superseded by restorations in the Gothick style, but the substructions will still be found to demonstrate the original Norman plan of the whole building. Salisbury is, perhaps, the only entire exception. Most of the great churches, both in France and England, have been the work of several ages. The disparity is, in general, great, as each architect has a plan according with his own time.

" The Anglo-Norman style, consisting of enormous circular pillars bearing round arches, with indented mouldings, distinguishes the nave,* which is the chief part of the original structure, begun, according to Florence of Worcester, in 1057, by Aldred, bishop of that see, but more generally attributed to Abbot Serlo, in 1088. The north aisle is of contemporary architecture, which is observable in the round arches of the windows, and the pilasters, which have very elaborate capitals. Two centuries later, the opposite aisle was finished by Abbot Thokey in another manner, as the windows bear the nail-head moulding, which is repeated on either side, and the heads are of the obtuse lancet form.

" At Ely and Peterborough the aisles are divided into two tiers of arcades, one above the other, but both communicating with the nave. The nail-head moulding was an early deviation from the true Norman, when pointed arches were first intermixed. It appears to have had a long usage, as this building was probably erected in the early part of the reign of Edward II.† In the western front, and the additional arcade, we must observe a much later style, as the nave was

---

* King determines, in pursuit of his own hypothesis, this arcade, with those of Tewkesbury and Pershore, to be nearly contemporary, and certainly Saxon. *Godwyn Vita Aldredi. Leland, Itin.* v. viii. f. 75. These pillars are six feet nine inches in diameter, twenty-one feet eight inches in girth, and the intercolumniation twelve feet four inches. The comparatively good effect of a Norman arcade (when extended to the termination of the building, as this originally was,) may be seen by the intercolumniation, which is so much narrower, at Tewkesbury.

† The Register of Abbot Walter Frocester, with a chronicle, which begins with the foundation, and closes with his death, in 1412, is still extant in the

considerably lengthened by Abbot Horton, at the close of the fourteenth century.

" It is scarcely possible to enter the choir of Gloucester, which includes every perfection to which the Gothick had attained during the fifteenth century, without feeling the influence of veneration. In the nave,

> ———" the arch'd and ponderous roof
> By its own weight made stedfast and immovable,
> Looking tranquillity,"   CONGREVE.

immediately engages the attention, and by its heavy simplicity renders the highly-wrought ornaments of the choir more conspicuous and admirable.

" At the termination of the nave, under the tower, is the approach to the choir; and above the great arch is a window between two vacant niches, richly sculptured.

" On the north and south sides are the arches which support the vaulting of the transepts. Both of these are intersected at the springing by a flying arch with open spandrils, each spanning the space of the tower. The brackets are figures of angels, with escocheons of the abbey, Edward II. and the munificent Abbot Sebroke, the founder.

" Upon the exact point of these intersecting arches is a pillar, forming an impost of the great vaulted roof, which is then divided into sharp lancet arcades, and has an air of incredible lightness.* From this part there are five more arcades divided by clusters of semi-columns, which reach from the base to the roof; and the ribs are infinitely inter-

archives of the Dean and Chapter. A duplicate of the lives of the Abbots is in the Cotton Library (*Domitian,* viii. p. 128), and another in the library of Queen's College, Oxford. John Thokey was Abbot from 1307 to 1329; " cujus tempore constructa est ala australis, in navi ecclesiæ, expensis," &c. His successor was John Wygmore, who died in 1337. " De oblationibus ibidem oblatis infra sex annos prelationis suæ, alam Sancti Andreæ (the south transept) à fundamentis usque ad finem perduxit."

* King *(Munimenta)* remarks that this mode of construction is without example or imitation. Both at Salisbury and Wells the towers are strengthened internally by an arcade, the upper arch being inverted, and resting on the other.

sected and variegated with the most elaborate trellis-work, composed of orbs and rosettes, which, although they are so thickly studded, are not repeated in a single instance.*

" Over the high altar are angels in full choir, with every instrument of music practised in the fifteenth century. This is an extremely interesting specimen, if it be remembered that we have no more accurate knowledge of the musical instruments of the Greeks and Romans, than that which may be collected from their bas-reliefs and statues. Coins and gems sometimes exhibit them, but little is to be learned respecting their form, from the ancient treatises on music. Of the same æra are figures of minstrels, with their different instruments, placed over the pillars on either side of the nave of York cathedral ; and others, of ruder workmanship, on the outside of the church of Ci-encester, Gloucestershire.

" It is probable that the whole vaulted ceiling was at first painted of a deep azure colour, with stars of gold, and the ribs or intersectors gilded, which were condemned at the Reformation, and concealed by a thick wash of lime. Such have been restored at Westminster by Sir Christopher Wren.

" At Orvietto, Sienna, and many of the Lombard churches, roofs, both of the naves and choirs, so ornamented, are still perfect. That the architecture has been restored to its native simplicity of colour, is a circumstance of truer taste : indeed, the incongruous and accumulated decorations of churches on

---

* Sir H. Englefield, in his description annexed to the Engravings published by the Society of Antiquaries, entirely coincides with the author's opinion, that the choir was begun by Abbot Boyfield, and mentions this sketch with respect.

In *Warton's Observations on the Fairy Queen of Spenser*, vol. ii. p. 195, it is said, that " the Florid Gothick distinguishes itself by an exuberance of decoration, as in the roof of the choir of Gloucester, where it is thrown like a web of embroidery over the old Saxon vaulting." Upon the slightest inspection of the external elevation of the choir, this circumstance will be discovered not to be founded in fact; as it is a superstructure, more than forty feet high, upon the ancient Saxon choir. Warton's remark is applicable to the nave, excepting that the Gothick roof is of the plainest kind. The date of the first vaulting is 1242. It was originally of rafters only.

the Continent, disturb the harmony of the design, by crowd-
ing so many adscititious parts, and the repose of it, by masses
of raw colours and gilding. The coincidence of the purity of
the Protestant worship with the chasteness which pervades its
temples (more especially in some which have been lately reno-
vated), is a certain criterion of national good sense.

" There are thirty-one stalls of rich tabernacle-work, carved
in oak, on either side, little inferior in point of execution to
the episcopal throne at Exeter, or to the stalls at Ely, erected
in the reign of Edward III., and allowed to be some of the
finest pieces of Gothick carving in wood now remaining in
England of that early date.*

" This choir was built in the grand æra of stained glass, when
it was more frequent and excellent than at any other period.
It was indispensably necessary to architectural effect, according to the prevailing style, which gave to windows a disproportionate space. But the sombre tints reflected from them
modified the light, and contributed to blend the whole into
one mass of exquisite richness. For, the general effect was
consulted by the Gothick, as well as the Grecian artists.

" At present the naked transparent window destroys the
intended harmony, and the primary idea is sadly impoverish-
ed.† How this incredibly light roof was constructed, may
puzzle modern imitators as much as the vault of King's College chapel. The analogy between these roofs must be confined solely to construction, for each has a style of ornament

---

* I observed, when at Rome in 1796, that the high altar of the church of
St. John Lateran had a Gothick canopy, composed of rich pediments and
finials, in the florid style of the fourteenth century, exactly like those of that
date in England. It is the only specimen of true Gothick now remaining in
Rome.

† Milton, who was educated at St. Paul's school, acquired a veneration
for the Gothick style by constantly frequenting the great cathedral in his early
youth. In his " Il Penseroso" we have almost as exact a description of that
majestic pile, as that given by Sir W. Dugdale. The cloisters, "the high
embowed roof of the choir," the " massy proof pillars of the nave, which was
in the Norman style," and " the storied windows, richly dight," are particu-
larized by both.

essentially differing from the other.   Certain it is, that the
cross-springers* are of very solid stone, and the vault which
they support of a petrifaction, called provincially the tough,
or toph-stone,† specifically lighter, in a great degree, than the
other. Chalk was used where easily procured, as at Chichester.

   " The two farthest arcades are splayed about a yard from
the right line, instead of forming a section of a hexagon, and
are connected with the great east window, which is embowed
in a slight degree, and occupies the whole space of the end of
the choir, almost to the floor.   It is said to be of the largest
dimensions in England,‡ for the arch has three chief divisions
or mullions, terminating in pointed arches, the middle of which
includes six tiers of stained glass," and those on either side,
four each, " now so extremely decayed and mutilated, as to
appear like the tissue of a carpet, to any but the eye of an
antiquary.   Nothing like a regular Scripture history can be
discovered, but a long series of portraits, larger than life, of
saints, prophets, and Jewish kings.   It was put up in Richard
the Second's time, when the price of stained glass was one
shilling a square foot, so that it originally cost 139l. 18s.§.

   " There is reason to presume that this very splendid work
was prosecuted through many years in succession, not only on
account of its elaborate difficulty, but of the vast expense

   * They have been so termed by Bentham (*Hist. of Ely*), and if not sufficiently scientific, may be further described, as the principal ribs of groins
springing from the angles, and crossing each other at a common centre.

   † See *Leland's Itinerary*, vol. vii. p. 2, f. 73, and *Harrison's Introduction
to Holinshed*, p. 14 ; who both observe, that this " toph-stone" is found in
great abundance at Dursley, in Gloucestershire.   But a more ancient
authority is Gervase of Canterbury, who, speaking of the vault of the
choir, " hæc fornix ex lapide et *topho levi* decenter composita est." *Decem
Scriptores*, c. 1292.   In no instance has disproportion been more happily
converted into gracefulness.

   ‡ The glass occupies a space of 78 feet 10 inches, by 35 f. 6 in.:—2798
square feet.   The great east window at York is of the same kind and æra;
but it is only 76 feet 6 inches, by 32 feet.   It is inferior in point of effect.

   § The western windows of Windsor, King's College, and Henry the Seventh's chapels, have three chief divisions, and occupy the whole space of
the nave.

which was necessary to its completion. During the abbacy of Adam de Staunton, the plan of improving the ancient choir was first suggested, and had probably commenced before his death in 1351. His immediate successor, Thomas de Horton, who died in 1377, was a great contributor to the fabric: but to John Boyfield* we may fairly attribute the stupendous vault of the choir, and he lived to see it finished before 1381. That of Trinity chapel at Ely, though of much inferior dimensions, has a precise resemblance to it in general form and ornament; and the date of either is the same. Perhaps, if we may judge by similarity of workmanship, he had projected the cloisters, which were undertaken by Walter Frocester, the next abbot. The arches, and the tower which rises upon them, were the work of Abbot Sebroke, 1457.

" Our Lady's chapel was originally added to the choir in 1228.† It was totally rebuilt, between the years 1457 and 1498, by the abbots R. Stanley and William Ferleigh. The

* The *Cotton. MS.* (Domitian, A. viii.) appears to give the original, or rather the incipient, construction of the present choir, to Abbot John Wygmore, (1329—1337), and its continuation to Adam de Staunton (1337—1351). There is another transcript in the library of Queen's Coll. Oxon., and in the archives of the Dean and Chapter are still preserved the Chronicle of the Abbey and other MSS., as the Register of Abbot Frocester, 1381—1412. But the Monkish Annalists, when they treat of architecture as applied to their convents, are perpetually falling into inaccurate, at least into indistinct definitions. The word " *construxit*," as frequently occurring in this MS., by no means confirms the completion of any part of the conventual building. Sir H. Englefield, as before observed, adopts my opinion, that the whole choir had not reached its present state till the time of Abbot Boyfield, who died in 1381; and for that reason, the particular style of architecture of which it consists, was probably one of the earliest known instances, the groining of the roof, with its intersections, being no less complicated and enriched, than any since constructed. It is worthy observation, that in many instances, the original plan of ecclesiastical buildings having been begun under the patronage of any prelate or abbot, was adhered to by his successors, without deviation, until its final completion. We have satisfactory evidence of this fact at Salisbury, Exeter, and other cathedrals, which are remarkable for uniformity of style.

† *Wharton, Ang. Sac.* vol. i. p. 487.

interior is peculiarly elegant, though it loses much effect from
the concealment of the altar, of the finest tabernacle-work,
which was covered over, some years since, by a raw white
stucco, resembling a radiation.* The extreme eastern window of this beautiful chapel, with part of its fretted roof, is
now seen in a pleasing perspective, through the alcove of the
heavy unsuitable altar-piece of the choir, placed there in the
last century.† When the reformers, with indiscriminating zeal,
destroyed so many fine specimens of art, merely as the gaudy
appendages of popery, to introduce within plain unembellished
walls their own simpler worship, somewhat of ancient ornament still remained for the fanatic adherents of Cromwell to
destroy. Soon after the establishment of Charles II. on the
throne, the clergy exerted themselves, with more piety than
taste, to restore their altars and choirs to their former beauty,
and, generally speaking, without success. When we know
that the rich canopies and shrine-work, instead of being renewed, were partially injured, were chipped away to make
room for plain oak wainscot, pilasters, alcoves, and carvings
of heterogeneous shape, we must regret a misapplication without remedy. There are too many of our cathedrals to which
this observation applies.

" Originally, and prior to this injudicious interruption, the
continuity must have produced a striking idea of space and
grandeur, as may be remarked at Ely and Wells. The ancient rere-doss and high altar did not obstruct the view, as
they now remain concealed by the wainscot of oak, and may
be examined from the side galleries of the choir. Such a
specimen of exuberant foliage anterior to the reign of Henry
the Seventh, as these roofs display, is unique ; particularly in

* Removed in 1811, and the mutilated altar restored to view.

† I am gratified by observing, that the wainscot was removed in 1807,
and a chaste architectural effect produced by a stone skreen, designed by
R. Smirke, and that these objections are thus obviated. The removal was
suggested by my late valuable friend, Samuel Lysons, Esq. whose " Gloucestershire etchings" (including several portions of this cathedral) are a
lasting monument of his ingenuity and taste.

contrast with the other parts of the church. As a certain
degree of confirmation of the opinion, that the roof of the
choir is not of a later æra than the close of the fourteenth
century,* the pendents, which were so universally introduced
afterwards, as the utmost effort of architecture, are totally
omitted. It is evident, that Bishop Aldred's fabric consisted
of dimensions as extensive as the present, of which the vast
substructions, still retaining many members of early Norman
ornament, afford a sufficient proof. The whole choir, indeed,
as to its ground-plan and side-walls, is contemporary with
the nave. When the new work was adopted, half the circumference of the Norman pillars was cut away. "The heavy
tower † at the west end was taken down in the reign of
Edward III. when Abbot Horton's addition and accommodation of the nave, in its whole roof, to the Gothick style,
were made. He built likewise the north transept, which, we
collect from the MS. Lives of the Abbots, cost 781*l.* of which
Horton contributed 462*l.*, no inconsiderable sum in those
days. The passages and oratories by which the choir is surrounded, are all of Saxon, or, at least, of early Norman archi-

---

* " Tempore cujus opere et industriâ ejusdem magnum altare cum pres-
biterio cum stallis ex parte abbatis fuerunt incepta et consummata. Et ala
Sancti Pauli quæ incepta fuit in monasterio B. Petri in crastino Epiphaniæ
Domiui, anno regis Edwardi III. post conquest. XII. (1339); et in vigil.
Nat. Domini, anno regis supradicti XLVII. (1375), cum gratiâ plenarie est
consummata. Cujus operis expensæ cum omnibus suis expensis extendunt
se ad DCC.LXXXI. libras et ij den., quarum dictus abbas solvit CCCC.LXII.
prout patet in rotulis supradicti operis." — MS. ut sup. Abbot Horton
presided from 1351 to 1377.

† This western tower was rebuilt during the abbacy of John de Feldâ,
1250, which had fallen in 1116 : it resembled that at Hereford, which fell in
1786. Florence, the historic monk of Worcester, in his Annals, gives the
date of the building of the present nave 1058, and of its dedication, 1100.
The roof was renewed in 1242, as we learn from the MS. of the Lives of the
Abbots already referred to. " A. D. 1242, completa est nova volta in navi
ecclesiæ, non auxilio fabrorum ut primo, sed animosâ virtute monachorum
tunc in ipso loco existentium." May we conclude from this passage, that
the monks finished it with their own hands ? See *Whittington's Account
of the building of the Church of Nôtre Dame de Dunes in Flanders*, p. 37.

tecture. It is constructed within them ; the side-walls and low circular pillars having been reduced, and the whole lined with facings of elegant pannels. These are placed within arcades of semi-mullions, resembling windows, which are open to the choir from the galleries before mentioned. During the grand ceremonies of the church, the ladies of superior rank, and their attendants, surveyed them from above.

" In the pavement before the high altar we may notice a singular curiosity—being entirely composed of painted bricks, which were prepared for the kiln by the more ingenious monks,* who have discovered accuracy in the penciling of the armorial bearings, and fancy in the scrolls and rebus, which are the usual subjects. Most of these repeat the devices of Edward II., of the Clares and De Spencers Earls of Gloucester, Abbot Sebroke, and his immediate predecessors. †

" The rich workmanship of the cloisters, which elucidates my former remark on their general construction, is well worthy attention. One side of the square, extending a hundred and forty-eight feet, with a window of stained glass at the termination, attracts the eye immediately upon entering the cathedral, as the very striking perspective is admitted through an iron grate. It is a happy illustration of the picturesque principle in Gothick. These cloisters, begun by Abbot Horton in 1351, and left incomplete for several years, were finished by Abbot Frocester about the year 1390. All the windows were formerly filled with stained glass, which, being placed low, was the more easily taken away or destroyed.‡" In the

---

* Of Abbot Wygmore it is recorded in the same MS. " Tabulam ad altare prioris cum ymaginibus politis et deauratis sumptibus suis adornavit. Et aliam tabulam, quæ nunc est in capellâ abbatis, de eodem opere composuit. Qui in diversis artibus multùm delectabatur, ut ipse sæpissime operetur, et multos diversos operarios in diversis artibus percolleret tam in opere mechanico, quam in texturâ."

† *Carter, Ancient Sculpture and Painting,* vol. i., has given a coloured etching of this pavement.

‡ The cloisters of Peterborough and Canterbury were long celebrated for the beauty of their painted glass, afterwards broken by the Puritans. See

roof, of fan-tracery, we have one of the first and best instances. Subsequently, as in the Divinity School at Oxford, and in other buildings during the reigns of Henry the Seventh and Eighth, pendents were introduced, with an effect of surprise rather than beauty. The original and simple idea became overcharged, and lost its primary character.

" Lord Bacon mentions the whispering gallery as remarkable. It is a narrow passage, formed by five parts of an octagon, and is twenty-five yards in extent. On the outside, it appears to have been merely a second thought for the purpose of communication.

"With the variety and magnificence of ancient decorations, as well architectural as sepulchral, the antiquary will be much gratified. But the man of taste must regret that the good Bishop Benson, distinguished by Pope for his " manners and candour," should have wasted his munificence upon ill-conceived and unappropriate ornaments — upon works which are neither Gothick nor Chinese.* Kent, who was praised in his day for what he little understood, designed the skreen.†

" When Edward II. lay murdered at Berkeley Castle, Abbot Thokey ventured to show that respect for the royal corpse which had been refused to it by other ecclesiastics. He re-

Gunton and Battley. But the more common destination of windows in cloisters was to convey moral and religious instruction, in various scrolls, each bearing a scriptural text, or monkish rhymes with ethical maxims.

* We may trace to a book on architecture, written by Batty Langley, who invented five new orders of Gothick, all the incongruities which may be seen in the renovations of parish-churches. This most absurd treatise is unfortunately much approved of by carpenters and stone-masons. Kent sanctioned such gross deviations from taste by his own practice. It will be scarcely credited in this age, that Kent recommended to the good bishop to have the Norman pillars of the nave channeled or fluted; and that nothing but their being found to be unsolid, prevented this *bizarrerie* from taking place.

† Removed in 1820, and another substituted in a style of correspondent and good taste by Dr. Griffith, a prebendary, who died before its completion, having greatly contributed to the expense.

moved it to Gloucester, and performed the funeral obsequies with the accustomed splendour. Near the high altar is the monument of that inglorious prince, still in the highest preservation, with the figure finely carved. Rysbrack visited this tomb with professional veneration, and declared the recumbent figure to be the best specimen of contemporary sculpture in England,* and certainly the work of an Italian artist. I conjecture that it was executed by some of those who accompanied or succeeded Pietro Cavallini.

I noticed in Italy three tombs much larger, composed of verd-antique and various marbles, all of similar form to that of King Edward, and with equally elaborate canopies. They are the tombs of the Scaligeri, lords of Verona in the fourteenth century, where they stand exposed to the open air, at the angle of a street, as entire as when first erected.†

" Soon after Edward III. was seated on the throne,‡ he made a progress, attended by his whole court, to pay the customary honours to his deceased father, for whom the con-

---

* This tomb has been frequently the subject of very good engravings, which are well known, and casts have been taken from the head. In Smyth's *History of the Berkeley Family*, (a MS. now preserved in the Castle,) is an account of the expenses incurred for the removal of the King's body to Gloucester, which were inconsiderable, as they were chiefly defrayed by the Abbot.

† They contain equestrian figures, which are amply described and delineated in the *Archæologia*, vol. xviii. p. 186.

‡ Adam de Staunton, elected in 1337, ob. 1351 — " Cujus tempore constructa est magna volta chori magnis et multis expensis, et sumptuosis cum stallis ibidem ex parte doni et oblationis fidelium ad tumbam regis confluentium, quæ ut opinio vulgi dicit, quod si omnes oblationes ibidem collatæ, super ecclesiam expenderentur, potuisset de novo facillime reparari." The offerings of Edward III. Queen Philippa, Edward Prince of Wales, and the nobility, are all distinctly noticed in the MS. above cited.

John Boyfield was elected abbot in 1377, and died in 1381 — " Et in alâ Sancti Pauli juxta tumbam Thomæ Horton abbatis in australi parte sepelitur; quia, dum esset præcentor hujus loci, supervisor fuerat ejusdem operis."—Id. MS. I presume, in this and a foregoing quotation, that " ala" means " ala transepti," in distinction to the " ala navis ecclesiæ," though they are not specified.

vent, in gratitude for the oblations made at his tomb, soli-
cited canonization a century afterward, but without success.

So large was the fund of wealth they acquired, that it furnished supplies for the rebuilding of the whole church beyond the nave, under the auspices of succeeding abbots, who
did not materially deviate from one plan.*

The following very characteristic description, not originally intended for Gloucester, is extracted from a poem of no
common merit.

> ———— " Doom'd to hide her banish'd head
> For ever, Gothick architecture fled :
> Forewarn'd, she left in one most beauteous place
> Her pendent roof, her windows' branchy grace,
> Pillars of cluster'd reeds, and tracery of lace."

FOSBROKE'S Economy of Monastic Life, p. 73.

---

* Hearne has published a poem on the foundation of the Abbey of Gloucester, which he has attributed to William Malverne, otherwise Parker, the
abbot, who survived the dissolution in 1541.   Speaking of Edward II. he
observes:

> " By whose oblations the south isle of thys church
> Edyfied was and build, and also the queere."—*Stanza* xv.

DISCOURSE IV.

ANALYSIS OF CATHEDRAL, CONVENTUAL,

AND

PAROCHIAL CHURCHES

IN

𝕰𝖓𝖌𝖑𝖆𝖓𝖉.

" We admire commonly those things which are oldest and greatest; old monuments and high buildings do affecte us above measure—and what is the reason? Because what is oldest, cometh nearest to God for antiquity; and what is greatest, cometh nearest his works in spaciousness and magnitude."

BISHOP CORBET.

ANALYSIS OF CATHEDRAL CHURCHES

IN

ENGLAND.

BEFORE I enter upon a more minute and systematic description in a tabular form, a few remarks may be necessary concerning internal composition and appendages.

I. The WESTERN FRONT or FAÇADE has, from the first, occupied a pre-eminent part of every large church. It exhibits a gradual alteration of style, from the early Norman at Colchester, Malmsbury, and Castle Acre, to the front of Windsor chapel, at the close of the fifteenth century. In the chief feature, the entrance door-way, there is a remarkable difference between those in England and upon the Continent. We give the preference to very spacious windows above doors so small as to have no relative proportion. The French and German portail forms nearly half of the total space, whilst a circular or rose window, (as already particularised,) of vast diameter, proudly surmounts it.

Yet ornament was not neglected by our own architects. In the doorcases, a series of statues, in small niches, is sometimes carried up like a hollow moulding; and in others, double foliated tracery, branching freely from one of the outer mouldings, gives a richness superior to any other decoration. Canopies, each being formed of four segments of arches inverted, having crockets with a large finial at every point, were not uncommon. The south door of Lincoln, one in the cloisters at Norwich, and the north entrance of Lichfield, cathedrals, are of this description.

II. Of CLOISTERS I have already spoken incidentally. They were first introduced as an appendage to the larger monasteries, and their use, in our climate, is obvious, which will account for their greater frequency in England. Some notice of three of the more remarkable may suffice. Those of Salisbury (1240) form an exact square of 181 feet 9 inches withinside, by 18 feet wide. The ambulatory is rendered beautiful, having windows open to the air, and the dividing mullion brought down to the floor.—At Norwich are some of the most spacious in England (f. 176. 8 E. and W.; f. 177. 2 N. and S.; and f.12 only wide.) The window-heads are each wrought in a distinct pattern, (as they are likewise at Exeter cathedral, and the chapel of Merton College, Oxford,) and the mullions do not reach to the floor by several feet. Begun in 1320.—At Gloucester, finished in 1390: a perfect inclosed square, originally glazed, (f. 144.3 by 148, and f.18.6 in width.) None in England present so perfect an example of the fretted roof, as it springs from circular groins, at each angle; it is also of the earliest date, and one of the most complicated specimens of that manner.

As cloisters were more particularly adapted to conventual life, no doubt can be entertained but that many attached to the greater abbeys at least equalled those above-mentioned —indeed, many of the cathedrals were likewise conventual. This assertion is confirmed by the remains at Fountains, Yorkshire; Tewkesbury, Gloucestershire, and many others.

III. CRYPTS were an essential and constituent part of the churches built by Normans, both in France and England. They were used for the celebration of masses for the dead, and are always excavated under the choir or chancel. They are sometimes called "undercrofts," and are of nearly parallel dimensions with the upper end, always semicircular. The most ancient in England is said to be that of St. Peter's church in Oxford. Under the whole eastern extremity of Canterbury cathedral is one of extraordinary loftiness. In both these remain curious hieroglyphical sculptures on the capitals of the pillars.   At Rochester, Winchester, Gloucester, and particularly at York, they are still perfect, and worthy of curious investigation.   All these have their date from the eleventh to the earlier half of the twelfth century, if not before, and are contemporary with the most ancient cathedral and conventual churches in England.

IV. PORCHES, distinct from the great western entrance, are attached to the aisles or transept.   The north porch of Salisbury, and the south of Lincoln cathedrals, are the most spacious and beautiful.   Of a later age, others, at Doncaster; Cirencester, Gloucestershire; Hitchin, Herts ; Thaxted, in Essex ; Redcliff, Bristol, north porch ; Hereford and Gloucester cathedrals, are worthy of selection.

V. CHAPTER-HOUSES, from the best evidence, are coeval with the building of any cathedral or monastery, certainly with the early Anglo-Norman bishops.   They were not only built as necessary to the conventual establishment, for assembling the members of the church in council at their elections, and for other purposes, but were likewise the depositories of the deceased superiors and noble benefactors.   The most ancient of them now existing, and others taken down, were erected, as above stated ; but an entirely new and more beautiful form was

invented early in the thirteenth century. At
first they were, in general, oblong, having in
certain instances a round end like the choir.
That at Christ-Church, Oxford, gives an excellent example of the lancet arch. Most of these,
as in the subsequent manner, were panneled
around the base with interlaced Norman arches
in the walls; within them the monks sat in
full chapter. They are always approached
from the cloisters, and in several instances, as
at Chester and Bristol, had large vestibules.
Several, which were built as early as the twelfth
century, have windows with a central single
column. But early in the next, the parallelogram was abandoned for the polygonal form,
probably after the model of the round churches
which had been introduced by the Knights
Templars. Those of the chapter-houses, the
dates of which may be referred with certainty
to the fourteenth century, or even later, abound
in the most beautiful forms, and the richest
style of decoration, by which that æra in particular may be discriminated. The insulated
shaft, apparently, but not really, supporting the
concentrated springings of the groins, has thus
suggested a more bold attempt to produce surprise; or the deeply-pendent bosses from the
roof, which became so frequent during the
reign of the Tudors. Perhaps the vault of the

Divinity School at Oxford, finished in 1480, was the prototype. I do not recollect an earlier instance of that latest Gothick invention.

The art of sculpture (more properly perhaps to be denominated carving), as applied to, indeed a constituent of architectural design, was the constant ally of the Gothick in its gradual changes, and profusely contributed, when on a smaller scale, to the embellishment of the interior parts of a structure. I will therefore advert briefly to its history and application.

VI. SHRINES and ALTAR-SKREENS admitted a very wide scope for design and embellishment. Their composition included many large and small receptacles for the standing images of saints, with pedestals and canopies, capable of exhibiting an exhaustless variety of architectural decoration. Sometimes they were mural, and occupied the whole end wall of the choir ; in other instances they divided the choir from the transept.

The most memorable are those already mentioned in this work—at Winchester, St. Alban's, and Neville's skreen at Durham. This was discriminated by the old master-masons as " shrine or tabernacle work."

Crockets, so called by Norman architects, and invented by them, were universally applied. They are composed of curled pieces of foliage, placed at the angles of spires, canopies, tabernacles, and turrets externally, as well as to the shrines within the church; and they contribute to all a remarkable richness or elegance. The flying buttresses are finished by crocketed pinnacles.

VII. STALLS are of the same early introduction, and partook of every variety in architectural form and ornament. They were, when composed of stone, first used near the altar by the officiating priests in choirs, and as subsellia in parish chancels. Many still, only partially mutilated, may be inspected, and are beautiful from the excessive delicacy of workmanship apparent in their canopies, and other internal parts of the most intricate design. The statues are destroyed, almost without exception. In choirs, where many were united in one general plan, carved oak was soon substituted, as a material affording greater facility for the most elaborate carvings. The episcopal throne at Exeter has never been surpassed; and the stalls of Salisbury, York, and Exeter, with the Garter stalls at Windsor, furnish us with unrivalled examples. Both for quantity and excellence of this complex workmanship in wood, the more perfect specimens were finished between the commencement of the fourteenth and the end of the sixteenth century. There are very fine stalls at Beverley, placed there as late as 1520—those at Winchester College, not long before. The cathedral of St. David's, and some others in Wales, contain large and beautiful specimens.

Imitations of the "boisseries" invented and brought to absolute perfection in France, were likewise adopted in England, of which the oak skreen which separates the choir from the chapel of King's College, Cambridge, (1524,) may vie with any other example of its partial adoption.

But as exhibiting one entire design, both as to extent of dimension and finishing, is a complete oratory or private chapel, formed of the heart of oak, late in the fifteenth century, and now in a state of original perfection at Luton, Bedfordshire, the seat of the Marquess of Bute. The infinite variety and the richness of execution abounding in the scrolls, friezes, inscriptions, and tabernacle work, is nowhere exceeded; and its present state is not its least remarkable singularity. "Ornaments cannot be more profuse, beauty of carving more evident, or unpainted oak more to be admired."

VIII. NICHES OF STONE WITH PEDESTALS AND CANOPIES. That the art of sculpture was well known to the Norman architects of the second school, the evidence is incontrovertible. I advert to that mode of it, as it first appeared in the greatest beauty, in the statues of Eleanor queen of Edward I., which have been previously noticed. There is scarcely a cathedral in which, (before the destruction wrought by the icono-clastic fanatics,) many which equalled them did not abound ; and sepulchral effigies were spared to confirm this assertion. Several vo-lumes are extant relating only to sepulchral monuments, to which plans and engravings are annexed, with sufficient attention to their true forms.

Carved figures in freestone, placed within niches, were no less numerous externally than within the church ; as at Wells, Lincoln, and Lichfield, in their façades. The bas-reliefs at Ely and Lincoln are singular. At Exeter and Lincoln there are many figures standing in a row, as if playing in concert, with such instru-ments of music in their hands as were then in usage, certainly borrowed from very curious instances in Normandy. Invention and skill were no less exerted in the complex design and ornaments of niches, consisting necessarily of a canopy and pedestal. These more especially presented a beauty of form in the minute and natural representation of leaves and vegetable substances, particularly the vine. Nor was ca-pricious fancy unexercised, when we observe the soffits of the arches of doorcases composed

of a series of similar niches, upon a small scale,
made to follow into the curve of a Gothick
arch, from the base to the centre. This conceit we borrowed from France, as at Rouen, &c.

> " Habenries and pinnacles,
> Imageries and tabernacles."
>   CHAUCER.

and there they are exuberant. In the south
porch of St. Ouen at Rouen, the entrance is
surrounded within by pendent trefoil arches,
which spring from carved bosses, and form an
open festoon of tracery. In that of St. Maclou,
in the same city, the bosses of the groined roof
are wrought and perforated into filligrain, the
work extending over the intersections of the
groins, which are seen through its reticulations.
The vault within is ornamented with pendentives. Similar members of architecture are
found in many churches in France, to which
additions were made at the close of the fifteenth century.

IX. BAPTISMAL FONTS. The variety shown
in the shape and design of these is infinite;
and upon no subjects did the sculptors exert
more fancy or taste, both in the shape and design of ornament. No genuine Saxon work
is so frequent as the font, in those parochial
churches in counties which the Saxons principally inhabited. They have frequently survived dilapidations, and have been religiously

preserved. The shape is a large basin for immersion, standing upon low pillars. Of such, the carvings are not unfrequently rudely copied from Roman designs, and sometimes a series of figures representing a legend. Those in Winton and Lincoln cathedrals are well known. Among the Norman and in the successive æras, the respective styles may be traced so far, as that they may be easily discriminated as to date. Many exhibit a richness, and even elegance of fancy, and nicety of execution, when detached from coats of white lime subsequently laid over them by the village beautifiers of country churches.

After the large hollowed basin for total immersion was superseded, about the fourteenth century, it would appear that the first ambition of the sculptors was to invent a new design for a baptismal font. One was very rarely a copy taken from another; and in this novelty the most expensive workmanship was not spared. Few subjects of Gothick art have been made more familiar by engravings.* Towards the close of that century, a very ornamental appendage to fonts was introduced, and chiefly

* See *Archæologia*, vol. vi. p. 37, &c.; *Lysons' Gloucestershire* etchings; and *Magna Britannia*. " Of Norman fonts, that of Aylesbury is the most classically designed; and of later invention, the most beautiful, those in Norwich cathedral, Ufford, and St. George, Sudbury, both in Suffolk."

in the eastern counties : these were, covers of carved oak, exquisitely wrought and embellished, which were suspended from the ceiling, moveable at pleasure, and not unfrequently consisting of a pinnacle or frame several feet high.*

X. SACELLA, or ORATORIES, were introduced as an appendage to churches, for the purpose of receiving the tombs, and celebrating prayers for the dead. In France, they are numerously attached to the choir and chevet; and not unfrequently to the choir and transept, in England. About the fifteenth century, they were erected withinside the church, and sometimes rose to the height of forty feet, with sufficient internal space for the officiating priest. The windows were filled with stained glass, and the roofs painted, with gilded bosses and emblazonings. Upon these subjects, the ingenious architect displayed his best talents; for the sculptor worked only in subordination to his plan, which afforded an ample scope for the invention and application of minuter ornaments. It is remarkable, that while the great structures bore a general, and sometimes a near analogy to each other, as far as accordant style; scarcely any two of these sacella, although of the same æra, are strictly similar.

* A Series of Baptismal Fonts, lately published by F. Simpson, 4to. 1829, classifies them—1. Saxon ; 2. Early English ; 3. Decorated English of the lower æra.

For size and magnificence, I select the series
of prelates' oratories at Canterbury and Winchester, so well known. The little chapels
surrounding the tomb of Henry V. at Westminster, and that at Worcester of Prince
Arthur, are singularly fine. To these may be
added, without farther enumeration, Lord La
Warr's at Boxgrove, Sussex; and that of Poyntz,
attached to the Gaunt's chapel at Bristol.

Of the exterior parts of the elevation, after
the façade or western front, the DOORCASES
and WINDOWS, in their gradual change of position, form, and embellishment, are worthy observation. Of these, satisfactory accounts are
given in the various descriptive treatises upon
Gothick architecture. In the thirteenth century, the doorcases at the north-west end of
Salisbury, the south entrance of Lincoln, and
the west of Lichfield, may be selected. Windows of the same period, equally to be remarked, are those called the Four Sisters, at York;
Exeter cathedral, and Merton College, Oxford,
where the ramifications of the heads of each
exhibit a distinct pattern, and are of the succeeding century. As late as the fourteenth,
windows of enormous breadth and height, as
at York and Gloucester, had their first introduction. They occupied so vast a space in the
whole front, as to destroy that rich and harmonious effect which is admirable in the French

cathedrals; and though they originally presented a blaze of light through the stained
glass, yet they were not so striking as the circular or rose-windows, which are better adapted
to such a display.

XI. GALILEES were larger porticoes or chapels, always placed at the western entrance:
they are peculiar to England, and there not
often applied. We now see them at Durham,
Ely, Peterborough, and Lincoln. They were
intended to receive such of the congregation
as were under censure, and prohibited from
entering the church.

XII. EASTERN and TRANSEPT FRONTS. Principal examples are those of Ely and Lincoln in
thirteenth century; York and Beverley in the
next; and those of Norwich, Winchester, and
Gloucester, with Tewkesbury abbey, in the
fourteenth; which last-mentioned were all of
them superstructures upon the Norman choirs.
Of northern transepts, those of Westminster
and York are the best examples.

XIII. WESTERN TOWERS. Upon most of
these were superadded spires of great height,
constructed with timber-frame, and originally
covered with lead placed octangularly in ribs.
I have incidentally mentioned, that these were
introduced into England as early as the beginning of the thirteenth century, but from their
greater insecurity and danger, were succeeded

by others of stone. The Chronicles frequently give us the date of their destruction, from the effects of wind or conflagration. Old St. Paul's, Lincoln, and Ely, were very remarkable, as being of the first description; and those of Salisbury, Chichester, and Norwich, are the boldest instances of construction with stone. The western towers, both of Lincoln, York, and Beverley, are of beautiful forms.

XIV. CENTRAL TOWERS are erected upon the great arcade by which the transept is divided, and the nave from the choir.* They formed an integral part of the scheme or plan of a cathedral church, as designed by the Norman architects, and were massive and low, as at Winchester; not intended to contain bells, but to give light to the transept, having many windows, and being open to the vaulting, at York, Lincoln, Peterborough, and Norwich. Such have since been differently built, and, as at Ely, called louvres. In several instances, they have served as the bases both of towers and spires, which, in subsequent ages, have risen above them. Lincoln claims precedence, both in point of time and beautiful elevation. But the zenith of perfection in towers, was the reign of Henry VII., amply displayed in those of

* The finest remaining Norman specimen is at Tewkesbury, built by Robert Consul, 1130. It was equalled by that, now a ruin, at Malmsbury, of the same age.

Gloucester and Canterbury. Numerous specimens of the same age and style are seen more particularly in the western division of the kingdom, even in obscure villages, the work of munificent bishops, or of richly-endowed abbots. In Lincolnshire, the most lofty and best constructed spires enrich the views of a flat country: those of Lowth, Grantham, and Newark, rise immediately from the ground, with greater advantage.

XV. OCTANGULAR TERMINATIONS OF THE EASTERN END. Such were, from the earliest time, common in France, but they have only obtained partially in England. At Canterbury, Peterborough, Westminster, Lichfield, Norwich, and Gloucester, they vary from the angular to the circular form, which, without doubt, was suggested primarily by the Roman basilicæ.

XVI. SUPERSTRUCTURES. Of choirs, upon the original Norman walls: — at Gloucester, 1330; Norwich, 1480; Winchester, 1510; Oxford, 1530; each in the style of its age.

XVII. FLYING ARCHES, or, as they are with greater propriety styled by the French, from whom we have borrowed them, " Arcs boutans." But to fix the precise æra of their earliest usage might be a difficult investigation, because they have been necessarily added to churches having loftier superstructures upon the original

walls, to support which they were then required. At first, they presented a simple diagonal
form ; afterwards, when connected with ornamented pinnacles, the lower sides of them were
enriched with segments of open circles, crocketed at each termination. One of the most
elaborate specimens is now seen in the exterior
of Henry the Seventh's chapel, which has been
lately so well restored. Of the most ancient
and simple instances, are those at Caen in Normandy, and, in England, at Salisbury cathedral. An anonymous modern critic* has given
the following judicious opinion concerning
them. " Flying buttresses, as they are called,
have an elegance in their form that may please
the eye, examining them severally; and in their
construction they have ingenuity, the idea of
which may amuse the fancy. And there rests
their merit : they seem hardly right appendages of stone-work ; props of cane for a giant,
who ought to be able to stand by himself.
Thus, in the lateral view of a cathedral, neither
length nor breadth can be measured by the
eye."

XVIII. CONSTRUCTION OF ROOFS AND
VAULTS. More anciently, one vault runs longitudinally along the church, and the upper
windows open into the sides of this longitudinal vault by shorter vaulted spaces, which,

---

* *Principles of Design in Architecture*, 8vo. 1809. p. 125.

running perpendicularly to the length of the building, may be called transverse vaults. The mode of vaulting with semicircular arches both ways, and with no diagonal ribs, appears to have succeeded to the wooden roofing of the first Norman cathedrals. Arcades were surmounted by triforia, and small single windows, sometimes doubled, were inserted into the clerestory walls.

Advancing to later examples, these differences become more complicated, consisting of a very great variety of mouldings. The vaulting shaft rises from the floor to the vault, and is there reticulated into an almost infinite diversification of forms, which are objects of sight rather than description. In these cases, the vaulting is modified by the introduction of the pointed arch, and both the longitudinal and transverse bands become pointed also. " These have been discriminated as having cells or hollow spaces, which may be called quadripartite; sexpartite, and octopartite. The diagonal ribs of pointed vaults are never flat and square-edged. Rolls, or bent cylinders, constitute these lines, which are afterwards clustered, and then the clustered parts are separated and ramified, and thus assume any of the endless forms of Gothick architecture."*

* *Professor Wheley's Essay.*

XIX. SPIRES, considered separately, and as accessories to towers. The most ancient spire of stone is that of Sleaford in Lincolnshire, for in the instances both of Old St. Paul's and Salisbury, they were after-thoughts, or subsequent additions. Many others were erected in the thirteenth century, which commence distinctly from the parapet. They were constructed with timber-frame, and covered with lead. In the fourteenth century, they were composed of stone only, when their sides began to be purfled with crockets, and the pinnacles connected with the spire by flying buttresses. Those of the cathedrals of Sarum and Norwich have fillets or bands of open quatrefoils. Of crocketed spires, the singularly beautiful are those of Whittlesea, Cambridgeshire, and Lowth in Lincolnshire ; but instances abound more, certainly, in some counties than in others.

The roofs, suspended by invisible support ; the columns and arcades of incredible lightness ; the towers gaining symmetry by their extreme height ; but, more than all, " the heaven-directed spire," elevated the mind of the devout spectator to the contemplation of the sublime religion which he professed.

The intention of the following arrangement is to submit to the reader, under one view, a scheme of every cathedral in England, exhibiting the date of each component part now in existence. These have been collected from ecclesiastical records, in which notices are found, not only of dimensions, but of bishops, abbots, and priors, who contributed to the several buildings. Whether we are to consider them, in every instance, as architects and designers, may admit of doubt; but some are known to have been skilled in architecture, and may be ranked as professors in the English school. Many of the great parts of the cathedral churches, which are attributed to one prelate or abbot, may have required more money to complete them than could have been collected in one lifetime; in which case, the name recorded is frequently his who began or completed the structure, and sometimes that of him who contributed the largest sum of money, or who gave the plan. The date of foundation, not that of completion, is the true æra of the style of architecture by which it should be designated. This fact is not commonly attended to, particularly where the first plan has been scrupulously followed; and we are aware that contradictory statements abound. " Classifications should give clearness and connexion to descriptions in detail, without which they are rarely intelligible, and observations are rendered uninteresting." An attentive investigation of the history of the early English architecture has scarcely been rewarded with more than the discovery of a solitary name, or the confirmation of a dubious date. The art, of all others, which flourished most in the dark ages, has been involved in the deepest obscurity, not only with respect to its principles, but its history. Gundulphus, Henry of Blois, Grostête, William of Wykeham, Alan de Walsingham, and Robert Tulley, shine conspicuously in the Gothick night. It is a well-founded tradition, that these were equally versed in the science and practice of architecture. The master-masons, and the fraternity which accompanied them, and over whom they exercised a kind of jurisdiction, executed these stupendous works, and not unfrequently designed them. They had many archetypes and plans to follow, if they wanted skill to invent. It has been questioned, by those who wish to consider the history and principles of our early architecture as involved in more mystery and obscurity than they really are, whether or not these magnificent piles were raised without system or detailed plans. Such a circumstance is scarcely probable, even in the earlier centuries; but in the fifteenth, there is positive proof, from the wills of Henry VI. and Richard Duke of York, that a plan of their intended colleges had been laid before them for approbation.

The plans and working-drawings first made, and decided upon by the founders of the cathedrals of Salisbury, Exeter, Lichfield, and Wells, were uniform, and were strictly adopted by their successors, for centuries, till the whole structures had reached eventual perfection in the state we now see them. Can any doubt be longer entertained respecting their preservation among the church records, and their probable destruction at the Reformation, when all graphic or illuminated MSS. or rolls were cut into pieces and dispersed? But in libraries on the Continent many are still preserved, perfect, and upon an extensive scale.*

* *Moller.*

APPENDIX OF ILLUSTRATIONS

TO

THE FOURTH DISCOURSE.

BATH—CONVENTUAL CHURCH OF THE BENEDICTINES.

Dates.	Founders.	Nave.			Choir.			Aisles.			Transept.			Our Lady's Chapel.	Cloisters.	Chapter-house.	Tower.		
		L.	B.	H.	L.	B.	H.	L.	B.	H.	L.	B.	H.				L.	B.	H.
1495–1502	Oliver King, bishop	.	.	.	75	35	73	of the nave			46	48	74	None	None	None	20	30	150
1532	Bird ⎱ Priors							112	21	38	46	28	74						
	Gibbes ⎰	136	72	78	.	.	.	of the choir											
1570	Inhabitants of Bath							80	21	38									
1609	Sir J. Harrington, &c.																		
	James Montague, bishop.																		

Remarkable parts of the Structure.—The building was left unfinished at the Reformation, and was finally completed by Bishop Montague and the executors of Lord Treasurer Burleigh. Oliver King, bishop, and Priors Bird and Holeway, gave the plan and carried it to a certain point. The tower has four turrets without pinnacles, and is an oblong of the proportion of 35 to 25 feet, north and south. The transept is narrow and the aisles very low. The tower is narrowed to the transept. To the extremities of the west end is attached a continued alto-relievo, representing "Jacob's ladder," with the angels ascending and descending, as in the founder's dream. There is no triforium nor ornamented band with perforations, but a plain string course only. The upper tier of windows is lofty beyond proportion, and the aisles are little higher than a cloister. Plans and Sections published by the Society of Antiquaries. Total dimensions 210–126.

BRISTOL—CONVENTUAL CHURCH OF ST. AUGUSTINE.—Barret's History.

Dates.	Founders.	Nave. L. B. H.	Choir. L. B. H.	Aisles.	Transept. L. B. H.	Our Lady's Chapel.	Cloisters.	Chapter-house. L. B. H.	Tower. Height.
1160	Robert Fitz-Harding	. . .	. . .	. . .	. . .	Elder Lady's Chapel.	Square 103 Partly destroyed	46 26 – Vestibule	. . .
1230	Robert, third Lord Berkeley .	75 73 43	Originally included	. . .	128 – 43	. . .	. . .	. . .	. . .
1311–1332	Maurice, fourth Lord Berkeley, and Edmund Knowles, abbot								
1463	Elliot and William Hunt, abbots	. . .	100 – 43 Our Lady's Chapel	. . .	North Tr.	. . .	. . .	. . .	127
1481–1500	John Newland, or Nailheart, abbot. Completed .								

Remarkable parts of the Structure.—This church displays two distinct species of beautiful architecture. The Chapter-house and Elder Lady's Chapel were built at the beginning and close of the twelfth century; and the present nave and choir in the beginning of the fourteenth. There are several accounts given of its imperfect state. It is probable that it was never completed after the plan of Abbot Knowles, and not destroyed either at the suppression or by Cromwell. The tower has been the base of an intended spire. In *Lysons' Gloucestershire Etchings* are many interesting prints of this cathedral. The parapet and pinnacles are of disproportionate size, unaccordant with the original plan, and probably added as a hasty completion. This has a singularity, that there are no external flying buttresses. The side walls of the nave are strengthened by the roofs of the aisles, formed by complicated open arches, which have a very beautiful effect. The aisles and nave are of equal height—only forty-three feet.

CANTERBURY—CATHEDRAL CHURCH.—From Wild's History.

Dates.	Founders.	Nave.			Choir.			Aisles.			Transept.			Our Lady's Chapel.			Cloisters.			Chapter-house.			Towers.
		L.	B.	H.	L.	B.	H.	L.	B.	H.	L.	B.	H.	L.	B.	H.	L.	B.	H.	L.	B.	H.	
1070 Archbishop Lanfranc 1090 Archbishop Anselme.		The second Church			Destroyed by Fire 1174																		N.W. 100 ft. high
1100 Ernulphus } Priors Conrade																							
1122 Archbishop W. Corboil. 1174 W. Senensis } Architects W. Anglus		Present Church			150	40	71	Included			Upper 154			Becket's and Trin. Chapels.									
1304 Henry de Estrey, prior.																							
1379 S. Sudbury to W. Courtenay } Archbishops 1431 T. Arundel		Improved and ornamented									Lower 124												N.W. spire of lead added 100 ft. high, taken down 1705. S.W. 130
1420 T. Chittenden } Priors T. Goldstone		214	94	80																92	37	52	
1468 W. Sellinge 1490 W. Morton, Archbishop.																	134 square						Central 234 high; 35 diameter.

Remarkable parts of the Structure.—The original Anglo-Saxon structure of Archbishop Lanfranc was rebuilt after the canonization of T. à Becket. The church was newly modelled in all its parts in the fourteenth century. Archbishop Courtenay expended 300*l.* on the cloisters.—Archbishop Arundel contributed 1000 marks to the nave, which Chicheley completed. He likewise built a tower, and furnished it with bells.—The exquisitely beautiful central tower was finished by Archbishop Morton, 1500. Our Lady's Chapel, built by Prior Goldstone, between 1449 and 1468, is particularly fine. The crypt is of greater extent and more lofty than any other in England. The Norman imitations of Corinthian columns in the choir, and the alternate circular and pointed arches in Becket's crown, are the earliest and most curious instances. The central tower beautiful. Total dimensions: extreme internal length 514 by 154.—*Canterbury Cathedral, by C. Wild,* fol. 1807.

CARLISLE—CATHEDRAL CHURCH.—From Nicolson's History.

Dates.	Founders.	Nave.			Choir.			Aisles.			Transept.			Our Lady's Chapel.			Cloisters.	Chapter-house.	Tower.		
	Bishops.	L.	B.	H.	L.	B.	H.	L.	B.	H.	L.	B.	H.	L.	B.	H.			L.	B	H.
1150 1270	Henry Murdac, abbot of Fountains	82	–	71 originally 164	.	.	.	Included			.	.	.	.	.	.	Destroyed	Destroyed			
1353–1363	Gilbert de Wilton, bishop	.			137	–	71	71	–	–	124	28	71	.	.	.	.	.			
1363–1397	T. de Apylby.																				
1400–1419	T. de Strickland	.															.	.			128

Remarkable parts of the Structure.—The greater part of the nave was taken down by Cromwell's soldiers to erect barracks. The opening has been closed by a wall. The eastern window is large and beautiful.—Total dimensions 219–124.

CHESTER—CONVENTUAL CHURCH OF THE BENEDICTINES.

Dates.	Founders.	Nave.			Choir.	Aisles.			Transept.			Our Lady's Chapel.	Cloisters.	Chapter-house.			Tower.
		L.	B.	H.	L.B.H.	L.	B.	H.	L.	B.	H.			L.	B.	H.	Height.
1128 1210	Ranulf Earl of Chester	.	.	.	.	.	.	.	Transept dissimilar. North, a parish church 180 — -			.	.	50	26	36	Finished in 1508.
1320	.	.	.	.	.	.	.	.	.	.	.	.	.	.	.	.	127
1485	Simon Ripley, abbot —— Oldham, abbot.	Upper part - 73 73			.	of the Choir			.	.	.	.	.	Vestibule 33 27 12,9			
1508	.	The western front			.	.	.	.	.	.	.	.	.	.	.	.	

Remarkable parts of the Structure.—The lower part of the nave and the north transept are the more ancient parts of the church. The chapter-house was built by Ranulf Earl of Chester; and many of his descendants are interred there. It is a specimen of the architecture of his day. The refectory of the abbey still remains—98 feet by 34. The whole roof is of timber-frame. There is a north transept only, of large dimensions.—Total dimensions 348–180.—*Illustration of Chester Cathedral, by C. Wild*, fol. 1813.

CHICHESTER—CATHEDRAL CHURCH.—From Dallaway's History of Western Sussex.

Dates.	Founders.	Nave. L. B. H.	Choir. L. B. H.	Aisles. L. B. H.	Transept. L. B. H.	Our Lady's Chapel. L. B. H.	Cloisters. L. B. H.	Chapter-house.	Tower and Spire.
	Bishops.	First Church							
1094	Ralph, 2 . .	105 95 61		Included					At the west end 95
1125	Siffrede, 2 .			− 91 −					Bell Tower 107
	Abbot of Glastonbury			There are four aisles,	North . .				Spire added to
1217	Ralph de Warham .	· · ·	100 64 61	two on either side	South with	47 21 22	W. 84 14		the tower
1282	Gilbert de St. Leofard	· · ·	· · ·	the nave: the outer	the window		S. 198 10		271 high.
1329	John de Langton .	· · ·	· · ·	were added. It is			E. 122 10		
				the only instance in					
				England					
1520	Robert Sherbourn .	Repairs and embellishments of the choir, &c.							

Remarkable parts of the Structure.—The early Norman style of the original building has been in several instances accommodated to the Gothick of the thirteenth century. There is a great resemblance between this spire and that of Salisbury, as well as a coincidence of date; from which circumstances they have been attributed to the same architect. R. Poore had been bishop of this see before Salisbury.—Total dimensions 407–131.—This structure was much dilapidated during the siege, 1642: unskilfully repaired after the Restoration: again, internally, with worse taste, in 1816; and, in 1829, restored to its ancient forms and colour, by clearing the sculpture of ochre and white-lime, &c. The present church may be considered as having been founded by Siffrede 2, upon the ruins of the church built by Bishop Ralph the second in 1094.

DURHAM—CATHEDRAL CHURCH.—Account by the Society of Antiquaries.

Dates.	Founders.	Nave.			Choir.			Aisles.			Transept.			Our Lady's Chapel.			Cloisters.			Chapter-house.			Towers.		
	Bishops.	L.	B.	H.	L.	B.	H.	L.	B.	H.	L.	B.	H.	L.	B.	H.	L.	B.	H.	L.	B.	H.	L.	B.	H.
1093	William de Carilelpho	260	74	69																					
1128	Ralph Flambard.																								
1230	Richard Poore, and							Included			176	57	–												
1233	Melsonby, prior																						Western towers – – 143		
	Bertram Middleton and Hugh Darlington, priors }				120	74	71				90	18	–	Chapel of Nine Altars											
	Nicholas de Farnham, bishop.																								
1295	Richard de Houton, prior													135 35 – Built as a transept at the end of the choir.			A quadrangle of 147 feet			Taken down in 1797			Central tower – – 214		
1390	Walter Skirlaw, bishop																								
1420	T. Langley, bishop.																								
1438																									

Remarkable parts of the Structure.—The pillars of the nave are curiously striated, with lines drawn in various figures. The galilee or chapel at the western front is 50 feet by 78. Total dimensions 420–176.—Bishop Nicholas de Farnham (according to *Spelman*, annexed to *Speed's History*) vaulted the whole church; and Bishop Langley finished the galilee in 1430, which had been originally constructed before the great western entrance in 1180, by Bishop Hugh Pudsey, (at an expense of 500*l.*) in which he was buried. Its removal was intended under the direction of the late James Wyat, who was employed by the Dean and Chapter to reform (*more suo*) and beautify their cathedral. The galilee, however, eventually escaped demolition. The re-modelling by Wyat took place in 1795, under the patronage of Bishop Barrington, who first engaged him at Salisbury.

EXETER—CATHEDRAL CHURCH.—Account by the Society of Antiquaries.

Dates.	Founders.	Nave.			Choir.			Aisles.			Transept.			Our Lady's Chapel.			Cloisters.			Chapter-house.			Towers.		
		L.	B.	H.	L.	B.	H.	L.	B.	H.	L.	B.	H.	L.	B.	H.	L.	B.	H.	L.	B.	H.	L.	B.	H.
	Bishops.																								
1100–1128	W. Warlewast	180	40	68																			28	28	145
1280–1293	Peter Quivil																								
1293–1307	Thomas Bytton										140	32	68	65	35	40									
1307–1318	Walter Stapyldon				132	34	68	148	20	35															
1340	Edmund Lacy							132	20	35															
1290–1380	Thomas Brentingham																133	133	–	55	32	50			

Remarkable parts of the Structure.—The western façade was built, and two arches added to the length of the nave, by John Grandison, bishop, about 1360. The towers are placed at either end of the transept. The cloisters are perfect only on one side: the other three, with all the sculpture, were destroyed by Cromwell's soldiers. The aisles are continued collaterally with the choir. The plan of this whole church is that originally designed by Bishop Quivil, from which none of his successors have deviated in their completion of it. Two hundred and eighty years in building. Total dimensions 390–140. Bishop Grandison (according to *Speed*) completely vaulted the church, who says that the chapter-house, begun by Bishop Lacy, was finished by Bishop Neville, and that the north tower was built by Bishop Courtenay (1478–1487). Bishop Grandison's skreen is known to antiquaries as displaying a series of statues, more numerous and entire than any other cathedral. The gallery, in the transept, has figures of many men with the musical instruments of the age, as playing in concert. They rank among the few instances of sculptured groups still remaining.

ELY—CATHEDRAL CHURCH.—From Miller's and Briton's History.

Dates.	Founders.	Nave.			Choir.			Aisles.			Transept.			Our Lady's Chapel.			Cloisters.			Chapter-house.	Tower.		
	Bishops.	L.	B.	H.	L.	B.	H.	L.	B.	H.	L.	B.	H.	L.	B.	H.	L.	B.	H.		L.	B.	H.
1109–1133	Hervey . .																						
	Nigillus . .																						
1174	Id. Geoff. Ridal	203	–	104							N. 178		6				100	–	150	.	–		210
1174–1380	—	{	Presbytery made the														Destroyed			.	in the centre of the western front		
1235–1252	Hugh Northwold		choir in 1769.																				
1320	John Hotham				Octagon.									Attached to the north transept									
1337	Simon Montacute				101	34,6	70							100	46	60							
	J. Wisbich, prior													Sepulchral chapel.							A spire of wood 60 feet high was added by Bishop Northwold, and lately taken down.		
1349	Thomas Lisle .													The same.									
1488	John Alcocke .													The richest specimen of tabernacle-work in England.									
1530	Nicholas West																						

Remarkable parts of the Structure.—From *Bentham's Ely.*—The octangular louvre, or lantern, is 71 feet 6 inches in diameter, and 142 high from the floor. It was built in 1328; the architect was Alan de Walsingham, a monk of Ely. The space between the octagon and the ancient presbytery, now the choir, is 53–73–6, and was built by John Hotham, lord treasurer. The diameter of the lantern is 30 feet, and the external height 170; it was repaired by James Essex, 1757–1762. The north-west angle of the north transept fell down in 1699, and cost in rebuilding 2637*l.* 6s. 4d. Turrets on the south side of the façade are 120 feet high. The lofty stone tower in the centre fell down February 12, 1322, when the octagon was built in its place. Total length and breadth 517–178–6.

One of the most ancient instances of the Pointed arch is in the tower and transept, 1180. The western portico, or galilee, which is the most perfect remaining specimen in England, was finished by Bishop Hugh Northwold, in 1252. Attached to the pillars of the octagon, higher than the spring of the arches, are eight singularly curious and well-executed bas-reliefs, relating to passages in the life of St. Etheldreda. It is not equilateral, having four longer and four shorter sides. The longer are to the others as ten to six.

The expenses of several parts of this cathedral have been preserved, which present an accurate estimate of the value of labour, materials, and money.

Stow and *Speed* inform us, that Bishop Hugh Northwold expended 5350*l.* 18*s.* 8*d.* in seventeen years (between 1220—1254). He began the presbytery, and added the spire, of timber frame and lead, to the great tower erected by Geoffry Ridal. Bishop John Hotham finished the presbytery (now the choir) at the cost of 2034*l.* 12*s.* 8*d.* and the octagon, of 2406*l.* 12*s.* 0*d.*—Total 4441*l.* 4*s.* 8*d.* Between 1316-1337.—Prior J. Wisbich built Our Lady's Chapel in twenty-eight years and eleven weeks.—*Leland, Collectanea,* vol. ii. page 606.

Evidence of the money expended before the close of the fourteenth century :—

Henry III.	Bishop Northwold	. . .	£5350
Edward III.	Bishop Hotham	. .	2034
	The Convent .	.	2406
			—————
			£9790

Which sum Adam Smith, the present oracle of calculation, estimates at 80,000*l.* of present value.

Alan de Walsingham was not only the architect of the louvre, but likewise of Bishop Hotham's presbytery and of Trinity Chapel, which latter is justly considered as one of the most perfect buildings now to be seen of its style and æra. Walsingham laid the first stone in 1321.—*Leland.*

GLOUCESTER—CONVENTUAL CHURCH OF THE BENEDICTINES.—Antiq. Society's Account.

Dates.	Founders.	Nave. L. B. H.	Choir. L. B. H.	Aisles. L. B. H.	Transept. L. B. H.	Our Lady's Chapel. L. B. H.	Cloisters. L. B. H.	Chapter-house.	Tower. L. B. H.
1057–1089	Aldred Bishop of Worcester	171 41,2 67,7							
1089	Id.								
1310	Abbot J. Thokey			N. 171 20,10 40,6					
1330	Abbot J. Wygmore			S. 171 22 40					
	Id.								
	Adam Staunton.								
	T. de Horton.								
	J. Boyfield.				S. 66, 43,6 78				
1330–1357	Walter Frocester	Clere story and vaulting	140 34,6 86						
	Hugh de Morton.								
	John Morwent.								
	Reginald Boteler.								
	Thomas Sebroke.							Now the Library	
1351–1390	Thomas Horton.								
	J. Boyfield						144 19 18,6		
	Walter Frocester				N. 66 43,6 78		148		
1369–1375	Ut supra.								
1457–1498	Richard Hanley.								
	W. Ferleigh.					92,1 24,4 46,6			
1457–1518	Id.								
	John Malverne.								
	Thomas Braunch								
	John Newton.								24 22 224
	W. Parker.								

Remarkable parts of the Structure.—The north transept cost 781l. of which Abbot Horton paid 462l. (MS. Lives, &c.) The western façade and two arches were added to the nave by T. Horton, about 1370. The library was built by T. Horton for a chapter-house in 1351. A parliament was held there. Length 72 9, breadth 33 8, height 31 6. The tower rises from the centre of the building, above the entrance into the choir. Robert Tulley, afterwards Bishop of St. David's, architect. The cloisters are the most perfect and beautiful in England, but not the largest. They are unusually placed, on the north side of the church.—Total dimensions 426 by 152.

HEREFORD—CATHEDRAL CHURCH.—From Duncumb's History.

Dates.	Founders.	Nave.			Choir.			Aisles.			Transept.			Our Lady's Chapel.			Cloisters.	Chapter-house.	Tower.		
		L.	B.	H.	L.	B.	H.	L.	B.	H.	L.	B.	H.	L.	B.	H.			L.	B.	H.
	Bishops.																				
1079–1095	Robert de Losinge	144	68	68	.	.	.	.	.	.	140	–	–	.	.	.					
1101–1115	Rainelm	.	.	.	125	20	64	.	.	.				.	.	.			Ancient spire		
1131–1148	Robert de Bethune, prior of Llanthony }	.	.	.	.	.	.	144	.	.	Lower			.	.	.		.	–	–	240
1190	De Vere	.	.	.	.	.	.	.	.	.	111	–	–	.	.	.					
1200–1216	Giles de Bruse	.	.	.	.	.	.	.	.	.	.			.	.	.			Western tower was 130		
1287	Cantelupe	.	.	.	.	.	.	.	.	.	.			.	.	.		.			
1492–1502	Edmund Audley	.	.	.	.	.	.	.	.	.	.			73	30	28 and a sepulchral chapel	Destroyed in the rebellion—115 square.	Destroyed. Octagon with a single pillar 37 diameter.	The spire was taken down 1790		
	Restoration by James Wyat.																				
1786	John Butler. The chapter, nobility, and clergy of the county.																				

Remarkable parts of the Structure.—The great west tower fell in 1786, and destroyed the greater part of the nave and aisles; which, when rebuilt, were shortened 15 feet. The architecture of the chapter-house was particularly beautiful, unnecessarily taken down by Bishop Egerton. The expense of rebuilding amounted to more than 17,000*l.* A very complete specimen of the nail-head moulding is still exhibited in the central tower, and other parts of the original church. The porch on the north-west side of the church was attached to the former by Bishop Boothe, in 1520, and is of very correct design and masonry for so late a period, being a good specimen of the last style of Gothick. The window at the north-east end of the Lady Chapel affords one of the most complete examples of the Early English, or Pointed manner, after the introduction of the nail-head moulding in the grooves, which is still to be seen in its original state.—Total dimensions 325–100.

LICHFIELD—CATHEDRAL CHURCH.—Illustrations, &c. by C. Wild, fol. 1813.

Dates.	Founders.	Nave.			Choir.			Aisles.	Transept.			Our Lady's Chapel.			Cloisters.	Chapter-house.	Tower.		
		L.	B.	H.	L.	B.	H.		L.	B.	H.	L.	B.	H.			L.	B.	H.
1295	Bishops. Walter de Louton, or Langton And his successors	213	67	67	120	33	67	Included	88	—	—	55	—	—				Western spires 183	
1430	To William Heyworth, who died in 1447	Western front 78	—	—								Presbytery 35	—	—				Total of the central spire 258	

Remarkable parts of the Structure.—This much-admired church has great uniformity, and, like Salisbury and Exeter, was completed upon one plan. The style is elaborately ornamental. Bishop Langton expended 3000 marks, according to *Leland.* It was so much injured by Cromwell's soldiers, that in 1662 the estimate of repairs amounted to 9092*l.* 1*s.* 7*d.* the greater part of which was contributed and procured by John Hacket, bishop, in ten years. Mr. Wyat's alterations were adopted in 1788. The arches of the triforia show the moulding called the dogtooth, in great perfection, the whole nave exhibiting a remarkable purity of style. A criticism upon these alterations, which is dictated by judgment and good taste, is given by Mr. Wild in his account of *Lichfield Cathedral,* which I copy, as being entirely the same opinion which I have ever entertained of James Wyat's system:—" The interior of the choir has undergone great alterations, under James Wyat since 1788. Before that time the choir and Lady Chapel were separated by a rich altar-skreen, erected by W. de Langton, and containing the shrine of St. Chadd, which being removed in the last decorations, was employed to form the present altar-skreen, at the extreme end of the church. That much accommodation has resulted from these alterations must readily he admitted, yet not without great regret for the sacrifices by which it has been obtained; since the church has been deprived of an interesting relick of antiquity; the choir of an appropriate termination, and of that uniformity and proportion, which it originally possessed: its complete inclosure likewise deprives it of that grand effect which a partial view of the nave and aisles, aided by the magic of light and air, must formerly have produced."—Total dimensions 411–88.

LINCOLN—CATHEDRAL CHURCH.—Illustrations, &c. by *C. Wild,* fol. 1819.

Dates.	Founders.	Nave.			Choir.			Aisles.			Transept.			Our Lady's Chapel.	Cloisters.			Chapter-house.			Towers and Spires.
	Bishops.	L.	B.	H.	L.	B.	H.	L.	B.	H.	L.	B.	H.	None.	L.	B.	H.	L.	B.	H.	H.
1184	Alexander Normannus, rebuilt.																				
1186–1200	Hugh de Grenoble	240	80	80	140	40	72	Included										A decagon diameter 60 feet.			Central 288
1240	Robert Grostête																				West 260
1254	Henry Lexington																				
1279	Oliver Sutton.																				
1286–1300	Hugh Burgundus				Presbytery 106 82 72						W. 220 63 74 E. 166 63 72				120 feet by 100.						West front 173 and 83 high.
1306	John D'Alderby.																				
1361	John Sinwell.																				
1438	William Alnewick, built the great west window and porch.																				

Remarkable parts of the Structure.—The great western front was built by Remigius, bishop, and finished by Hugh Burgundus. In 1254 H. Lexington added five arches beyond the upper transept. The central tower and choir were the work of Bishop Grostête, and the whole structure completed by John D'Alderby in 1306, when leaden spires were placed upon each of the three towers. The central, higher than Salisbury, was blown down in 1547. The others were removed in 1808. The roof between the upper transept and the east window is peculiarly rich. There is a curious bas-relief of the Deluge over the west door, and another of the Last Judgement over the south porch. No other cathedral in England has such a display of finely-wrought sculpture of the earliest intro-duction, and in a profusion upon every member of its architecture, which equals its excellence. There are many statues holding musical instruments as in concert, placed longitudinally, like those at Exeter. The eastern façade of singular beauty.—Total dimensions 498 by 227.

LONDON—OLD ST. PAUL'S CATHEDRAL CHURCH.—Dugdale's History.

Dates.	Founders. Bishops.	Nave. L. B. H.	Choir. L. B. H.	Transept. L. B. H.	Aisles.	Our Lady's Chapel. L. B. H	Cloisters. L. B. H.	Chapter-house. L. B. H.	Tower. L. B. H.
1086	Mauritius	335 91 102			Included		These cloisters were double, one above the other. The north side taken down in 1549. They were only 91 feet square.	The chapter-house remained perfect after Inigo Jones's repairs. It was octangular.	Height of the tower 260, of the spire 274. The spire was burned down in 1561.
1120	Richard de Beaumes			297 – –					
1220	William de St. Maria		163 – 88						
1260	Henry de Wingham								
1312	Henry de Lacy, Earl Lincoln					92 - -			
	Hugh de Baldock.								

Remarkable parts of the Structure.—Dugdale has written a minute history of this sumptuous church, embellished with numerous plates by the accurate Hollar. The whole space it occupied in 1309, was three acres and a half, one rood and a half, and six perches. The cloisters were taken down by the protector Somerset, to build his palace in the Strand. Inigo Jones began his restorations in 1633, and the whole was entirely taken down by Sir Christopher Wren in 1675. *Dugdale* (page 17) states the following dimensions of this cathedral in 1309:—length of the nave 290 feet, breadth 120; height of the vaulting of the western part 102 feet, of the eastern 188; of the tower 260 feet, and of the spire, which was made of timber-frame and covered with lead, 274.

Speed mentions Richard Fitz-Nele, bishop, as completing the work of Beaumes before 1199. Eustace de Falconburg was likewise a great contributor to the fabrick. Ralf de Baldoc gave 2000 marks to the building of Our Lady's Chapel, in 1310. Towards the repair of the spire, burned down by lightning in 1561, 1460*l.* were collected by the clergy, and 1312*l.* 12*s.* 8*d.* by the bishop, dean and chapter, and others.—*Stow's Annals*, p. 646. But the spire was never rebuilt. In 1636, when almost a rebuilding (in a most incongruous style) was designed by Inigo Jones, 5410*l.* were raised. Charles the First contributed the whole expense of the portico. Sir Paul Pindar, who had been ambassador to the Porte, gave 4000*l.* more.—Total dimensions 631–130.

LONDON—NEW ST. PAUL'S CATHEDRAL CHURCH.

Dates.	Founders.	Nave.	Choir.	Aisles.	Transept.	Our Lady's Chapel.	Cloisters.	Chapter-house.	Dome.
									Height and diameter.
1675 to 1710	Charles II. by act of parliament, imposing a tax upon coal imported into the city of London. Henry Compton, bishop, and the English clergy at large, by various contributions to the amount of 126,604l. 6s. 5d. Architect Sir Christopher Wren. The first stone was laid June 21, 1675 ; the building was completed in 1710, and the whole of the decorations in 1723.	L. B. H. 107 130 88 Diameter of the cupola 106	L. B. H. 166 42 88	Included	L. B. H. 250 – 88	None.	None.	In the façade.	Internally. 356 106

Remarkable parts of the Structure.—The whole expense was 736,752l. 2s. 6d. The breadth of the façade, or western front, is 180 feet, height of the towers 221. Comparisons are usually made between St. Peter's at Rome and St. Paul's. The former is 229 feet longer in the whole. The transept 260 longer. The nave 208 feet wider. The cupola 97 feet higher, and the difference of the vaulted roof the same. The façade of St. Peter's is 215 feet wider than that of St. Paul's. The circuit of St. Paul's church 112,292 feet, containing two acres, sixteen perches, twenty-three yards, and one foot. The western pediment is 120 feet high.

COMPARISON WITH OTHER GREAT CHURCHES.

St. Peter's, Rome, stands on an area of feet superficies, 227,069 ; of which area the points of support occupy 59,308 feet. Proportion of the latter to the former 261.

St. Mary, at Florence, 84,802—17,030—201. St. Paul's London, 84,025—14,311—170. St. Genevieve, Paris, 60,287—9269—154. Supposing sections to be made from north to south, through the transepts of each of the four churches above mentioned, their areas, including the thickness of the walls, piers, &c. will be in the following ratio:—

St. Peter's 10,000   St. Mary's 5358   St. Paul's 4160   St. Genevieve 3363.

Britton's Public Buildings of London, vol. i. pp. 20, 21.

NORWICH—CATHEDRAL CHURCH.—From Britton's History.

Dates.	Founders.	Nave.			Choir.			Aisles.	Transept.			Our Lady's Chapel.	Cloisters.			Chapter-house.	Tower.		
		L.	B.	H.	L.	B.	H.		L.	B.	H.		L.	B.	H.		L.	B.	H.
	Bishops.																		
1096	Herbert Losinga	140	71	—								None	.	.	.	.	.	Tower.	
1171	Eborard	.	.	.	165	—	—	Included	191	—	—								
1197	John of Oxford	.	.	.															
1272	Walter de Suffield																		
1278	William Middleton, and																		
1297	W. de Kirkby, prior	.	.	.	.	.	.	.	.	.	.	.	.	.	.	Destroyed.	.	.	.
1361	Ralph Walpole																		
	Thomas Percy	.	.	.	.	.	.	.	.	.	.	.	.	.	.	.	Spire 317		
1420	John Wakering	.	.	.									174 ft. square.			.	.		

Remarkable parts of the Structure.—Before the year 1272 this church was dilapidated, and was nearly rebuilt by succeeding bishops and priors. The present central spire was erected since 1361, by Bishop Percy, who contributed 300*l.* and his clergy granted an aid of nine-pence in the pound, according to the value of their benefices. It is, internally, of brick. The end of the choir is octangular. The clere-story and vaulting added to the choir by Bishop Goldwell, are of most light and elegant construction. The cloisters are the most spacious in England. The windows are more diversified and elaborately wrought in the heads, and do not reach the floor by several feet. The Norman arcade in the interior of the tower is remarkable, but in its plan resembling that of Ely. —Total dimensions 414—191.

OXFORD—CONVENTUAL CHURCH OF ST. FRYDESWIDE AUG. CANONS.—From Britton.

Dates.	Founders.	Nave. L. B. H.	Choir. L. B. H.	Aisles.	Transept. L. B. H.	Our Lady's Chapel.	Cloisters. L. B. H.	Chapter-house.	Tower. L. B. H.
1050	Guymond, prior of St. Frydeswide	74 54 41½	80 37 –	Included.	102 – –		54 24 –	…	Tower.
1120	.		. .	. .	. .	.	. .	…	
1192	.	. .	. .						
1216									
1270						Latin Chapel.			
1528	Cardinal Wolsey	. .			. .		. .	…	Spire.
1545	Robert King, first bishop		Clere-story						

Remarkable parts of the Structure.—The church was built by the priors of St. Frydeswide between the years 1120 and 1270. The spire was added by Cardinal Wolsey in 1528, who took about fifty feet of the original nave. It is uncertain whether the beautiful pendent roof of the choir was made by Cardinal Wolsey or Bishop King. The chapter-house is of perfect Anglo-Norman architecture, built in the reign of Henry the Second. Total dimensions 154—102.

PETERBOROUGH—CONVENTUAL CHURCH OF THE BENEDICTINES.—From Britton.

Dates.	Founders.	Nave. L. B. H.	Choir. L. B. H.	Aisles.	Transept. L. R. H.	Our Lady's Chapel. L. B. H.	Cloisters. L. B. H.	Chapter-house. L. B. H.	Tower. L. B. H.
1160 temp. H. II.	William de Watteville, 21st abbot		138 78 78				Destroyed 138 131 –	Destroyed 84 33 –	
1175	Benedict, 22nd abbot	231 78 –		Included					
1272	Richard de London, 32nd abbot				69 203 78	Taken down in 1651. 80 – –			
1295	William Parys, prior, or								Spires. Two 156
1300	W. de Woodford, abbot								Unfinished tower 120
1330	Geoffry Croyland, 34th abbot								Louvre 150
1496	Robert Kirton, 44th abbot, built the chapels at the end of the choir.								

Remarkable parts of the Structure.—The grand façade and portico, the proportions of which are the most perfect and beautiful in England, were begun by Abbot Benedict, and completed by Abbot London, according to conjecture. It is 156 feet broad, and consists of an arcade of three arches 82 high, and is finished by two spires, each 156 feet high. In the original plan four were intended. The louvre between the nave and choir was probably built by William Parys. It is square, and 136 from the pavement. The cloisters were most remarkable for the finest stained glass. Many of the ancient conventual buildings are still entire. Total dimensions 460–203. The roof of the nave is probably contemporary with the nave itself. It is composed of wainscot divided into three chief compartments, running for the whole length and subdivided into pannels, all of which were gilded and painted with various devices and figures with musical instruments. Originally with resinous varnish, but since painted over with oil.—See *Archæologia*, vol. ix. p. 148.

ROCHESTER—CATHEDRAL CHURCH.—From Hasted's History.

Dates.	Founders.	Nave.			Choir.			Aisles.	Transept.			Our Lady's Chapel.	Cloisters.	Chapter-house.	Tower.		
	Bishops.	L.	B.	H.	L.	B.	H.		L.	B.	H.				L.	B.	H.
1080	Gundulphus	150	75	–					122	–	–	.	.				
1115	Ernulph																
1227	Henry Sanford	.			156	–	–	Included	.			.	.	Destroyed by Cromwell's soldiers.	Spire 156		
1270	W. de Hoo, Prior																

Remarkable parts of the Structure.—The front of this cathedral is one of the most perfect specimens of early Norman architecture in England, particularly the hatched ornament in the arcade of the triforia. The crypt extends equally with the choir and eastern transept. Bishop Gundulph, who rendered himself so famous by his skill in military architecture, in the Tower of London and the contiguous castle, has left no other specimen of church-building. When the choir was rebuilt in 1227, it was extended to a greater length, by several feet, than the nave itself. The choirs, indeed, of all the Norman churches, were disproportionately short. It has been remarked, that the door-way of the chapter-house at Rochester, is the finest specimen of canopied niches and effigies in the architrave to be seen in England. Total dimensions 306–122.

SALISBURY—CATHEDRAL CHURCH.—From Britton, &c.

Dates.	Founders.	Nave.	Choir.	Aisles.	Transept.	Our Lady's Chapel.	Cloisters.	Chapter-house.	Tower.
	Bishops.	L. B. H.	L. B. H.		L. B. H.	L. B. H.	L. B. H.		
1217	Richard Poore	229 76 81	140 — 84	Included	230 60 84	69 37 —	160 feet sq. 18 wide.	Octangular	To the parapet of tower 207 feet. Spire 404 high.—Ancient campanile or bell-tower taken down under the direction of J. Wyat, architect.
1230	Robert Bingham								
1274	Robert Wikehampton								
1280									

Remarkable parts of the Structure.—This church can boast a greater degree of uniformity than any other. In 1737 it was found that the entire roof contained 2641 tons of oak timber. From the account delivered to King Henry the Third, it appears that 40,000 marks (22,666*l.* 13*s.* 4*d.*) had then been expended on this structure. Bishop Poore gave the original plan, from which his immediate successors made not the least variation. There were two consecrations of this church: one on September 30, 1268, and the other September 29, 1280, probably when the spire was finished. Great repairs have been made by Sir Christopher Wren; by Price, in 1726; and by J. Wyat, in 1784. This was the first scene of Mr. Wyat's improvement, which has rendered the interior more picturesque, by sacrificing the original character and distribution of parts. Total dimensions:—interior 450 feet; total length 474 feet; western front 112 feet.

The spire is banded with three rows of lozenge-shaped compartments. "Molem propinquam nubibus arduis." Under three arches of the central tower, each of them are filled up with one of half its height, upon the crown of which rests another pointed arch inverted, having the groins perforated by a large quatrefoil, and the upper space clear. It appears to have been an expedient, and evidently an afterthought to give strength, and to better support the incumbent weight of the tower with the addition of the spire. *Leland (Itin. v. 3, p. 120,)* records a similar circumstance as having been adopted in the great church of Glastonbury Abbey. "Abbate Bere made the vaulte of the steeple in transepto, and under two arches like St. Andrewe's crosse, els it had fallen." At Wells there is a correspondent instance. "The height of the spire is of no settled proportion; sometimes the height to the breadth of the base, is as eight to one. The spire of Salisbury is only seven inches thick, so that if we reasoned of construction from theory, it would be inadequate to sustain its own weight."—*Murphy's Batalha, Introduction.*

WELLS—CATHEDRAL CHURCH.—From Britton, &c.

Dates.	Founders.	Nave.			Choir.			Aisles.	Transept.			Our Lady's Chapel.			Cloisters.	Chapter-house.	Tower.		
	Bishops.	L.	B.	H.	L.	B.	H.		L.	B.	H.	L.	B.	H.			L.	B.	H.
1205–1239	Joseline Troteman	191	67	67	108	67	–	Included	135	–	67	47	33	–			Western		
1293	W. de March.											Space between					234	–	130
1366	John Harwell.											the choir					Central		
1450	Thomas Beckington											22	–	–			–	–	160
1465	Robert Stillington																		

Remarkable parts of the Structure.—The western façade of this church is singularly adorned with statues in a more perfect state than is seen in any cathedral, excepting that of Lincoln; they are of kings, bishops, and warriors. The original plan, as at Exeter, appears never to have been departed from, but to have been followed by successive bishops, till its completion by Bishop Stillington. Ralph de Shrewsbury, bishop, who died in 1363, is said, by *Speed*, to have continued the original plan, and to have been a great benefactor. Total dimensions 371–185. The cloister has three sides only; the east and west are joined to the church. Under the central tower, three sides each contain a strong insulated arch, which supports another arch inverted on its point, all uniting with the side-piers, and having perforated spandrils with circles. A more effectual and scientific support could not have been invented. That at Salisbury has been previously noticed, the plan of which is slightly different.

WESTMINSTER—CONVENTUAL CHURCH.—From Neale and Brayley's Account.

Dates.	Founders.	Nave.	Choir.	Aisles.	Transept.	Henry VII.'s Chapel.	Cloisters.	Chapter-house.	Western towers.
		L. B. H.	L. B. H.	L. B. H.	L. B. H.	L. B. H.			Height.
1250	King Henry III.	166 38 101	155 38 101	166 16 101	136 40 78				To the top of the
1300	King Edward I.	Extreme breadth							western turrets
		of the nave and							102 feet 6 inches.
1490	King Henry VII.	aisles 71ft. 9in.				103 35 60			addition 225 feet
						Aisles			in the whole.
						62 17 –			

Remarkable parts of the Structure.—A singularly fine specimen of what has been termed the "Transition style." The most beautiful arcs-boutants in England are those of Henry the Seventh's Chapel. The triforia are lighted from the back wall by a range of windows, each consisting of three circles, inscribed within a spherical triangle, externally; the circle or cinquefoil only, being the upper one, withinside. The architect was Thomas Fitz-Otho, the King's mint-master.—*Whittington.* This peculiar shape occurs in another instance only, at Lichfield.

WINCHESTER—CATHEDRAL CHURCH.—From Milner's History.

Dates.	Founders.	Nave.			Choir.			Aisles.	Transept.			Our Lady's Chapel.			Cloisters.			Chapter-house.	Tower.		
	Bishops.	L.	B.	H.	L.	B.	H.		L.	B.	H.	L.	B.	H.	L.	B.	H.		L.	B.	H.
1070	Wakelyn								186	—	—								—	—	150
1190	Godfrey de Laci														179	179	—				
1350	W. de Edynton											54	—	—		Destroyed.					
1394	William de Wykeham	300	86	78																	
	Cardinal Beaufort.				Presbytery 93	86	78											Destroyed — was formerly 90 feet square, with a central column.			
1493	T. Langton							Included in the whole breadth.				Enlarged by Prior Silkestede, and T. Langton, bishop.									
	J. Silkestede, prior.																				
1510	Richard Fox																				

Remarkable parts of the Structure.—The western front was completed by Edynton. Wykeham's nave is considered as one of the finest in England, and longer than that of York. The exterior of the choir and Lady's Chapel is of most beautiful Gothick workmanship of the fifteenth century. There are four very fine sacella or sepulchral chapels for the Bishops Wykeham, Wayneflete, Beaufort, and Fox. Wykeham is said to have surrounded the piers erected by Wakelyn with pilasters. The choir is under the tower, as at Gloucester. The exquisite screen behind the altar was the work of Bishop Fox, to whom Speed attributes, not only the additions to the choir, but the vaulting and glassing (with stained glass) of the whole church. Total dimensions 545—186.

WINDSOR—COLLEGIATE CHURCH.—From Lysons's Berkshire.

Dates.	Founders.	Nave.			Choir.			Transept.			Cloisters.			Tomb-house.		
		L.	B.	H.	L.	B.	H.	L.	B.	H.	L.	B.	H.	L.	B.	H.
1100	Henry I.	Rebuilt														
1345	Edward III.	118	30	—	80	30	—	110	25	—	70	65	—			
		Aisles			Aisles											
		90	15	—	110	15	—							70	30	—
1480	Edward IV. vaulting, &c.															
1488	Henry VII.															
1503	Sir Reginald Bray, vaulting, &c.															
1516 to 1540	Henry VIII. completed the whole structure }															

Remarkable parts of the Structure.—The octangular terminations of the transept, and two octangular chapels at the west end. The flying arches are finished by tall pinnacles only, with flat heads, upon which were originally placed figures of cognizances, composed of copper gilt. Similar devices were placed above the balustrade of the Beauchamp Chapel at Warwick. The western windows of Windsor, King's College, Cambridge, and Henry the Seventh's Chapel, have three chief divisions, and occupy the whole space of the nave. Total dimensions 210–100.

WORCESTER—CATHEDRAL CHURCH.

Dates.	Founders.	Nave.	Choir.	Aisles.	Transept.	Our Lady's Chapel.	Cloisters.	Chapter-house.	Tower.
	Bishops.	L. B. H.	L. B. H.		L. B. H.	L. B. H.	L. B. H.		L. B. H.
1218	W. de Blois	212 78 72	80 36 61	Included	Lower 128 32 –				
1224									
1327	T. Cobham					60 49 –			
1372	W. de Lynne						120 125 –	Decagon 58 diameter.	
1374					Upper 120 25 –				
1380	Henry Wakefield								– – 162

Remarkable parts of the Structure.—The original church was built before 1150, parts of which may be traced. In Green's Survey of Worcester is a very curious statement of the relative proportions of the different constituent parts of this cathedral. The refectory of the convent is still perfect. It is 120 feet long by 38 broad. The nave is extremely beautiful, both in style and proportions. Total dimensions 410–130.—*Illustration of the Architecture and Sculpture of Worcester Cathedral, by C. Wild,* fol. 1823.

YORK—CATHEDRAL CHURCH.

Date.	Founders.	Nave.			Choir.			Aisles.			Transept.			Our Lady's Chapel.			Cloisters.			Chapter-house.			Towers.		
		L.	B.	H.	L.	B.	H.	L.	B.	H.	L.	B.	H.	L.	B.	H.	L.	B.	H.	L.	B.	H.	L.	B.	H.
	Archbishops.	250	103	92	150	43	101	250	–	47	222	–	103	65	30	50	None.			Octagon 57 57 66,7			Western Façade and Towers 196 feet high.		
1227	Walter Grey																						Central 44 42 182		
1291	John Romain																								
	W. De Melton																								
1340	W. Zouch.																								
1361	J. Thoresby																								
1300 to 1420	J. Bermingham, treasurer, completed the façade.																								

Remarkable parts of the Structure.—In 1171, Roger, the archbishop, laid the foundations of the present church. The central lantern, or steeple, built by J. Le Romaine, was taken down by Walter Skirlawe 1380. Archbishop Romaine began the nave, which was completed by Archbishop Melton with the façade. The aisles surround the whole church in every part, and are of the same dimensions in each, and built at the same time. "Archbishop J. Thoresby built the transept and choir, who laid the first stone in 1361, contributed towards the work 1670*l*. and completed the external walls in about nine years." The open central tower or louvre is 188 feet from the floor; the choir with the terminating chapel is exactly co-extensive with the nave, 222 feet. The rose window (the finest in England) is 22 feet 6 inches in diameter.—*Wild's Perspective Views of York Cathedral,* fol. 1809.

The spire of Strasburgh is exactly twice as high as the highest pinnacle of the towers of the façade of York.— *See Moller's print.*

CORRESPONDENT DIMENSIONS OF THE SEVERAL .
COMPONENT PARTS OF CATHEDRAL CHURCHES.

TOTAL LENGTH.

Chichester	.	410 feet.
Norwich .		411
Worcester	.	410
Durham .		420
Gloucester	.	420

HEIGHT OF NAVES. STYLE.

Salisbury .	.	84	. Pointed arch.
Lincoln.	. .	83	. Pointed arch.
Canterbury	.	80	. Pure Gothick.
Peterborough	.	78	. Norman.
Winton	.	78	. Pure Gothick.
Durham	.	71	Norman.
Ely .		70	Norman.
Exeter .		69	Pointed arch.
Gloucester		67	Norman.
Wells .		67	Pointed arch.

BREADTH OF NAVES AND AISLES.

Norwich 71, Bristol 73, Chester 73, Ely 73, Canterbury 74, Exeter 74, Sarum 76, Peterborough 78, Worcester 78, Durham 80, Lincoln 83, Gloucester 84, Winchester 85.

A SCALE OF CATHEDRALS, &c.

Naves and Aisles.	L.	B.	H.	Spires and Towers.	
London (ancient) .	335	91	102	London . .	534
St. Paul's (modern)	200	107	88	St. Paul's cupola .	356
Ely . . .	327	73	70	Salisbury . .	387
York . .	264	109	99	Norwich . .	317
Lincoln . .	—	83	83	Ely . . .	270
Winchester . .	247	86	78	Lincoln, west .	270
Salisbury . .	246	76	84	Chichester . .	267
Peterborough .	231	78	78	Lichfield . .	258 W. 183
Norwich .	230	71	—	Peterborough .	186
Canterbury . .	214	74	80	Rochester . .	156
Lichfield . .	213	67	—	Oxford . . .	184
Worcester . .	212	78	—		
Chichester . .	205	91	61	TOWERS.	
Wells . . .	191	67	67	Lincoln . .	260
Gloucester . .	174	84	67	Canterbury . .	235
Exeter . . .	173	74	69	York . . .	234
Rochester . .	150	65	—	Gloucester . .	225
Hereford .	144	68	68	Durham .	214
Bath . . .	136	72	78	Ely . .	210
Westminster .	130	96	101	Worcester .	196
Bristol . . .	100	75	73	Ely louvre . .	170
Oxford . . .	74	54	41	Bath . . .	162
Chester . .	—	73	73	Wells . . .	160
Carlisle . .	—	71	71	Peterborough louvre	150
				Exeter . .	130
				Chester .	127
				Bristol . . .	127

This parallel will afford us, at one view, authentic information concerning the proportion of one constituent part to another of every cathedral in England, which is worthy the notice of an architect. Such a coincidence of dimensions as that which is found in many of them, can scarcely be supposed to be the effect of chance, especially where the buildings are contemporary, and of an exactly correspondent style. May we not fairly conjecture, in these several instances, that they have been designed by the same architect? To avoid repetition, I refer my intelligent reader to the tables, where he will find the equality of proportions to be confined to each æra and style of ecclesiastical architecture, in a remarkable degree. The constant rivalry which subsisted between the magnificent prelates, was excited upon the erection of any part of a cathedral of superior beauty, and imitated in those of the same kind which were then undertaken; and the architect, who had once displayed great talents, was invited to repeat the more perfect performance, upon which he had rested his professional fame.

It is a distribution of parts which will hold almost generally, that the width of the nave is that of both the aisles, measured in the plan to the extremity of the buttresses externally, and that the breadth and height of the whole building are equal. In the more ancient churches, the aisles are usually of the width of the space between the dividing arches.

A SCALE OF THE CATHEDRALS IN ENGLAND,

COMPARING

THE DIMENSIONS OF THEIR SEVERAL INTERNAL PARTS.

Total Internal Length.		Transept.		Internal Breadth.	Choir.		L.	B.	H.
London . .	631	London . .	297		London . .	163	91	88
Old St. Paul's	500	Old St. Paul's	248		Old St. Paul's	165	42	88
Winchester .	545	Lincoln . .	227		Norwich . .	165	—	—
Ely	517	York . . .	222		Rochester .	156	—	—
Canterbury .	514	Salisbury . .	210		Westminster	152	—	101
York . . .	498	Peterborough	203		Canterbury .	150	74	80
Lincoln . .	498	Norwich . .	191		Gloucester .	140	—	86
Westminster .	489	Westminster	189		Salisbury . .	140	—	84
Peterborough	480	Winchester .	186		Carlisle . .	137	71	—
Salisbury . .	452	Ely	178		Winchester .	138	—	78
Durham . .	420	Durham . .	176		Peterborough	138	—	78
Gloucester .	420	Canterbury .	154		York . . .	131	—	99
Chichester .	401	Gloucester .	144		Exeter . . .	131	—	69
Norwich . .	411	Hereford . .	140		Worcester .	126	—	74
Lichfield . .	411	Exeter . . .	140		Durham . .	117	33	71
Worcester .	410	Wells . . .	135		Lichfield . .	110	—	67
Exeter . . .	390	Chichester .	131		Wells . . .	106	—	67
Wells . . .	371	Worcester .	130		Hereford . .	105	—	64
Hereford, anc.	370	Bristol . . .	128		Ely	101	73	70
Chester . .	348	Bath . . .	126		Bristol . . .	100	—	—
Rochester .	306	Rochester . .	122		Chichester .	100	—	—
Carlisle . .	213	Oxford . . .	102		Oxford . . .	80	—	37½
Bath . . .	210	Lichfield . .	88					
Bristol . . .	175							
Oxford . .	154							

CONTEMPORARY ARCHITECTURE OF CATHEDRAL CHURCHES IN ENGLAND.

ANGLO-NORMAN.

Before 1100, *to* 1170, *during the reigns of King Henry I. and Stephen.*

Oxford : nave and choir. *Rochester :* western front and nave. *Gloucester :* nave, north aisle, and the chapels round the choir, with the whole original substruction. *Exeter :* transept towers. *Winton :* central tower and transept. *Chichester :* nave. *Ely :* north transept. *Peterborough :* choir. *Lincoln :* older part of the western front and central tower. *Durham :* the entire church, excepting the additional transept to the east. *Worcester :* many arches. *Norwich :* nave and tower.

SEMI OR MIXED NORMAN.

From 1170 *to* 1220. *Henry II. Richard I. and John.*

Ely : western towers and nave. *Bristol :* elder Lady chapel and chapter-house. *Canterbury :* choir, and the round tower called Becket's crown. *Norwich :* nave and choir finished. *Hereford :* transept, tower, and choir. *Wells :* nave and choir begun. *Chester :* chapter-house. *Chichester :* presbytery. *Peterborough :* transept.

LANCET ARCH GOTHICK.

From 1220 *to* 1300. *Henry III. Edward I.*

Oxford : chapter-house. *Lincoln :* nave and arches beyond the transept. *York :* north and south transept. *Durham :* additional transept. *Wells :* tower and whole western front. *Carlisle :* choir. *Ely :* presbytery. *Worcester :* transept and choir. *Salisbury :* uniformly. *Rochester ;* choir and transept.

TRANSITION STYLE, OR PURE GOTHICK.

From 1300 *to* 1400.　*Edward I. II. III.　Richard II.*

Exeter : nave and choir.　*Lichfield* : uniformly.　*Lincoln* : additions to the central tower.　*Worcester* : nave.　*York* : nave, with the choir and the western front.　*Canterbury* : transept.　*Gloucester* : transept.　*Norwich* : spire and tower. *Sarum* : spire and additions.　*Gloucester* : cloisters begun. *Bristol* : nave and choir.　*Chichester* : spire and choir.　*Ely* : Our Lady's chapel, and the central louvre.　*Hereford* : chapter-house and cloisters (now destroyed).

DECORATED GOTHICK.

From 1400 *to* 1460.　*Henry IV. V. VI.*

Gloucester : choir.　*Canterbury* : nave.　*Wells* : Bishop Beckington's additions.　*Lincoln* : from the upper transept to the great east window.

TUDOR STYLE, OR FLORID GOTHICK.

From 1460 *to the close.　Edward IV. to Henry VIII.*

Gloucester : Our Lady's chapel.　*Oxford* : roof of the choir.　Alcocke's chapel at *Ely*.　Exterior of the choir at *Winchester*.　Our Lady's chapel, *Peterborough*.　North Porch, *Hereford*.

It is well worthy of observation, that though the ground plans of sacred edifices are, generally speaking, similar and systematic, yet in no single instance which occurs to my memory do we find an exact and unvaried copy of any building which preceded it, in every part of the structure.　A striking analogy or resemblance may occur, but *that* rarely.

In Greece, all the temples were constructed after a few great models, and were discriminated only by their relative dimensions: they are, upon that account, less impressive on the imagination than the infinite variety which, in a Gothick edifice, is constantly presenting itself to our view.

Gothick buildings should be referred to their places in the order of art, instead of a succession of extracts relative to particular churches. Architectural chronology is not to be determined by any single church; but rather the age is to be inferred from many which are similar. When the Puritans seized upon the cathedral churches, every particle of ornament accessible to the hand of violence suffered a destructive injury. The iconoclastic bishops, after the Reformation, had nearly removed many beautiful but superstitious objects; and the ignorance of true style, with the prevalence of false taste, increased instead of mending these defects, by injudicious repairs.

But during the late reign, the justly-celebrated architect James Wyat contributed principally to the introduction of more correct principles of repairing the decayed structure of several cathedrals; yet he was unmindful of true restitution, indulging, in some instances, a love of mere picturesque effect, foreign to the original character of the church, in the disposition of its internal parts.

RESTORED CHURCHES.

Durham,
Salisbury,
Lichfield,   } James Wyat.
New College Chapel, Oxford,

PARTIAL RESTORATIONS.

Winchester.	Canterbury.
Peterborough.	Chichester.
Ely.	Worcester.
Gloucester.	

Choir of York, (burned down in 1829.)—R. Smirke.

WESTERN AND EASTERN FAÇADES OF CATHEDRAL CHURCHES.

1	Rochester	As the most ancient specimen.
2	Lincoln	The original part.
3	Peterborough	The timber-frame roof of the nave.
4	Gloucester	The arcade of the nave.
5	Ely	Two parts of three finished.
6	Salisbury	Simple pointed, style Gothick.
7	Peterborough	The whole western façade.
8	Wells	Most rich in niches and statues.
9	Lichfield	Of a similar character.
10	York	Most beautiful in point of proportion and finishing.
11	Exeter	Remarkable for uniformity and sculpture.
12	Bath	The same in the latest style and æra.

EASTERN.

1	Lincoln	The finest in England.
2	York	Similar, with a certain inferiority.
3	Salisbury	Of smaller dimensions, but perfect in its own style.
4	Beverley Minster	In the style of York, and scarcely inferior.
5	Gloucester,	Above the roofs of the choirs and the
6	Norwich,	chapels of Our Lady, upon the ancient choirs, as a superstructure.
7	Winchester,	

PECULIARITIES OR SINGLE INSTANCES IN THE INTERNAL OR EXTERNAL ARCHITECTURE.

1	Bath	The extreme height of the clere-story above the arcade.
2	Bristol	Had no nave in the original structure. The present choir is the Lady Chapel. It is supported internally in the aisles by the construction of their roofs, which are of equal height with the nave.
3	Canterbury	The grand portal is under the south tower of the façade. The octangular chapel at the east end, called Becket's Crown. The marble columns of the choir, with their romanesque capitals, are the earliest specimen now to be seen in England.

4	Chester	A north transept of the largest dimensions.
5	Chichester	Double aisles to the nave.
6	Durham	Our Lady's Chapel, placed at the east end as a second transept. The Galilee chapel placed before, and distinct from the façade.
7	Ely	A single western tower connected with the nave; an octangular tower; and Our Lady's chapel, detached from the choir. A portico called a Galilee in a perfect state.
8	Exeter	The skreen before the western front, and the towers at either end of the transept. The ramifications in the heads of the nave windows are all of them dissimilar. Completed according to the original plan.
9	Lichfield	Three spires of stone.
10	{ London, St. Paul's	The cupola and hemispherical porticoes attached to the transept.
11	Norwich	Roof of the nave and east end.
12	Peterborough	The triple arcade before the west end, eighty-two feet high: double towers with spires attached to the west end.
13	Rochester	The choir longer than the nave.
14	Salisbury	Complete uniformity of style, and the height of the central spire. A double elliptic inverted arch under the tower, as at Wells.
15	Winchester	The longest nave.
16	York	Double aisles to the transept. The largest window, of seven divisions of lancet arches. The square louvre. No cloister.

Lincoln and York are remarkable for the variety and exquisite finishing of all the sculptured ornaments, as attached to the columns, and the tabernacle-work of the choirs and skreens. The space of the arcade of the upper transept of Lincoln is filled up about the middle with a row of niches and canopies, as if resting upon a beam of stone, but in reality supported by the side walls.

CATHEDRALS, OF WHICH THE SUPERSTRUCTURES OF THE LATER GOTHICK STYLE HAVE BEEN INTRODUCED UPON THE EARLY NORMAN.

1	Gloucester	ThomasBoyfield, abbot, finished before 1381 the complete vaulting of the nave, which, with the upper tier, had been begun in 1461. The choir, with its lofty roof, was introduced within the old Norman walls by the same abbot.
2	Oxford	By Cardinal Wolsey, or John King, the first bishop.
3	Norwich	By Bishop James Goldwell.
4	Winchester	By Bishop Richard Fox.

ABBEY CHURCHES.

| Malmsbury | Clere-story of the nave. John de Tyntern abbot, 1340. |
| Tewkesbury | The choir. |

NAVES OF CATHEDRALS IN THE TRANSITION OR GOTHICK STYLES.

BEFORE THE YEAR 1400.—Salisbury; Exeter; Worcester; Winchester; York; Lichfield; Lincoln; Wells; Chester; Westminster.

AFTER 1400.—Canterbury.

CHOIRS.

BEFORE 1400. — Sarum; Wells; Lincoln; York; Lichfield; Ely, with the louvre and octagon; Exeter; Gloucester begun; Worcester; additions to Norwich.

AFTER 1400. — Windsor; Henry the Seventh's chapel, Westminster; King's College chapel; Winchester and Oxford raised upon the ancient walls.

CHAPTER-HOUSES.

LONGITUDINAL.

	LENGTH.	BREADTH.	HEIGHT.	
	ft. in.	ft. in.	ft. in.	
Bristol .	46	26	—	—
Gloucester .	72	33	—	—
Peterborough	84	33	—	—
Chester .	50	30	—	Vestibule 35—35.
Oxford .	54 6	23 9	35	—
Durham .	75	35	—	Circular end taken down 1785.
Exeter .	55	32	50	—

OCTAGON—DECAGON—POLYGONAL.

York . .	57	57	66 7	Octagon, without a central column.
Lincoln .	60	60	42	Octagon.
Worcester .	57 .	57	—	Circular decagon.
Lichfield .	42	27	23	Square within circular terminations.
Salisbury .	58	58	62	Octagon.
Westminster .	60	60	—	Octagon.
Wells . .	53	53	—	Octagon.
Hereford .	40	40	—	Decagon. Taken down.

CONVENTUAL ARCHITECTURE.

BOTH as to the churches and the habitable parts of a large monastery, Conventual architecture is of sufficient importance to merit a distinct investigation; I shall therefore select two instances, from which their whole plan may be deduced, because these accounts authenticate sumptuous buildings in the state in which they were found immediately before their final dissolution, when they were very generally consigned to a total ruin. The number, large dimensions, and designation of the chief apartments, did not vary greatly in most monasteries of the higher order.

Glastonbury and Reading are examples.

The whole site of *Glastonbury*, within the walls, was sixty acres. Dimensions of the church:—nave, f. 228 long; choir, 159—79; transept, f. 220; chapel of St. Joseph, f. 117; total length, f. 594. Chapter-house, f. 90. Breadth of the tower, f. 45. Quadrangle, f. 491—224. There were twelve apartments belonging to the abbot, including state chambers, abbot's hall, and private chapel. His great chamber was f. 111—51; and his stables always contained forty-four horses, &c. The abbey kitchen f. 40 square.*

Sir H. Englefield † gives the following measurements of *Reading* Abbey:—the nave, f. 215 long; choir, f. 98—34; transept, f. 196—56; aisles, f. 19 wide; cloister, f. 148 square; chapter-house, f. 78—42; abbot's refectory, f. 72—38. Extreme length of the church, exclusively of the transept, f. 420 by 92.

The ground-plan of the habitable portion of conventual buildings was usually, though not without exception, quadrangular; and in the later ages partook of improvements in domestic architecture, as in the colleges built by Wykeham and Waynflete, and many of the episcopal residences. As several of these abbeys had buildings recently erected at

---

* *Hearne's Hemingford*, Appendix.   † *Archæologia*, vol. vi. p. 63.

the dissolution of monasteries, the grantees of their sites, in many instances, retained, and made them their own habitations. In the two instances I have cited, the Visitors recommended that they should be kept in the King's hands, as palaces, and their dilapidation was respited till the subsequent reigns. Of the halls and other large apartments of. which they were composed, the laborious destruction, and the immediate sale and dispersion of their materials, have scarcely left us any remains: even of the cathedrals to which monasteries were annexed, and the conventual churches, now become cathedrals, the surrounding buildings have been in a great measure removed. Those at Durham and Peterborough, and the conventual halls of Worcester and Chester, must be excepted. The hall of the former measures one hundred feet by forty; and at Peterborough the abbot had a hall, the dimensions of which were ninety-six feet by thirty-six, and his great chamber, ninety-nine by thirty. How great must have been the profusion of examples of architecture, in the richest variety, during the zenith of the Roman Catholic religion, when the cathedrals, or parts of them, which we now admire as almost solitary instances, could be compared with numerous conventual structures without inferiority, and which imitated or rivalled them in dimensions or grandeur. Such was the visible employment of their great wealth, which modern calculators condemn, as having been injuriously misapplied. Yet the ingenious man was patronised, and the artisan was fed.

The liberality of founders and benefactors was without bounds. It is recorded, that the abbey of Vale-Royal in Cheshire had cost King Edward I., before its completion, no less a sum than 3200l. sterling; a sum scarcely credible if estimated in modern money; but the extreme difficulty of conveying the materials from Wales caused this expense. Our authority is that of an historic monk of Abingdon, in the *Cotton MSS.*

Even the churches of the Mendicant Friars were singularly rich in every species of embellishment; as they were selected in preference, for their sepulture by noble and opulent persons. Of these, the most eminent was the church of the Franciscans, near Newgate, London, (the site of Christ's Hospital,) the length of which was f. 300, width f. 89, and height f. 64. Margaret, second queen of Edward I., built the choir at the expense of 2000*l*., besides other very large contributions to the fabric. In the satirical poem called *Pierce Plowman's Crede*, is a lively description of one of these magnificent convents of the " mendicants," frequently quoted.

Several of the conventual kitchens were of a peculiar and excellent construction, the roofs being groined with stone, and having an octangular opening to the middle of the roof, which sprang from the angles, rising like a louvre. Those at Glastonbury and Durham still remain, and are equally perfect and curious. The former is forty feet in diameter, and the latter, thirty-six.

The castellated, or at least embattled, country-houses, both of bishops and abbots, for retirement, and the reduction of their large retinue, during summer residence, resembled colleges, upon a smaller scale. They were very frequent, and several were attached to one monastery.

According to the subsequent division of style in which parish churches and their parts have been designed and executed, individual instances are found in every county in England, and many of them are equal to those which I have adduced. This list is intended merely to communicate a general idea and classification. To the credit of the laborious piety of our ancestors it is worthy of remark, that in certain counties where the materials of architecture least abound, the beauty of parish churches is the more frequent and conspicuous; and whilst the monastic institution is so generally scandalised on account of the unprofitable expenditure of enormous wealth, it is a known fact, that the chief number of handsome churches have been built from their funds, either totally or by munificent benefaction. They have the merit likewise of the architectural plan, as suggested by the more scientific of the fraternity.

ABBEYS FOUNDED BY THE SAXONS.

The rule of St. Benedict obtained, almost universally, under the dynasty of the Saxon kings. To each of these monasteries, without doubt, large buildings of a requisite kind were annexed ; but it would be difficult to decide upon the genuineness of any remains. The crypts, as being the least subject to demolition from fire or rebuilding, have the best claim. The ambition of the Norman prelates to reconstruct their cathedrals upon much more expensive plans, superseded those of true Saxon architecture. All the subjoined, which were founded previously to the Conquest, were BENEDICTINES.

Abingdon.	Rochester Cathedral.
St. Germain's Cathedral, Cornwall.	Westminster (1049), Edw. Confessor.
Barking nunnery.	Peterborough.
Colchester.	St. Frideswide, Oxford.
Gloucester.	Glastonbury.
Tewkesbury.	Bury St. Edmund's.
Winchcombe.	Malmsbury.
Rumsey nunnery.	Evesham.
St. Alban's.	Pershore.

Besides these, several of inferior consequence may be found in the different counties, which are traditionally of Saxon origin, but it is not probable that their structures had any degree of splendour.

CONVENTUAL CHURCHES MADE EPISCOPAL OR PAROCHIAL.

CATHEDRALS.

Peterborough,
Bristol,
Gloucester,
Westminster, now Collegiate only, } Entire.

PAROCHIAL.

St. Alban's, Waltham, Malmsbury, Shrewsbury, Thorney and Croyland, Tewkesbury, Pershore; Christ-Church, Hants; Winbourn, Dorset.

Of these, some are nearly entire, and others have escaped only the almost total dilapidation.

AT THIS TIME IN RUINS. — Glastonbury, unquestionably the most magnificent; St. Mary's, York, a most beautiful structure.

THE FOLLOWING ARE KNOWN ONLY BY THEIR SITES, AND BY ANCIENT DELINEATIONS OR DESCRIPTIONS:—St. Augustine's, Canterbury ; St. Edmundsbury ; St. John of Jerusalem, London ; St. Benet's, Hulme ; St. John's, Colchester ; Evesham, Abingdon, Reading, Cirencester, Winchcombe, Hayles, Bardsey, Hyde, Tavistock, Reading ; Hulme, Yorkshire.

Of these, the greater number enjoyed the privilege of the mitre, and are selected as having been, when entire, the most remarkable for architecture and extent. Other, and not greatly inferior, instances may be found in several counties of England.

CONTEMPORARY ARCHITECTURE OF CONVENTUAL CHURCHES IN ENGLAND, NOW APPLIED AS CATHEDRALS OR PARISH CHURCHES, OF WHICH THERE ARE REMAINS OR AUTHENTIC ACCOUNTS.

SAXON.

A. D. 800 *to* 870 *and* 1000.

Waltham Abbey, Essex. Transept arches of *Southwell*, Notts. The nave of the abbey church of *St. Alban's*, Herts. *St. Augustine, Canterbury*, west front. *St. Frideswide's, Oxford*, nave. Remains of the west front and porch of *Malmsbury*. Tower of *Caystor Church*, Norfolk.

ANGLO-NORMAN.

Before 1100 *to* 1150.

The destroyed abbeys of *Abingdon*,[a] *Reading*,[b] and *Cirencester*.[c] *Malling*, Kent. *Tewkesbury*,[d] nave, aisles, tran-

---

* The churches marked * are now used as parochial.

[a] Is described by Leland to have resembled the cathedral of Wells. The choir was of the early Norman. T. de Salford and R. de Hamme, abbots,

sept, and west front. *Malmsbury,[e] nave and west front. Buildwas, Salop. St. Botolph, Colchester. Bolton,[f] Yorkshire. * Winborn Minster, Dorset.[g] Castle Acre, Norfolk. Hagmon, Salop. *Dunstable, Bedfordshire. *St. Cross, Hants. * Romsey, Hants. Furness,[h] Lancashire — the more ancient parts. Lindisfarne, Northumberland. Byland, Yorkshire. Lanercost, Cumberland. * Sherbourn, Dorset. Southwell, Nottinghamshire. Kirkstall,[i] Yorkshire, nave. Christ-Church, Hants, the more ancient part.

SEMI OR MIXED NORMAN.

From 1150 to 1220.

Lanthony,[k] Monmouth. Fountains,[l] Yorkshire, nave and west front. Glastonbury, nave, and the chapel of St. Joseph. Selby,[m] Yorkshire, west front. * St. Alban's,[n] Herts, many

1426—1435, built the nave; which, with the western front and towers, was finished by their successor, W. de Ashenden.

[b] The church was dedicated by T. à Becket, 1164, and was constructed upon the plan of Durham. Total dimensions, f. 420—196; nave, f. 215; choir, f. 98—34; transept, f. 196—56; eastern or Lady's chapel, f. 102—55.

[c] According to the measurement made by W. Wyrcester in 1440, the total length was f. 280; nave, f. 92 broad with the aisles; choir, f. 132—66; cloister, f. 104 square; chapter-house, f. 42—30.

[d] f. 324—136; nave and aisles, f. 70; west front, f. 100.

[e] f. 100 by 60, tower and choir destroyed.   [f] Total length, f. 261.

[g] f. 180 by 60.

[h] Ruins of the transept and east end, with a few arches of the west; chapter-house, single shaft in the centre, built in 1200; choir in 1460.

[i] f. 224—118; transept built by Henry de Laci and Alexander, abbots, from 1147—1182. The tower built in the reign of Henry VIII. by W. Marshal and John Ripley, the last abbots.

[k] Total length, f. 212. Transept, f. 100.

[l] f. 351—65, nave and aisles; transept, f. 186. In 1204, John de Ebor, abbot, began the fabric. John Pherd, afterward bishop of Ely, and John de Cancia (who died 1245, 29 Hen. III.) finished the whole structure. The chapter-house was f. 84 by 42. Refectory, f. 108 by 45. The tower stood at the north end of the transept, and is f. 166 in height.

[m] f. 267—100; nave and aisles, f. 50. West end built 1180; nave and transept, 1090; choir, 1390.

[n] f. 550—217; f. 65 high; nave and aisle, f. 72.

parts. *Wenlock*, Salop, choir. *Cartmell*,[n] Lancashire. *Furness*,[o] the more modern parts. *Byland*, west end, with the wheel window, and the south transept.[p] *Bolton*, Yorkshire, in parts. *Brinkbourn*, Northumberland, in part. *St. Edmundsbury*, Suffolk, in part. *St. John's* church, *Chester*.

LANCET ARCH GOTHICK.

From 1220 to 1300.

Lanercost, Cumberland. *Rivaulx*, Yorkshire. *Westminster* abbey. *Fountains*, choir and east end. *Tinterne*,[q] Monmouthshire. *Netley*,[r] Hants. *Whitby*,[s] Yorkshire. *Valle Crucis*, Denbighshire. *Ripon* minster, Yorkshire. *Beverley* minster,[t] Yorkshire, south transept. *Milton* abbey,[u] Dorset. * *St. Alban's*,[x] part of the nave. *Tinemouth*, Northumberland. *Brinkbourn*, Northumberland. *Vale Royal*, Cheshire. Eastern façade of *Howden*, Yorkshire.

PURE GOTHICK.

From 1300 to 1400.

Western façade of *Howden*, 1320. *Merton College*,[y] Oxford, chapel. *Gisborne* priory, Yorkshire. *New College*,[z] Oxford, chapel. *St. Stephen's* chapel,[a] Westminster. *Kirkstall*,[b] Yorkshire, additions to the pediments of the choir and

---

[n] Built 1188, semi-Norman, as Selby and Fountains.   [o] f. 287—130.

[p] Nave roof, f. 38; transept, f. 73; choir, f. 50; nave and aisles, f. 68 wide. Total length, f. 323.

[q] f. 225—150; nave and aisles, f. 40 in breadth, thirteen arches on the south side, with an intercolumniation of fifteen feet. Begun in 1239.

[r] f. 200—160; breadth of the nave and choir with aisles, f. 60. Begun in 1239, by the same architect.

[s] The choir, north aisle, centre tower, and north transept, remain. The nave was blown down in 1702.

[t] f. 333 by 165; nave and aisles, f. 63 wide; western towers, f. 198 high.

[u] Built by Walter Archer, prior, 1320—1330; f. 132—107; f. 55 high; tower, f. 101 high, resembling Merton College, Oxon.

[x] The church is f. 550 long by 72: and 65 high: transept, f. 217.

[y] Built by W. Rede, bishop of Chichester, and T. Rodeborne, warden.

[z] Finished 1379.   [a] Built by Edward III.

[b] By W. Marshall, abbot.

' north transept. *St. Mary's*, in *York.* *Kirkham*, Yorkshire. *Selby*,[c] Yorkshire, choir.

PURE GOTHICK DECORATED.

From 1400 *to* 1460.

Tewkesbury, Gloucestershire, choir.[d] *St. Mary's* chapel, *Ely* cathedral. Façade of *Croyland*, Lincolnshire. *Beverley* minster,[e] Yorkshire. *Magdalene College, Oxford*, chapel. *Eton College* chapel,[f] Bucks. Chapel on the Bridge,[g] *Wakefield*, Yorkshire. *Beauchamp* chapel,[h] Warwick.

FLORID GOTHICK AND TUDOR STYLE.

From 1460 *to* 1540.

St. George's chapel,[i] *Windsor.* *King's College* chapel,[k] *Cambridge.* *King Henry the Seventh's* chapel,[l] *Westminster.* *Great Malvern*, tower and choir,[l] Worcestershire. Roof of *Christ-Church* choir, *Oxford*.[m] Campanile and gateway of *Evesham* abbey, Worcestershire.

---

[c] In 1390.

[d] Built by the Despencers, earls of Gloucester, during the thirteenth century.

[e] f. 333 by 165; nave and aisles, f. 63; western towers, f. 198 high. They were the model of those added by Sir Christopher Wren to Westminster Abbey.   [f] Begun and finished by Henry VII.

[g] Built by Edward IV. in memory of his father, Edward Duke of York.

[h] Built by the executors of R. Beauchamp, Earl of Warwick.

[i] Begun by Edward IV. and finished by Henry VII. and VIII., under the superintendence of Sir Reginald Bray and Cardinal Wolsey.

[k] Founded by Henry VI. upon the plan of Nicholas Cloos, but not completed till the reign of Henry VIII.

[l] Built by Sir R. Bray.

[m] Added by R. King, Bishop of Oxford.

COMPARATIVE DIMENSIONS OF CONVENTUAL
CHURCHES, MANY OF WHICH ARE IN RUINS.

	L. ft.	B. ft.	H. ft.
St. Alban's	550	217	65
Glastonbury	420	220	—
St. Edmund's Bury	506	240	—
Reading	420	196	—
Tewkesbury	300	120	—
Fountains	351	186	—
Beverley	323	165	—
Selby	267	100	—
Kirkstall	224	118	—
Lanthony	210	100	—
Tintern	225	40 nave.	

We must not confine the progress and perfection of our
early architecture to such specimens as are presented to our
view in perfect cathedrals. Some of the grandest of them
were conventual, and several were connected with a monastic
establishment whose funds were dedicated to architecture.
This view of such ruins, and authentic documents concerning
them, in which the original measurements are given, would
afford convincing proof that many destroyed conventual
churches were not inferior to the existing cathedrals.*

VAULTED ROOFS IN THE FOURTEENTH, FIFTEENTH,
AND SIXTEENTH CENTURIES.

	A.D.	Feet.
Choir of Lincoln Cathedral	1306	200—40
Our Lady's Chapel, Ely	1349	100—46
Choir of Gloucester Cathedral	1360	140—34
Do. of York	1373	135—45
Chapel at Windsor Castle	1508	260—65
Do. Henry VII., Westminster	1508	99—65
Do. King's College, Cambridge	1516	291—45½
Choir of Winton Cathedral	1525	138—86
Do. of Christ-Church, Oxford	1535	80—20

* See new edition of Dugdale's Monasticon

PAROCHIAL CHURCHES.

SAXON.

Tickencote, Lincolnshire ; *Stewkeley*, Bucks ; *Barfreston*, Kent,—as the most decisive instances. Many Saxon door-cases and heads of arches have been preserved and inserted, when other parts of the churches have been rebuilt, and fonts, for their sanctity and curious carvings and bas-reliefs.

ANGLO-NORMAN.

Melton, Suffolk. *Sotterton* and *Sleaford*,[1] Lincolnshire. *Christ-church*,[2] Hampshire. *Sherbourn* minster, Dorset. *Winchelsea*, Sussex. *Steyning* and *New Shoreham*, Sussex. Chancel of *St. Peter's, Oxford*. *Earl's Barton* tower, Nor-thamptonshire. *West Walton* tower, Norfolk. *Eifley*, Ox-fordshire. *Castle Rising*, Norfolk. *St. Margaret's* porch, *York*. *St. Peter's* church, *Northampton*. There are several round or polygonal bell-towers both in Suffolk and Norfolk.

SEMI OR MIXED NORMAN WITH THE LANCET STYLE.

Winbourn minster, Dorset. *Rumsey*, Hants. *Dorchester*,[3] Oxfordshire. *St. Mary Ottery*,[4] Devon. *Howden*, York-shire. *Doncaster*, ditto, *Lynn*, Norfolk. *Stowe*, *Great Grimsby*, and *Sleaford*, Lincolnshire. *St. George's, Stam-ford*. Choir of *St. Mary's, Warwick*. *St. Mary Overy*, *Southwark*, choir. *Beverley*, Yorkshire.

PURE GOTHICK, OR TRANSITION STYLE.

Grantham,[5] Lincolnshire. *Attelborough*, Norfolk. *High-am Ferrars*, Northamptonshire. *St. Michael*,[6] *Coventry*.

---

[1] The western front of Sleaford is one of the largest and most ornamented of parochial churches in England which has not originally been conventual.

[2] f. 302—106. [3] f. 251—100.

[4] Two towers, one attached to each semi-transept, as at Exeter cathedral.

[5] f. 183—87. Tower, f. 180 high.

[6] The church of St. Michael, Coventry, f. 293—197 ; tower and spire, f. 272 high. They were twenty-two years in building, and cost 2100*l.*; 1372 to 1393.—*Dugdale.*

Truro, Cornwall. *Witney*, Oxfordshire. *Stratford-upon-Avon*, Warwickshire. *St. Peter Mancroft, Norwich. Boston,*[7] Lincolnshire. *St. Mary, Edmund's-Bury*, Suffolk. *Maidstone*, Kent. *Ludlow*, Salop.

PURE GOTHICK.

St. Mary Overy, Southwark. Thaxted[8] and *Saffron Walden*, Essex. *Lowth* and *Stamford*, Lincolnshire. *Campden*, Gloucestershire. *St. Mary, Redcliff;*[9] and the tower of *St. Stephen, Bristol. Taunton* and *Churton Mendip*, Somersetshire. *Lavenham*, Suffolk. *Manchester* College. *St. Mary's, Oxford. Whittlesea*, Cambridgeshire. *Wakefield*, Yorkshire. *Doncaster*, Yorkshire. *Newark-upon-Trent. Heckington*, Lincolnshire. *Mould, Gresford*, and *Wrexham*, in Flintshire. *Melton Mowbray*, Leicestershire. Octangular towers, *St. Margaret's, Norwich*, and *All-Saints, York.*

FLORID GOTHICK.

This style is principally to be referred to oratories, porches, and chapels annexed, or to sepulchral sacella, with their tombs included, in parochial churches. There is perhaps no parish church which exhibits a complete specimen of it in all its parts. The pulpit and skreen at *Dartmouth*, Devon, are a superior specimen.

Every observer knows, that it was a common practice in the thirteenth century, and perhaps earlier, to place pointed arches upon round Norman pillars, and to rebuild the zigzag mouldings in that form, especially in parish churches, where a saving of expense was necessary. It will not be easy, from that circumstance, always to discriminate the true æra and style of any parish church where it occurs. One fact is evident, that the building has been re-constructed, at least in several constituent divisions of it.

---

[7] The church at Boston, Lincolnshire, f. 280—99 ; f. 86 high, with its very remarkable lanthorn tower, rising f. 262 from the ground, was begun in 1309, and was in progress of building during the whole reign of Edward III. The expense was chiefly defrayed by the foreign merchants of the Steelyard   [8] f. 195—79. Spire, f. 273.   [9] f. 220—110.

DISCOURSE V.

MILITARY ARCHITECTURE OF THE FIRST AND MIDDLE
CENTURIES AFTER THE NORMAN CONQUEST; WITH
AN EXAMINATION OF CASTLES IN ENGLAND, AND
THEIR SEVERAL COMPONENT PARTS.

To enumerate or describe fortifications and
castles, such as are still seen in every nation of
Europe and Asia, would require a great length
of research: it is sufficient to observe, that in
the lower empire of Rome and Greece, no city
was undefended by castellated walls, and a
castle or citadel, the architecture of which was
successively renewed according to the general
plan practised during the Gothick ages.*

Referring generally to the very able investigations made by General Roy and Mr. King,
concerning the military erections of the Romans, and in what degree the camps and forts

---

* " The walls of Constantinople extend for more than three
miles on the western side—are triple and embattled. Its hundred towers, diminishing in perspective, offer a stupendous
scene. No single castle in England presents a continued
front of more than three hundred yards."—*Archæolog.* vol. xiv.
See Note [A] page 317.

of the Romans may be distinctly considered,* what is the description of the Anglo-Saxon tower, or the larger castle, built by Alfred, this review does not respect an earlier period than that of the Norman conquest. As military structures were necessary in all ages and nations, it is certain that the Romans built many in every province they conquered, which we can hardly suppose to have been either destroyed or dilapidated by time, when they quitted Britain; and their Saxon successors probably availed themselves of all the fortifications they found.† The application of Roman bricks and tiles, used as the materials of the walls in castles of their foundation, is remarkable at Colchester, and is likewise seen at Arundel, where, withinside, are placed rows of herring-bone masonry. Chaucer describes the composition of the fluid-mortar by which the grouting was made.‡

The Normans, who brought with them the feodal system in its greatest extent, knew that a castle must be attached to every lordship, and they either assimilated what they found of Saxon work, or constructed castles on new sites, according to their own peculiar plans of

---

* See Note [B] page 317.

† Launceston, Restormel, and Tintagel castles, in Cornwall, are said to have been erected by the aboriginal inhabitants.

‡ See Note [C] page 319.

building. They imported stone from Caen, but only for the casing of the walls, and the carved jambs of the doors and windows. The walls themselves, frequently from ten to fifteen feet thick, consisted of an indissoluble grouting, made with fluid mortar, mixed with pebbles, or small flints, or sea-shells.

Forty-nine castles are enumerated in Domesday Book, that of Arundel only as existing in the reign of Edward the Confessor. Eight of these were built by William the Conqueror, ten by the greater barons, and one by a tenant of Earl Roger Mont-Gomeri. There are eleven, the builders of which are not particularised.*

The leading discrimination of a Norman fortress is a lofty mound of earth, thrown up in the centre of the other works, and caused by the forming a very deep ditch, moat, or fosse, from the upper ballium or summit of which rose either a square tower of several stories and great height, or a circular one much lower, and of equal diameter, approached by steep unguarded steps on the outside. Other component parts were, the gateway, and the barbican or watch-tower, both of which communicated with the keep by sally ports.

During the lapse of centuries, from the earliest date of their foundation to their final

* *Introduction to Domesday Book*, lately published by Parliament.

decay or destruction, various styles of military architecture, by which the several parts of a castle were rebuilt or added, will afford a decided proof of the æra to which they belong: for it is certain, that deviations from the first building, by a new construction and forms of gateways, towers, and embattlements, may still be discovered, in castles of the larger extent, which have passed through many owners in succession. This discrimination is no less strongly marked, than in the several distinct æras of Church-architecture; and that to be as decidedly referred to its own proper period.

The prototypes of most of our English castles of primeval construction may be found in Normandy, in such parts of them as remain perfect, or nearly so.* Yet it is certain that the sites of numerous castles are now but green mounds or battered ruins; "and the place that once knew them, knows them no more." There are many too which exhibit vast fragments, and which have not been destroyed by time alone, from the mere adhesion of parts which pressure has rendered as indissoluble as the stone itself.

After having premised thus much, I would propose the subjoined classification.

1. SAXON, or of ROMAN foundation.

2. ANGLO-NORMAN, from 1070 to 1170.

* See Note [D] page 320.

3. NORMAN, from 1170 to 1270.

4. STYLE of the CRUSADERS, introduced by Edward I. in 1272.

5. STYLE of WINDSOR, by Edward III. 1350 —1400.

6. STYLE of the FIFTEENTH CENTURY, 1400 —1480.

7. CASTLES in the REIGNS of the TUDORS.

The purpose intended by this classification of castle architecture is, to convey a general view of its varieties, which were introduced in the course of successive centuries, by adducing such specimens only as remain to be inspected. Wherever dates of sufficient authority can be given, they are added in a note. Ocular demonstration will afford the most satisfactory proof of any hypothesis; it may therefore be superfluous to mention, by way of confirmation, the style of many castles of which there are accounts in Leland's Itinerary, and by other antiquaries, though they are now totally dilapidated by the injuries of war and time; purposely dismantled upon the suppression of feodal tenures, or by command of Cromwell, to pay his army by the sale of the materials. Ground-plans of several castles have been published by Grose. In the subjoined list,* I have mentioned those with which the antiquary is

* No. 1. Richborough, Kent; Castleton, Derbyshire; Porchester, Hants; Pevensey, Sussex; Castor, Norfolk;

best acquainted; for with instances of nearly
equal curiosity or consequence, we are embar-
rassed only by a facility of choice. This arrangement is governed by the æra when any
memorable change in the construction or more
habitable parts took place, and when one considerable castle gave the new mode of building
to several others. Such a progress made from

Burgh, Suffolk; Chesterford, Essex; Corffe, Dorset; Exeter castle gateway; Dover, Kent; Beeston, Cheshire.

No. 2. Launceston, Cornwall; Arundel, Sussex; Windsor, Berks, rebuilt; Tower of London; the square keeps
of Hedingham, Essex; Caer-Philly, Glamorgan; Carisbroke,
Isle of Wight; Porchester, Hants, 1160; Guildford, Surrey;
Bamborough, Northumberland; Kenilworth, Warwickshire;
Richmond, Yorkshire; Cardiff, Glamorgan; Canterbury, Kent;
Oxford, 1071; Newcastle, Northumberland, 1120; Gisbo-
rough, Yorkshire, 1120; Castle Rising, Norfolk, 11..; Mid-
dleham, Yorkshire; Cockermouth, Cumberland; Durham,
1153; Lincoln, 1086; Berkeley, Gloucestershire, 1153; Lancaster; Orford, Suffolk, 1120, polygon.

No. 3. Ludlow, Salop, 1220; Kenilworth, Warwickshire,
enlarged 1220; Warkworth, Northumberland, square, with
the angles canted off; Denbigh; Beeston, Cheshire; Har-
warden, Pembrokeshire.

No. 4. Carnarvon, 1280; Conway, 1283; Harlech, 1290;
Beaumaris, 1295—North Wales. Arundel, outward gateway and barbican tower; Pembroke, gateway and lofty circular tower; Leeds, Kent, 1300; Chepstow, Monmouthshire.

No. 5. Windsor gateway and towers, 1340; Warwick
gateway, a polygonal, and octangular towers; Cardiff, Glamorganshire, octangular tower; Amberley, Sussex, gateway
and round towers, 1390; Lumley, Durham, perfect, built
by Sir Robert Lumley, 1320—1360, where the walls of the
towers incline from the base to the battlement, for greater

rude strength to interior accommodation of plan, and even ornamental construction, became universal during the fourteenth and the century succeeding it, when spacious halls, *bowers* or parlours for the ladies, *alures* or broad pavement upon the walls, small *herbaries* or enclosed gardens, oratories with an oriel window, or larger chapels, and numerous small

strength; Brauncespeth ditto, four large square towers with deep machicolations, 1398; Alnwick restored, Northumberland, 13..; Raby, Durham, perfect, built by John de Neville, 1378: *Leland* calls it " the largest castle of logginges." Naworth, Cumberland, perfect; Saltwood, Kent, 1380, gateway with circular towers; John of Gaunt's hall and buildings, Kenilworth, 1382; Goodrich, Herefordshire, gateway and hall; Maxtoke, Warwickshire; Bodyam, Sussex, (gateway and towers,) which is unique from its uniformity, upon the exact model of castles in Gascony.

No. 6. Sudley, Gloucestershire; Wingfield Manor, Derbyshire, brick; Tattersal, Lincoln, ditto, 1440; Herstmonceaux, Sussex; Hilton, Durham, gateway with numerous carved escocheons; Hampton-Court, Herefordshire, 1400; Whitton, Durham, 1410.

No. 7. Thornbury, Gloucestershire, 1511; Framlingham, Suffolk, 1500; Raglan, Monmouth, 1520; Bury Pomeroy, Devon, south front; Lulworth, Dorset, 15..; Earl of Leicester's addition to Kenilworth, 1575.

Castles in a habitable state, or restored:—Windsor; Arundel, Sussex; Warwick; Alnwick, Northumberland; Powys, Flintshire; Lumley, Durham; Belvoir, Rutland; Berkeley, Gloucestershire; Raby, Durham; Naworth, Cumberland; Bamborough, Durham; Maxtoke, Warwick; Shirbourne, Oxfordshire; Leeds, Kent; Skipton, Yorkshire; Appleby, Westmoreland; Stafford; Broughton, Oxfordshire.

apartments for the reception of the lord and his numerous menials, were found in almost every castle of the higher and more opulent nobility.

1070 TO 1170.

An architect of the greatest celebrity in the reigns immediately succeeding the Conquest, was Gundulphus, bishop of Rochester,* who seems to have considered the lofty artificial mound, originally of Danish usage, as unnecessary.† His central towers are so lofty as to contain four several floors: the basement was the dungeon, without light, and the portal, or grand entrance, many feet above the ground. But his great merit consisted in various architectural contrivances, by which cautions, as much security during a siege was given to his keeps by stratagem, as by real strength. Holinshed records a memorable circumstance of Rochester castle, when besieged for sixty days by W. de Albini, Earl of Arundel, in the reign of King John.‡

---

* He died in 1108; but having completed the Tower of London and the castle of Rochester, he may be considered as having invented and left models of that kind of castle architecture. See Note [E] page 320.

† The terms *gros-mont*, *hou-mont*, and *beau-mont*, occur frequently in ancient descriptions, to denote the mounds of earth thrown up for the erection of keeps.

‡ *Holinshed*, vol. iii. p. 188, says, that " after all the limmes

In the construction of a castle, no ordinary skill was required. We may suppose a Norman castle, fully garrisoned, to resemble a modern man-of-war, in the arrangement of the different parts, the complete occupation of space, and the perfect command of every division of it, from the subordination of its crowded inhabitants. The subsistence and comfort of those who were enclosed within it, were not less to be provided for by the architect than mere defence, or the devices by which the assailants might be misled or defeated. Most of the keeps, of which an account is now offered, had four distinct stories, and the walls were not unfrequently from twelve to twenty feet thick, and the floors were massy planks, which were grooved into each other to prevent assaults from above. There were four turrets at the angles, many feet higher than the parapet, which was divided into broad battlements. One of the turrets had a considerable elevation above the others, and such were seen in the two square keeps built by Robert Consul of Gloucester, in the reign of Henry I.—one at Bristol, and the other at Cardiff.* In the thickness of the walls were placed winding

of the castle had been thrown down, they kept the master tower till half thereof was overthrown; and after kept the other half, till, through famine, they were constreined to yeild." * See Note [F] page 321.

staircases, the well for water, the vast oven, enclosed galleries and chimneys, with an aperture open to the sky, and communicating with the dungeon, in which prisoners were confined, and to whom it gave all the light and air they could receive. There was likewise a kind of flue for conveying sound to every part, not more than eight inches in diameter. Wells of great depth, even of several hundred feet, were so constructed as to communicate with each separate floor, and with the platform on the roof of the keep. At Conisburgh, a very ancient instance, it was placed in the centre of the circle. The passage, or narrow gallery within the substance of the walls, did not run horizontally, but rose unequally; and without were steep steps, leading to a false portal. This military stratagem appears in Rochester castle. The walls of the first-mentioned are nearly half as thick as its diameter within, which is twenty-one feet; and as they ascend towards the top, a few places are hollowed out and converted into closets with loop-holes. The state apartment occupied the whole third story, and the staircases leading to it were made much more commodiously than the others, some of which were even large enough to admit military engines. Adjoining to the great chamber was an oratory.*

---

* These oratories were lighted by a larger window, em-

From the earliest period of the Norman æra, the power of the Church was predominant. It had pervaded even the walls of castles, which, by its influence, were not solely dedicated to war, or purposes of defence or destruction. Included within the thickest walls, or more frequently forming a room of a tower of entrance, always attached to the gateway of a keep, was a small chapel or oratory. At Arundel, such a one occupied' the highest story. They were usually dedicated either to St. George or St. Martin, the two military saints.

In the Tower of London there is a chapel, fifty feet by forty, with aisles, divided by an arcade. That at Ludlow is circular, and has many Norman mouldings. At Brougham, Westmoreland, is one very remarkable for a curiously groined roof. At Caernarvon, a very beautiful one is undestroyed. In process of time, chapels within castles were so constructed as to admit of ten or twelve priests, who became collegiate. Memorable instances are, St. George's at Windsor, and those destroyed or suppressed at Wallingford, Berks; Arundel, Sussex; and Tickhill, Yorkshire. These

bowed withinside, and called an " oriel." *Lydgate,* describing a lady, says;

> In her orpall there she was
> Closyd well with royall glas.

were founded sometimes in the lifetime of the great barons, but more often by their last wills and testaments, " *in articulo mortis.*"

In Rochester castle, the chief room was thirty-two feet high, including the whole space within the walls. Moveable suits of arras were suspended from the circular arch which supported the roof, to make separate apartments, and attached against the walls as furniture, which were sometimes painted in fresco, as in the castle of Guildford. In the ground-floor there was no light; loop-holes, only, were allowed in the second; but in the third were three large round-arched windows, placed high, so as not to be looked through, and so defended by an internal arcade, that no missile weapon could enter, or fall with effect. Each floor had its communication with the well. The chimneys were very capacious, and projected considerably into the rooms, resting upon small pillars; and the sinks were so contrived, in an oblique direction, that no weapon could be sent up them.

Gundulph is said to have introduced the architectural ornaments of the Norman style into castles, both withinside and without. In the Norman keeps of Berkeley and Pontefract, the walls were constructed with semi-round towers only.

The use of battlements, loop-holes, and open galleries or macchicolations, was certainly known to the Romans.

——Troes contra, defendere saxis
Perque cavas densi tela intorquêre fenestras.

Æn. l. ix. 533.

The basement or ground-story was divided into dungeons to confine prisoners, who, in those barbarous times, were deprived of light and air. But they were universally applied to hold the instruments and engines of war;* and those used in the early Norman reigns, appear to have been all of them adopted from the Romans. *Catapultæ*, or *Mangonels* to cast large stones to a distance. *Balistæ*, slings, *(springals,)* to throw smaller stones or arrows against the besiegers. *Tribuli*, the same, but so contrived as to have a triple delivery of any missile.† *Arcubalistæ*, cross-bows of steel, which were wound up with a windlass. *Multones (moutons)*, battering-rams, used only by besiegers. *Barfreni (skaffauts‡)*, wooden towers,

* In *Grose*, " *upon Ancient Armour*," will be found a larger list of these inventions, many of which, from their names, appear to have originated in France. I have selected those which were most in usage.

† Interea grossos Petraria mittit ab intus,
Assiduè, lapides Mangonellusque minores.

W. Brito, *quoted by Du Cange.*

‡ Thep dradde none assaut,
Of ginne, gonne or skaffaut.

CHAUCER, *Rom. of the Rose.*

with scaling-ladders, used to bring the besiegers on a level with the garrison on the
walls and embrasures; introduced and much
used by King Stephen in his wars.*

Among other preparations of military engines to be taken into Palestine by Richard I.
in his crusade, was a high tower of timber-
frame, to be erected there. In the romance of
" Cœur de Lion," it is thus described as made
after a model in stone :—

> ———— A castel, I understond,
> That was made of timbere yn Englonde;
> Wyth sex stages ymade of tourelles,
> Wel and flourished with gode kernelles.

These required almost all the space of the
basement; but there were round openings, like
wells, in the thickness of the walls, through
which the engines might be lifted with cords
or chains to the roof and macchicolation. A
stone thrown by a mangonel of sixteen inches
diameter, and weighing 200lb. has been found
in the foss of Kenilworth Castle. These observations will be found to include nearly the
whole scheme of ancient military tactics.

* At the siege of Arundel Castle by King Stephen.—
History of Western Sussex.

SCALE AND DIMENSIONS OF THE PRINCIPAL KEEPS ERECTED DURING THE NORMAN ÆRA.

INTERNAL SQUARE OR OBLONG.			
Names.	Dimensions.	Division of rooms.	Dates and Founders.
	L. B. H.		
Tower of Lon-	116 96 —	By semi-circular	William Conqueror.
don		arches	
Porchester . .	115 65 —	Four floors.	
Canterbury . .	88 80 50*	Two walls continued from the base to the top.	
Rochester . .	75 72 104	By semi-circular arches	Gundulph, bishop.
Dover . . .	— — 92		
Colchester . .	140 102 —	Three large rooms upon every floor.	
Norwich . . .	110 92 70	. . .	Roger Bigod.
Ludlow . . .	— — 110	Four stories	Roger de Laci.
Hedingham . .	62 55 100	Three tiers above the basement.	
Guildford . .	42 47 —		
Oxford . . .	. . .	. . .	Robert D'Oiley.
Bamborough .	. . .	. . .	1070.
Richmond . .	. . .	Vault supported by a single octangular pillar	1100.
Newcastle-upon- Tyne	82 62 54	By internal arches and door-cases in the Norman style	Robt.Curthoise,1080
Corfe	72 60 80		
ROUND OR POLYGONAL.			
Arundel . . .	69 57 —	Roof open in the centre ; straight buttresses	Roger MontGomeri, 1070.
Conisburgh .	23 diameter	Three floors; two of them state apartments	W. de Warren, 1070.
York	64 45 —†	Four segments of circles	William Conqueror, 1068.
Tunbridge . .	64 50 —		
Berkeley . .	. . .	Circular, flanked by four small towers	Robert Fitz-Hard- ing. 1120.
Lincoln . . .	. . .	. . .	William Con. 1086.
Orford . . .	. . .	Polygon, flanked by three square towers	
Windsor . . .	90 85 —	. . .	Rebuilt by Edw.III.
Durham . . .	63 61 —	. . .	Heightened in 1830.

* Dilapidated.   † Largest diameter.

The component parts of a complete castle in the first Norman centuries, may be stated to consist of—

The barbican.

Outward vallum, or rampart.

Outward ballium, or ditch.

Middle vallum.

Inner ballium.

Mount and keep, and a square tower built before the entrance, containing secret passages, and other stratagems, sally ports, &c.

Upper ballium surrounding it.

Upper and lower wards.*

The ditch, moat, foss, vallum, a hollow space on the outside of the walls or ramparts.

Ballium is the space between the outer and middle ditches. Round the upper ballium were walls which circumscribed the keep. These were commonly flanked with towers, and had a parapet embattled or crenellated. There were flights of steps for mounting it, placed at convenient distances; and the parapet often had the merlons pierced· with long chinks, ending in round holes or œillets.†

The keeps were ascended by an unguarded flight of steps, from which the besiegers might be precipitated; and though their general plan was nearly the same, yet the military

---

* *Archæolog.* vol. xii. p. 196.

† *Grose* and *Archæolog.* vol. iv. p. 390, and vol. vi. p. 253.

contrivances were effected in a very different manner.*

That most ancient fortress of Falaise (traditionally the birth-place of William the Conqueror) appears to have furnished the model of most of the strong holds in England. It is still a most noble ruin. The square form of keeps, the more usual with us, is of rare occurrence on the opposite coast; but the appendages and outworks are of very great extent. Very deep macchicolations, after the return from the first crusade, more frequently finished their round or polygonal towers, than battlements or parapets.

A large portal and windows, with sculptures, similar to those used in ecclesiastical buildings, appear in most of them.

Castle Rising, Norfolk, and Norwich, and particularly Newcastle-upon-Tyne, abound in admirable specimens of Norman arcades and mouldings ; but particularly one in the castle of Durham, exactly resembling those in the cathedral, and as richly designed ; and the castle of Newcastle-upon-Tyne is even more remarkable for the number of internal arches and door-cases, which are decorated with Norman carved work.

In the circular, oval, or polygonal keeps, which usually occupied the whole area of the

* King.

mount on which they stood, a richly-carved door-case is to be discovered. Such are still remaining at Arundel and Berkeley. The remaining circular tower, flanked by four small ones, at Houdon, near Falaise, is the exact prototype of the latter. The great tower of entrance was built at the foot of the artificial mount, from which was a subterraneous sally-port with stone stairs leading to the keep. It contained the portcullis and drawbridge affixed to the archway, and several spacious chambers. In point both of the formation of the mount and keep, and their connexion with the entrance-tower, the remains of Tunbridge, and the more perfect state of Arundel Castle, exhibit a singular resemblance.* The walls were protected by very substantial ribs or buttresses, and the round keeps had a central space left open to admit the light and air. At Arundel, the corbel-stones which supported the beams of timber,

---

* The gateway of Tunbridge Castle is of the same form and æra. The base of the mound covers an acre of ground. (See the elevation and plan in *Carter's Ancient Architecture in England*, pl. lxi. a work to which the candid will allow a considerable degree of merit.) The fosse at Arundel is 110 feet deep on one side, and 80 on the other. Leland observes a peculiarity of Berkeley, " sed non stat in mole egestæ terræ." The excavations under the keep of Reigate Castle, now destroyed, made in the sand-rock, are most extensive. There was formerly a very large crypt, surrounded by stone benches.

The keep of Pembroke Castle, with walls fourteen feet

and which converged to an open centre, where was a subterraneous room, are still easily to be marked out.

The life of a chieftain during the first Norman reigns, appears to have been passed in building castles and defending them, when not actively employed in destroying those of others. Although constructed, as if to last for ages, the long reign of Henry III. spent in a ceaseless contest between that king and his revolting barons, affords numerous instances of fortresses which were scarcely finished, before the outworks, at least, were levelled with the ground. The keep more frequently escaped utter ruin, after a long and obstinate siege. This demolition was effected by means of vast military engines, such as *catapultæ*, *(espringals)* and battering-rams, the use of which had been retained, and applied according to the Roman system of war. These ob-

---

thick, has a circular form likewise, and a singularly curious arched roof, composed externally of stone. The diameter is 25 feet, and the height 75. It is probably of a later date, by a century, than the two before mentioned. " A tower in Pontefract Castle had a singularly narrow and irregularly winding staircase going down from the upper floor to a sally-port constructed within a solid wall, under the mount." " The old rounders of imperishable stone and cement, which last even hardens by time, contain in themselves no more principle of decay, than the rock on which they stand." — *Whitaker's Skipton.*

servations likewise belong to the barons' wars in the reign of the second Edward. We can-not indeed fairly account for the total subversion of so many castles as the chroniclers have asserted, but by concluding, that after a castle was taken, the whole soldiery engaged as victors did not leave it until the entire demolition was completed,—"*funditus demoliendum.*"*

In process of time, several improvements, in respect both of military strength and commodious habitation, were adopted, even in these Norman fortresses. The second ballium was protected by smaller towers, and those of the barbican and gate of entrance admitted of spacious rooms. In these the feodal baron resided with his family, who were driven to inhabit the keep merely as a place of refuge during a siege. Such castles were frequent in every county in England, as early as the reigns of Henry II. and his sons, and continued till the close of that of Henry III.

But the plan which allowed of enlarged dimensions, and greater regularity and beauty in the architecture of the towers, owes its intro-

---

* *Lydgate* very forcibly describes such total ruin—

Walls and towres and crestes embattailed,
And for war strongly apparailled,
Be firste down bete, that nothing be seen,
But all togedyr with the pearth plein
Below laid.

Story of Thebes, Part iii.

duction into England to King Edward I. We may, indeed, consider his reign as the epoch of the grand style of accommodation and magnificence in castle architecture. When engaged in the crusade, he surveyed with satisfaction the superior form and strength of the castles in the Levant and the Holy Land.* Every city he saw surrounded by lofty embattled walls, thickly studded with well-shaped towers, and crested with hanging galleries and macchicolations, which served the double purpose of military defence and great external beauty.† Of the five castles which he built in Wales, Caernarvon, Conway, Harlech, and Beaumaris, retain the vestiges of former magnificence; but Aberystwith has scarcely a ruin which remains at this time.

The castle of Caernarvon consists of two distinct parts, one of which was military, and adapted to receive a garrison, and the other was a palace. Of this celebrated castle, the ground-plan is oblong, unequally divided into an upper and lower ward. None of the towers

* The Norman croisaders, during the winter, fortified, in the manner of their country, every post they had gained. Our Richard I. built the walls of Acre, Porphyra, Joppa, and Askalon. *Fuller's Holy War*, lib. iii. chap. 2. from *Wilhelmus Tyrensis*.

† See an account of the walls of Constantinople, *Archæolog.* vol. xiv. 231. *Procopius, De Edificiis Justiniani*, mentions 500 "φρυρια," or embattled towers; an evident amplification.

are circular, or with macchicolations, but have five, six, or eight angles. The largest, called from some tradition " the Eagle tower," has three tall angular turrets rising from it, whilst all the others have but one of the same description. The inclosing walls are seven feet thick, with alures and parapets pierced frequently with œillet holes. A great singularity is observable in the extreme height both of the great entrance gate and that which is called the Queen's. Leland observes of the portcullises at Pembroke, that they were composed *ex solido ferro*. In confirmation of the opinion, that the Royal founder adopted the form of such gates of entrance, those similar are almost universal in the castles, mosques, and palaces of the Saracens, and which he had so frequently seen during the Crusades. The tower of entrance from the town of Caernarvon is still perfect, and is the most handsome structure of that age in the kingdom.* It is at least one hundred feet high ; and the gateway, of very remarkable

---

* *Lydgate*, in his *Troy Boke*, describes the fortification of his own times :—

> The walls were on height
> Two hundred cubits, all of marble grey,
> Magecolled without for saultes and essay.

Magècolles, or machecoulis, were the openings under the parapet of the gate, or other towers of salient angles. Some of these, of singular curiosity, are at Lumley and Raglan

depth, is formed by a succession of ribbed arches, sharply pointed. The grooves for three portcullises may be discovered, and above them are circular perforations, through which missile weapons and molten lead might be discharged upon the assailants. In the lower, or palatial division of the castle, stand a large polygonal tower of four stories, which was appropriated to Queen Eleanor, and in which her ill-fated son was born; and another to the king, of a circular shape externally, but square towards the court. The apartments in the last-mentioned are larger, and lighted by windows with square heads, and intersected with carved mullions. There is singular contrivance in the battlements, each of which had an excavation for the archers to stand in, pointing their arrows through the slits; and a curious stratagem, the carved figures of soldiers with helmets, apparently looking over the parapet. This device is repeated at Chepstow.

It has been happily conjectured, that the castles of Caernarvon and Conway were intended for different purposes; the one, as a capital

castles, two instances as early, and as late, as they were made in England. Of the first-mentioned, the buttresses are sloped from the base, and the turrets are finished by macchicolated galleries. Hanging watch-turrets, large enough only to contain one man, are suspended, as if by geometry, from an angular point of the macchicolation.

fortress to overawe North Wales; the other, as a pleasant residence,—so far as residence could be pleasant where precaution, such as its plan and locality indicate, was required for personal safety. All the ornamental architecture, in both, has rather the character of the conventual or ecclesiastic, than the military— in the pointed arches and the shape of the windows ; a circumstance perhaps rather of necessity than choice, from the short time for the construction, and the difficulty of procuring workmen versed in any other style. " At Conway," observes an anonymous author, "what is called the Queen's Oriel is remarkable for the fancy, luxuriance, and elegance of the workmanship. Nor is the contrivance of the little terraced garden below, considering the history of the times, a matter of small curiosity, where, though all the surrounding country were hostile, fresh air might be safely enjoyed ; and the commanding view of the singularly beautiful landscape around, from both that little herbary or garden, and the bay window or oriel, is so managed as to leave no doubt of its purpose."*

Conway has no resemblance to Caernarvon. It is built much more exactly upon the model of the fortresses erected during the last Greek emperors, or those of the Gothick chieftains in

* *Principles of Design in Architecture*, 8vo. 1809. See Note [G] page 322.

the north of Italy. Here all the towers, with their turrets, are round, with a single slender one rising from each of them, and the macchicolations, which are not seen at Caernarvon, are introduced ; and the hall, capable of containing numerous guests, appears, as a first instance, to have been within castle-walls. The roof was vaulted upon ribbed arches of stone. A peculiarity in the construction of the towers, all of which are either circular or polygonal, is, that that those containing the royal apartments are finished by small round turrets, rising many feet above that upon which they are placed, as a proud distinction. Almost all the castles built in order to defend the marches of Wales and Scotland, more numerous than in other parts of England, were founded in his reign. After the subjugation of Wales, and the partition of it into great lordships, among the followers of the victorious Edward, for their security and the preservation of their power, many castles were erected upon the general plan of those he had built, but varying in dimensions and situation.

Caer-Philly, in Glamorganshire, was the strong hold of the De Spencers in the reign of the second Edward, and so much increased by them, that its vallations and remains are much more extensive than any now discoverable. The hall was an immense room compared with that at Conway.* There was another at Chepstow. Castles had then become habitable, and in these apartments, having more and better accommodation, if not magnificent. The splendid reign of Edward III. was an æra still more favourable to these improvements. Many of his barons, who had acquired wealth by the ransom of prisoners taken in the fields of Poitiers and Cressy, were proud to apply it to the decoration and enlargement of their castles ; and the example the king had shown at Windsor, excited in them a rivalry of imitation. The original destination of protection and defence was never wholly sacrificed to convenience, but was consulted by many cautions of a warlike nature.

Various improvements extended themselves from this reign to the close of the contention between the houses of York and Lancaster. Within that period we may date the erection or renovation of the grandest castellated structures of which this kingdom could once boast : and whose venerable ruins are the most characteristic features of the English landscape. About this time, turrets, and hanging galleries, over the salient angles and the gateways, very various in their design, were added to the ruder architecture of impregnable strength; and, par-

* The hall was f 129 by 31, and only f. 22 high. See the plan in *Pennant's Tour.*

ticularly in the Welsh counties, conical buttresses were applied to round towers, reaching
to more than half their height, and spreading
at the base like a modern bastion. By these
additions the ruins are rendered extremely
picturesque.

Of the fortress built by William Rede, bishop
of Chichester, at Amberley, Sussex, about 1370,
its ground-plan describes nearly a parallelogram, having four large towers at the angles,
which do not project externally, but are, as it
were, dovetailed into the side-walls. He was
one of the most able geometricians of his age,
and applied his skill to this structure.

The lofty perforated parapet or arcade of
Swansea castle is of this æra. Through these
arches the water ran from the roof. Henry
Gower, bishop of St. David's in 1335, improved
upon this plan in his magnificent castellated
palace which he erected there, and in another
at Llanphey Court. So beautiful an effect was
not repeated, and we have no other instance in
Wales.*

As the circuit of many castles, with their outworks, frequently encompassed several acres
of ground, the base court was proportionably
spacious, and the halls and other large state

* The following dimensions show the extent of this curious
and singular edifice:—area of the great court, f. 120 square;
king's hall, f. 88—30; bishop's hall, 58—33.— *Wyndham's
Tour.*

chambers had the advantage of windows, of less magnitude, but similar form to those in churches. Other apartments and offices were almost unavoidably incommodious, as defence was the leading idea; symmetry therefore is very seldom seen in the smaller rooms, which were often without fire-places; and the œillet-holes and narrow windows served only to make darkness visible.

If the chief apartments in a castle of improved construction be here more minutely investigated, it may be considered as a digression necessary to their better classification. I have observed, that the inner court only was so occupied.

HALLS.—William Rufus constructed a hall in his palace at Westminster, which preceded all others both in point of antiquity and of dimensions. Hugh Lupus built one at Chester;* Robert Consul one in Bristol castle; and others were erected by his father, Henry I., at

---

* The hall at Chester, called Lupus' Hall, was 99 feet long, by 45 feet wide: taken down in 1790. Of that æra and equal dimensions was that in the castle of Bristol, built by Robert Consul (temp. Henry I.), and taken down in 1643. W. Wyrcestre, in 1480, gives the measurement 108 feet by 50, divided by upright beams of timber. Aubrey (*MSS. Ashmol. Mus. Oxford*) says, that in the hall of Henry the First's palace of Woodstock, there were two rows of pillars supporting circular arches with Norman zig-zag mouldings, dividing as now commonly seen in churches.

Woodstock, and Beaumont in Oxford. These were probably of rude construction, and were divided into two aisles by stone arches or upright beams of timber.* Others were contemporary, of which similar accounts are known to the investigating antiquary.

In the next century, castles began to be constantly inhabited; and the necessary resort to them of equals and feodal dependants, at solemn feasts and customary entertainments, required a large space, and soon admitted of internal architecture and characteristic ornament, more especially at the upper end, where were the " dais" and the high table.†

Edward I. erected a hall in his castle at Conway, in which are certain peculiarities.‡ From that period, no principal residence of the

* The halls of some of the earlier castles had arches of stone crossing them at every bay, with a timber-frame roof resting upon them, and seen betwixt them. Such were at Conway, Goodrich, and Mayfield, Sussex.

† The haut-pas, or dais, was a part of the floor elevated above it, and approached by three steps at least.

‡ This hall is 129 feet by 31, and 22 feet high. It is not oblong, but is built to follow the curvature of the rock.

Halls, in these and similar instances, were so spacious, as to admit of a knight's riding up to the high table ; as the champion of England was used to do at the coronation. The hall of Raby is sufficient for that purpose, f. 90—36; 34 high.

In at the halle dore al suddenlie
There came a knight upon a stede,
And up he rideth to the highe borde. CHAUCER

nobility or feudal lords was without one ; and though the general plan was correspondent with each other, they varied both in minuter parts, and in the degree of magnificent construction.

Edward III. gave a grand example at Windsor, which was followed with emulation during his own and the succeeding reign. The limits of this slight treatise will not allow of an extended enumeration. The following, however, must not be passed over. Westminster was rebuilt by Richard II., and Eltham, Kent; Kenilworth, by John of Gaunt; and Dartington, Devon, by Holland Duke of Exeter, all of them most remarkable. Crosby Hall, London, was finished by the Duke of Gloucester, afterwards Richard III. Of each of these, accounts have been published, which are scientific and satisfactory.*

There was a general plan, as to the internal arrangement of these halls. The high table was elevated upon a platform above the level of the floor, and was reserved for the lord and his family, with the superior guests. Around the walls were separate tables and benches, for the officers of the household and dependants. In the centre was the great fire-place, open on all sides, placed immediately beneath a turret in the roof, called a louvre, for the purpose

* See Note [H] page 323.

of conveying away the smoke : this was the most ancient, but a very imperfect expedient. We find from Leland, that chimney-places included within the walls were in Bolton Castle; but there are other, and perhaps earlier, proofs of this alteration, at Conway and Kenilworth.

The expansive roofs were made of timber-frame of oak or chesnut. Whether of the indigenous material oak or chesnut, or of the latter imported from Portugal and Castile, is a question which has been discussed, but not determined, by antiquaries. It was firmly compacted together with considerable geometrical skill, and admitting many of the ornamental forms, in carved wood, which abounded in the age in which they were erected.

Large corbels of stone and projecting trusses issued from the side walls, and were disposed in the bays (likewise called *severeys*) between each window. Upon the ends of these were carved demi-angels, each holding a large escocheon to their breasts. The vast superincumbent frame-work was thus supported, and was composed of open lattices, which gave much lightness by perforation, and were finished with pendants. Near to the high table was a projecting or bay window, fully glazed, and frequently with armorial stained glass, in which was placed the standing cupboard, to contain the splendid display of plain and parcel-gilt plate. The rere-doss was a frame with tapestry,* sometimes canopied, fixed behind the seat of the sovereign or the great chieftain, when he dined in public. Around the walls was wainscot of panneled oak, or strained suits of tapestry. I speak of the fourteenth century, the æra of their introduction.

PRIVY CHAMBERS, PARLOURS, AND BOWERS. —Castles, at least as early as the reign of Edward I., were not constructed merely for garrisons. At Conway there were several smaller apartments which admitted of accommodation and ornament from the introduction of carving, fresco painting, or tapestry. The two first mentioned arts were applied with a profusion and excellence in the royal palace at Westminster, of which sufficient evidence has been preserved.

Of the dimensions of these castles, and the infinity of small rooms in which they abounded, the number of retainers who were resident, and necessary to the state of a nobleman, will give a positive proof, exclusively of occasional garrisons in time of war.†

---

* Into a halle of noble apparaile
    With arras spread.   CHAUCER.

See Note [I] page 324.

† See the ancient Household Books of the nobility, particularly that of the Earls of Northumberland, lately republished, 1828.

Adjoining to, or nearly connected with the hall, was a spacious room, usually having a bay window, which looked into the quadrangle or court. Here the lord received his family or special guests before dinner, and retired into it when that ceremony was finished. It was adorned with the richest tapestry, and cushions of embroidery by the ladies themselves, and was distinguished as " the presence or privy chamber." For the females of the family there was another similar apartment, in which they passed their time, and which was dedicated to their occupations and amusements, known as " my lady's bower, or parlour," where they received visiters.

KITCHENS.—A great kitchen was an indispensable appendage, and was generally constructed with considerable skill. The shape was square or octangular. At Raby, for instance, it was of the former description, and the roof most elaborately groined, with an octangular aperture in the centre to convey away the steam and smoke. The fire-places in them and other apartments projected into the room, and were supported by small pillars, as in the keep of Conisburgh, and several others; and the chimneys, externally, were single and lofty, as those built in Berkeley Castle in the reign of Edward III. : afterwards they were enclosed in turrets. The windows of the hall were long and narrow, of two lights only, and a single mullion; and a larger one over the high table at the end, looking to the court-yard.* Bay windows were never placed in the outward wall, and seldom others, excepting those of the narrowest shape. But as the architects were most conversant with church building, we may observe a certain similarity of form in those parts of a castle where it could occur.

We will now examine the plan and constituent parts of the exterior of enlarged and habitable castles. In the course of these investigations, some readers may be inclined to know, by the most certain evidence we can acquire, what was the real state of the principal castles which were, in the far greater proportion, adjacent to the Marches of Wales and Scotland, in the time of their perfect repair and habitation, and what was more worthy of remark in many of them.

In the reign of Henry VIII. (1534), that intelligent and industrious antiquary, JOHN LELAND, was commissioned to collect, by an actual survey, certain information concerning them, in every county in the kingdom. No man

---

* In these windows were emblazoned the armorial ensigns of the lord and his connexions, in stained glass. Leland has noticed that those at Sudley Castle, Gloucestershire, were composed of "berals." Chaucer, in several passages, has the terms " burrell and crystal," meaning only very thick, but diaphanous, glass in knobs, and probably not stained with colour.

was more competent to such a task; and greatly we must regret that his notes, taken in this
Itinerary, are the only remains of his labours,
which were finally interrupted by sickness and
death; and what remains to us is still imperfect, although Hearne, who published them,
has done as much to connect and restore them
as could have been done. At all events, Leland has enabled us to see what has, in so many
instances, vanished from the earth, with *his
eyes*, and realise many ideas of their former
extent and magnificence, which we may have
pictured in our day-dreams, whilst we were
inspecting their ruins. With him, " we may
walk about their bulwarks, and tell the towers
thereof."*

This consideration will create an interest in
many towards the extracts which I purpose to
make in the Appendix, principally relating to
peculiar rather than to general construction·
When the lover of our old national architecture visits the remains thus presented to him,
he will enlarge his view by previous knowledge
of its history, and be furnished with a clue to
his investigations of the once enormous structure, which has passed away for ages. For
Leland himself enumerates many castles, of
which he remarks " that they be now clene
downe."

* See Note [K] page 324.

An account of all the majestic mansions in which our ancient nobility resided, now totally rased and dilapidated by war and time, and of others whose fate and grandeur we learn only from historians, will not be expected in a slight essay. But for excellence or peculiarity of architecture the following may be selected.* Windsor was left a complete castle by Edward III. Spofford, Raby, Kenilworth, Ludlow, Alnwick, Arundel, Lumley, and Goodrich, had each of them halls of good proportions, like those in the greater abbeys. Those of Raby and Lumley remain at this day. Warkworth had extraordinary carved devices and escocheons, placed in series on the outside, under the battlements; while the gateways of Raby, Lancaster, and Warwick, were remarkable, when many now dilapidated could offer a comparison. The external application of escocheons with armorial ensigns, was most frequent in the northern counties. Nothing can exceed the lightness and elegance of the polygonal tower, which stands singly, at

---

* Amid the ruins of castles, we are frequently shown one called the " Maiden Tower," as in Lord Surrey's sonnet at Windsor : —

" With eyes caste up into the mayden's tower."

T. Warton, in a note on this word, proves that it did not refer to the habitation of the fair sex, or to the towers never having been taken, but simply a corruption of the old French " magne," great.— *Hist. of Poetry*, vol. iii. p. 15.

Warwick, finished with macchicolations and projecting brackets.

The effect of these polygonal, lofty, and richly-macchicolated towers, is most interesting in the perspective view; and of this we have still an opportunity of judging at Warwick and Cardiff. They are very beautiful.

The ground-plots of castles were arranged chiefly according to their sites. When placed on a rock above a river, with the foundation rifted and appearing as a continuation of the natural fastness, an idea is communicated of impregnable massiveness, which is peculiarly striking at Durham, Warwick, Conway, and Chepstow. The ancient castle of Leeds, in Kent, was placed on an island in the middle of a lake; and that likewise of Bodyam, Sussex.

No castle which recurs to my memory is of so regular a construction, and so strictly correspondent in its plan, as that of Bodyam, last mentioned, so much so as to be nearly unique. It rose from its foundation in 1397—1400; square, with four circular towers at the angles, a stately gateway between two others, deeply macchicolated, and two more, all corresponding in their location. There are no carved devices, but escocheons of arms and crests over each gate.*

* A graphic and historical sketch of Bodyam Castle, in Sussex, by *W. Cotton, Esq. M.A.* 8vo. 1830.

Baronial fortresses, which had not such advantages of situation, were usually oblong squares, with lofty towers at each angle, connected by embattled walls or curtains, pierced only by œillet-holes. They had open galleries, or corridors, and bay-windows, opening to the court-yard, from which the ladies could view the military processions, and award the prize to the successful knight at jousts and tourneys.

The castle of Newark, Notts, has several small rooms or closets, projecting externally, like bay windows, at a great height from the ground.

At Caernarvon, in a niche over the doorway, Edward I. is represented as standing, and about to draw his sword; and at Pembroke is the Earl, in a sitting posture. In several of the northern castles we have a display of large escocheons, with armorial ensigns, affixed to the building. The drawbridge over the first vallum, or ditch, was never omitted; and when the castle was built on the banks of a river, a long arched bridge added to its security.

Usually at one of the angles arose a tower, (as *Leland* terms it, of "lodginges,") sometimes to the height of even five stories, with single apartments, always occupied by the lord or his family. At Wresil Castle, Yorkshire, the Earl of Northumberland had converted one of these rooms into a library, which he called " Paradise."

There was a mode of building a certain part of a castle for greater security, called " a Bastille." This was effected by raising the connecting walls almost to the height of two or three of the towers, and strongly embattling them. The origin of it was the great fortress at Paris, known emphatically as ' The Bastille,'* which had two courts and towers of uniform height. Its destruction in 1793 will be remembered. There was an instance in the destroyed castle at Bristol,† but another does not occur to my recollection.

---

* This was the largest and most complete. In the two courts there were eight towers, which, with the walls, were of uniform construction. It was founded by Charles V. King of France, in 1370, and finished in 1382.

The term " bastillé" is used adjectively in the *Roman de la Rose.*

> Je bey un bergier grant et le',
> Enclos d'un hault mur, bastille'.

Which Chaucer translates—

> Full wel about, it was battailed,
> And round environ eke were set
> Full many a rich and fayr turret,
> At every cornere of this wal,
> Was set a towr full principal.

† In W. Wyrcestre's survey of Bristol Castle, about the year 1480, " Item, a bastyle lyethe southward beyond the water-gate; containeth in length 60 yardes."

Itin. W. W. p. 260.

Barbican towers were of early introduction. They were always erected on the first ballium, sometimes on a mount, and serving the purposes of a watch-tower, to keep a constant guard.

Scotland, on the borders, had a peculiarity in the castles. Almost every chieftain's manor-house was built around one large and lofty tower, which was called a " peel ;" and as they were generally deeply bracketed, there was a superstructure of wood under a conical or pavilion roof.*   Several apartments were thus

---

* This plan of superstructure was introduced from France, where, in the thirteenth century, the larger castle towers were finished by high conical or pavilion roofs.   See ancient illuminations in *Froissart, MSS. Harl.* fol. No. 4350, in the British Museum.   Such were known as " bartizans," from the old French; but the wooden erections on them were called " breteskes," from the Italian " bretesche."

Lydgate says, in his account of Troy :—

𝕰𝖇𝖊𝖗𝖎𝖊 𝖙𝖔𝖜𝖗𝖊 𝖇𝖗𝖊𝖙𝖊𝖞𝖊𝖉 𝖜𝖆𝖘 𝖘𝖔 𝖈𝖑𝖊𝖓𝖊
𝕺𝖋 𝖈𝖍𝖔𝖘𝖊' 𝖘𝖙𝖔𝖓𝖊, 𝖙𝖍𝖆𝖙 𝖜𝖊𝖗𝖊 𝖓𝖔𝖙 𝖋𝖆𝖗 𝖆𝖘𝖚𝖓𝖉𝖗𝖊,

which seemeth to apply to battlements only.

" The King (Edward III.) went to Striveling, where, on a plott of grounde, where the destroied castell had stood, he built another fortresse called a Peele."—*Holinshed*.   *Leland* likewise has adopted the term : " the house called Clifton, like a ' pile or castellet ;'" by which term he means a single tower.   A Peel is described as such, elevated on a mound of earth, and surrounded by a high fence of sharpened stakes.

made, in which, in time of danger, the females of the family dwelt, or retired to them for protection.

We will now turn back to consider and investigate how far the opinion which might have been suggested by former discussions be correct. The royal palaces of Westminster and others were not, strictly speaking, castles. Although they were not actual fortifications in each instance, Windsor was decidedly so, and the Tower of London.

As late as the reign of Edward IV. before a new manor-place was built, a permission from the crown of a partial fortification, at least, called a " licentia crenellandi," was procured.* This appeared principally in the great gate of entrance, which had at this period an embattlement of larger dimensions than before, upon a very deep and overhanging bracket, by which an open gallery was formed. This licence was more frequently demanded for the small castles, or peel-houses, in those counties which border on the northern marches.

* Sir W. Hastings, of Ashby-de-la-Zouch, had " licentiam murillandi, tourellandi, kernellandi, embattellandi, et macchicolandi," and the following more minute statement includes a full description of castle walls. Patent to W. Earl of Southampton, to build Cowdray :—" cum petris calce et zabulo, muris et turribus includere, batillare vel turrellare, kernellare, et macchicolare."

The great variety of materials of which castles were composed, depended upon the soil and the nature of the country where they stood. Walls of the thickness of twenty feet were faced only with hewn stone; the intermediate part was composed of pebble, rubble stone, or flint, imbedded in an indissoluble mass of fluid mortar, which acquired, by time and pressure, such an induration, as scarcely to be separated by any possible means. Upon the sea-coast, squared flints were last of all used for the outward walls; but in counties which produced the better kinds of stone, the neatest and most regular masonry was not spared. Stone was procured from Caen.

Castellated structures of brick became more frequent in England, when habitable houses, upon the largest scale, were erected; sometimes entire, and at others, mixed with stone, in the more decorated parts. Michael de la Pole, Earl of Suffolk, in the reign of Richard II. erected a magnificent house in the town of Kingston-upon-Hull, and surrounded the burgh with walls and towers of the same material.*

When the jealous and fierce spirit of the feodal system prevailed in its full force, castles were necessary to repel warlike attacks or predatory violence; and whatever hospitality and courtesy were practised within their walls, they

* See Note [L] page 329.

frowned defiance upon all without them, whether uncivilised or hostile.

From reflections on the history of the early Norman warriors, we willingly turn to those of the middle centuries, when Chivalry had thrown her rays of refinement over domestic life. Castles then became the schools of the hardier virtues, and manners, which were once distorted by emulation and love of power, had acquired from her institutions a mild dignity, which has long since been lost in a higher degree of polish, in the gradual progress of refinement.

By far the most important part of a fortress was the great gateway of entrance, and combined with it were the chief materials both of architectural beauty and warlike defence. It occupied, with few exceptions, the central part of the skreen wall, which had that aspect from which the castle could be most conveniently approached. The whole exceeded the other parapets in height.* Two more lofty towers, flanked either side, and the whole had a very deep corbelling, a mode of building brought from the East, where it had its most early use. The Arabs brought it into Europe, in Spain, and it was afterwards adopted by the Lombards and Normans. Corbels are stones which are extended at regular distances from the

* Among the finest specimens of such gateways now remaining are those of Caernarvon, Pembroke, Raby, Windsor, and Warwick.

main wall, for the purpose of supporting* a projecting parapet, cornice, or entablature, by means of brackets, which are either simple, or connected with each other by arches. They were most common in the construction of castles, in parapets and galleries so thrown out, where perpendicular holes were pierced in the flooring, which thus enabled the besieged, under cover, to throw down missiles, or destructive molten metal, on the heads of the assailants. Gothic fancy was employed to add terror to the view, by exhibiting carved giants and monsters, as attached to the walls. John of Gaunt's entrance gateway at Lancaster† has a lofty pointed arch, defended by overhanging corbels, with pierced apertures. On either side are two light watch-towers, crested with battle-

---

* A bay-window, in common acceptation, means simply a projecting window, usually rising from a corbel or bracket, between buttresses, and more frequently at the end of buildings.

† And portkolis strong at everie gate,
    And many a gargoile, and manie a hidous head.

                                                    Lydgate.

Hawes, in his " Palace of Pleasure," (1505,) describes the improved architecture shown in the castles of his own age :—

    The fayre tower ————
    ——————————— strangled doubtlesse,
    Gargopled with greyhoundes, and with liouns,
    ———————— and with divers sundrie dragouns.

Which means, that the gargouils or waterspouts, under the parapet walls, were carved into the forms of those beasts— the cognizances of the noble house.

ments. It is the grandest and most perfect instance in England of its particular æra.*

The two remarkable towers of Warwick Castle will communicate a perfect idea of castle architecture. Thomas de Beauchamp, Earl of Warwick, erected them (1395) in the reign of Richard II. The taller of them, already noticed for its beauty, has twelve sides, rises 105 feet above its base, and is 38 feet in diameter, with five stories, separated from each other by groined ceilings. *Dugdale* says at the expense of 395*l*. 5*s*. 2*d*. Talbot's tower, in the castle of Falaise, in Normandy, built by the Earl of Salop, in 1430, was more than 100 feet high.

John of Gaunt's works of architecture were singularly good, in the examples of his great hall at Kenilworth, (now in ruins,) and a bay window of his palace at Lincoln, one of the most beautiful now remaining. In both of these, the ornaments of masonry were abun-

* The industrious brothers N. and S. Buck, published large views of several castles, as they were situated in the different English counties. They were faithfully, but very inartificially executed. Grose is more voluminous; but from the hasty manner in which his views are sketched, with no knowledge of perspective, and very coarse engraving, we may wonder how they became so popular. The works of Hearne and Byrne embellish truth by a very picturesque arrangement of subjects; they were, indeed, the authors of the present improved style of architectural landscapes.

dantly seen, and the contrivances for splendid residence consulted, by the introduction of more spacious and symmetrical rooms.

During the middle centuries, subsequent to the Norman conquest, 1300 to 1500, when the plans of mere defence were rendered subservient to those of more comfortable habitation within the walls of a castle, a certain degree of splendour in the partial decoration of the interior was a necessary consequence.

The walls of the state-chambers were painted,* and sometimes lined with wainscot, of curious carved *boisserie* on the pannels, which subsequently were more adorned and hung with tapestry. In the numerous castellated palaces of our earlier sovereigns, were apartments ornamented in all these different modes, even at periods when it would not be supposed that any arts subservient to them, existed in the lowest degree of perfection; certainly not before the reign of Henry III.

At Warwick there was a memorable suit of arras, upon which were represented the achieve-

---

* The practice was introduced into England at the beginning of the thirteenth century. It was frequently seen, as in the palace of Westminster, in the chief chambers of bishops and abbots, at first applied to the emblazoning of arms, but subsequently to portraits in series, and parts of scriptural history and romances. They were painted in fresco, or with colours mixed up with resinous gums.

ments of Guy, the valorous Earl of Warwick, whose legend was familiar to our old poets.*

As nearly approximating to the description of castles, the walls of cities, and their gates, require a distinct notice. Those of Constantinople, already alluded to, are the grandest and the most extraordinary in Europe.†

Modern convenience and ardour of improvement have, by rapid degrees, in the course of the past century, nearly completed the demolition of the first mentioned ;‡ and the latter, which had not been destroyed during the civil war, or rased by Cromwell, have fallen into total decay. Of those which remain, none equal the walls of York, nor were others to be compared with them, when in a perfect state. The most complete fortifications surrounding a town, and still to be seen, are at Conway

---

* See Note [M] page 330.

† When I frequently surveyed them, in 1795, I could compare them only to the appearance of Caernarvon Castle, if stretched out and extended for the space of three miles.

‡ In the walls of York, there still remain four principal gates. Mickle-gate Bar is the largest and most remarkable. Bootham Bar is the only one which has not been despoiled of its barbican towers. The Water-gate, at Southampton, was of superior design and architecture, and has been lately taken down. *Leland* observes, (vol. v. p. 115,) of Newcastle-upon-Tyne, " The strength and magnificence of the wauling of this towne, far passeth all the wauls of the cities of England and of most of the towns of Europe." We have the authority of *Leland* for this fact.

and Caernarvon; the walls of Chester are kept up in the most perfect condition in England;* whilst those at York and Chichester are partly preserved; and at Southampton, they rise very picturesquely above the river. Round the garden of New College, Oxford, they are in admirable repair, with several towers, which are open on the inner side, having parapets and steps, a plan universal in city walls, and not unfrequent in castles, as at Framlingham, Norfolk.

It may be a subject equally worthy of an inquiry with that employed in investigations of the origin of our ecclesiastical architecture, whether we are not as much indebted to the Orientals for the structure of our castles, or fortified towns? A very late and observant author says, " That the walls of the city of Delhi are sixty feet in height, embattled and macchicolated, with small round towers and two noble gateways, each defended by an outer barbican of the same construction. The whole is of red granite, adjoining to the palace, which nearly equals that of Windsor."†

To those cities which were founded on either side of large rivers, connecting bridges were appended. By the Romans and the Saxons

---

* The walls of Chester are one mile, six furlongs, and a hundred yards in circumference."—*Pennant.*

† *Bishop Heber's Journal,* 1828.

they were constructed with beams of timber, framed together. Early in the Norman reigns, particularly that of Henry III. several of the most remarkable for extent and architecture were built,—over the Thames, at London ; the Ouse, at York ; and the Avon, at Bristol ; and all of them upon a correspondent plan, between the years 1215 and 1250.* They have been all removed, within the last century, for others of modern architecture. Pointed arches, with a central of double width, were adopted, almost without exception. The piers were very large, and projected far on either side of them, and the tops were formed into recesses, with parapets, for the safety of the passengers. This refers to their general plan ; but upon the three I have selected, were streets, the houses resting upon beams of wood, suspended between the piers. Upon some one of the arches was a chapel, for the position of it was not always the same, at Bristol, in the midway; at York and London at one end, which were of rich masonry, in the best style of the times. That celebrated as the most beautiful, is the chapel on the bridge at Wakefield, which was probably the last, erected by Edward IV.

A great curiosity, in point of architecture, is the triangularly-formed bridge at Croyland, Lincolnshire, built probably in the fourteenth

* See Note [N] page 332.

century. It is erected over the confluence of
three streams, and has no excellence or difficulty of construction, or beauty of effect, but
is, perhaps, an unique instance. There are
" three arches, rising from three several segments of a circle, each arch having three ribs,
and the whole meeting in one centre." Of
modern bridges, which do not belong to this
inquiry, it is a national boast, that several in
England are not equalled by others in any
part of Europe.

ANNOTATIONS ON MILITARY ARCHITECTURE,
ILLUSTRATIVE OF THE FIFTH DISCOURSE.

[A] page 267.—" The military architecture of the Greeks and Romans consisted, from the earliest to the latest times, of walls and towers capped with battlements. The over-hanging battlements, now called Gothick, were certainly known to the Romans as early as the reign of Titus, as there are among the paintings of Herculaneum representations of walls and towers completely finished in this way *(Pitture d'Hercolano*, tom. i. tav. 49) ; and it is probable that this fashion continued down to the subversion of the empire, and was then adopted by the conquerors. It is indeed the natural mode of fortification for any people skilled in masonry, and not acquainted with artillery, to employ ; as it afforded the most obvious and effective means of at once guarding the defendants and annoying the assailants: wherefore it might have been used by different nations who had no connexion with each other, and which might, with equal justice, claim the invention of it."—*Knight's Inquiry into the Principles of Taste*, p. 160.

[B] page 268.—*Roy's Military Antiquities of the Romans in Britain*, fol. 1793. *Munimenta Antiqua*, vol. iii. fol. 1804, by *King*, in which the origin of the more ancient castles is referred to a higher æra than that cited by most historians. The tower of Richborough *(Rutupium)*, certainly Roman, is round, but unlike any of Norman construction. Many single towers were built during the Heptarchy, and by King Alfred. The castle at Arundel dates perhaps its true origin from that monarch. Canute is said to have founded Norwich ; and the high mound of earth both at Castleton and Conisburgh has been attributed, upon good evidence, to the Danes.

At Exeter, the Saxon princes occupied the castle as a palace. In the early chronicles, copied by Holinshed and Stowe, are scarcely-credible accounts, in point of number, of castles built and rased to the ground, during the ceaseless contests which took place between the Norman kings and the great barons, previously to the reign of Henry III. These, from the excellence of their construction, particularly that of the round flanking towers, with imperishable stone and cement, would have remained entire to our own times without intentional destruction.

Mr. King's opinion concerning what fortresses were certainly Roman, merits considerable attention. He has particularised Richborough, Kent; Porchester, Hants; Pevensey, Sussex; Caistor, Norfolk; Burgh, Suffolk; and Chesterford, Essex.—vol. ii. pp. 11. 146, &c. The palaces and fortresses of the first Saxons were at Bamborough, Durham; Porchester, Hants; Pevensey, Sussex; Castleton, Derbyshire; Guildford, Surrey; Corff, Dorset; Bridgenorth, Salop; Goodrich, Herefordshire; Penline, Glamorgan: in all of which evidences of Saxon architecture are to be discerned. He considers, that wherever courses of herring-bone work are seen in the walls internally, it is an indisputable mark of Saxon construction.—vol. iii., &c. In fact, such an investigation was new to English antiquaries, when King's observations appeared in a detached form. By the time he had collected and arranged all his materials for this and other inquiries, he had become completely mystified; and his facts, originally the result of very accurate investigation, were all bent, if not distorted, to one particular theory.

In *Maseres'* notes to *Excerpta ex Orderico Vitali*, p. 228.

Castles built by William the Conqueror.

1. Dover, built before the Conquest, but enlarged and rebuilt.

2. Pevensey, 1066 } Upon his landing.
3. Hastings, 1066 }

4. London, 1066.

5. Winchester, 1067.

6. Arundel,   ⎫   ⎧ Given to Earl Roger Mont-
7. Chichester, ⎬ 1067 ⎨   Gomeri.
8. Exeter, 1068.
9. Warwick, 1068.
10. Nottingham, 1068.
11. York, 1068.
12. Huntingdon, 1068.
13. Cambridge, 1068.
14. A second castle at York, 1069.
15. Chester.
16. Stafford, 1070.
17. Lincoln, 1086.

Ten castles were built by the greater barons, and one by a tenant of Earl Roger. There are eleven noticed in Domes. day Book, the builders of which are not specified.

William appears to have been engaged in these buildings almost contemporaneously. The English were not completely subjugated before their entire completion, when they were furnished with garrisons. During his reign, his nobles had not obtained the privilege of building or fortifying castles, which was greatly extended in those of his immediate successors.

[C] page 268.—In " *The Romaunt of the Rose*" as translated by Chaucer, we have minute descriptions of the plan of contemporary castles, and of the materials with which they were built; and the subjoined very curious account of the particular cement which was then used. He says, that it was made—

      ——of licoure, wonder dere, *(very costly)*
    Of quicke lime persaunt *(piercing)* and egre, *(sharp)*
    The which was tempered with vineger.

Certain castles were remarkable for their towers and external fortifications, in the early Norman age, beyond comparison with others. Nor were they less so for their various means of defence by military stratagems, in which they abounded; such as concealed sally-ports, galleries of secret communica-

tion, or sometimes blocked up half-way ; doorways and staircases which literally " led to nothing;" excavations in the
solid walls; and dungeons which were accessible only by
trap-doors.

[D] page 270.—As tending to elucidation, I extract Mr.
Dawson Turner's account of ancient keeps in NORMANDY.
" *Gisors*, built from 1090 to 1100, a lofty octangular tower,
with strong projecting ribs, and a turret on one side, likewise
octangular, resembling *Conisburgh* very nearly, and standing
upon a high mount, chiefly thrown up.   *Galliard*, in 1196, a
cylinder placed upon a truncated cone, with many massive
perpendicular buttresses, which are ranged round the upper
wall, from which they project considerably, and lose themselves
at their bases in the cones from which they arise.   Attached to,
and hewn out of the rock on which it stands, are sally-ports,
staircases, and military stratagems.   *Arques*, in the eleventh
century.   The keep is quadrangular, and strengthened by
many upright ribs or buttresses, divided into two apartments,
each f. 50—20.   This mode prevailed generally in the first
Norman keeps erected in England.   *Lillebonne*, for extent
and massiveness with its round keep, and *Vire*, for its vast
ruin of a square one, are not less worthy of examination.
Falaise, of the same æra—interior, 50 feet square.   The walls
are from 15 to 20 feet in thickness, and have stones placed in
the herring-bone fashion."—*Tour in Normandy*, 2 vols. 1820.
Cotman.

[E] page 274.—Military architecture was applied in several instances by Gundulph's episcopal successors to castles on
their own domains, and for their occasional residence and
security.   At Durham, Winchester, and Farnham, were large
castles.   King Stephen's brothers — 1. Alexander of Blois,
bishop of Lincoln, built three castles, Banbury, Sleaford,
and Newark : 2. Henry Blois, bishop of Winchester, the
castle there, and at Farnham.   Roger, their nephew, bishop
of Sarum, at Devises, Marlborough, and Sherbourn, Dorset.

Newark is the earliest example of any departure from mere military architecture in the system of castles, by the introduction of ornamental forms externally, and of more commodious rooms. William of Malmsbury says : " Vernantissimum floridâ compositione castellum construxerat."

In the first æra of the Norman dynasty, bishops were architects for their own defence. To establish this fact, the following enumeration may suffice :

Durham, Pudsey bishop.

Ely, Nigellus bishop.

Winton, Farnham, Henry de Blois bishop.

Sherbourn, Devises and Marlborough, Roger Bp. of Sarum.

Wisbich, Morton bishop of Ely.

Banbury, Sleaford, Newark, Alexander bishop of Lincoln.

Amberley, Rede bishop of Chichester.

Bishop's Auckland, Durham, Antony Beke bishop.

Some centuries afterwards were built, Rose Castle in Cumberland, by Kirby bishop of Carlisle ; and Saltwood, Kent, by Archbishop Courtenay. It is hardly necessary to observe that the most ancient of these castles, having been erected before the wars between the empress Maud and Stephen, have been besieged and demolished. The remains of such as have been repaired and inhabited by the bishops to whom they have belonged, are still to be seen.

When these military residences were deserted, the bishops' palaces, usually contiguous to their cathedrals, were greatly enlarged, particularly by the building of very spacious halls. Those of Norwich, Salisbury, and Wells (all now in ruins) may be considered as the best examples. The bishop of Winton's hall at Southwark had a beautiful rose window at the end, of considerable dimensions, the only instance in England.

[F] page 275.—The more ancient word for keep was Donjon, or dungeon. Keeps are thus described by Chaucer :—

> The greate towere that was so strong,
> Which of the Castell was the chiefe dongeon.

Knight's Tale.

[G] page 290.—It is to be regretted that Leland has given us no account of Conway Castle in his *Itinerary*. Of architecture so peculiar, though his notes are very concise, it is probable that he would have given a more minute description as it stood in his time, and before it was dismantled by Cromwell. Warton (*Hist. of Poetry*, vol. i. page 84,) speaks of several romances in English verse, of the age of Edward I. which had the titles of "The Castle of Love," "The Tower of Beauty," &c. In all these, the construction and parts of a castle of that age in particular, are as circumstantially described as if they were not merely ideal edifices. Fancy has only given the command to a magician: the walls are of gold, set with precious stones, instead of common materials, but the turrets and macchicolations, then newly introduced, are always noticed as giving great beauty to the exterior view.

Chaucer's castles present to us the same ideas of an enchanted mansion, as having the precise form of a real one; but they are clothed in still brighter imagery. About his time it was common to place many gilded vanes on the turrets, of the distant effect of which he invariably avails himself in his gorgeous descriptions.

> For everie gate of fine gold
> A thousand fanes, aie turning.
> And of a sute were all the toures,
> Subtilly corben after floures;
> With many a small turret hie.
>
> CHAUCER'S *Dreme.*

The exact description of Conway and Caernarvon.

Chaucer was appointed "Clericus Operationum" (Clerk of the Works) of all the royal palaces, with a salary of two shillings a-day.—*Rot. Pat.* 13 *Ricardi Secundi*, p. 1. m. 30. From this grant, it is evident that he was paymaster or director only of the workmen — not that he furnished plans or designs, or, in fact, could be considered professionally as an architect; but his theoretical knowledge of it must be acknowledged, or it would not have appeared in his poems.

[H] page 296. — DIMENSIONS OF HALLS IN CASTLES
AND PALACES ERECTED BEFORE THE END OF THE
FIFTEENTH CENTURY, CHIEFLY DILAPIDATED.

	L.	B.	H.
Westminster (1397)	228	66	—
Bristol (divided by upright beams of timber)	108	50	—
Windsor (ancient)	108	35	—
Conway (the roof was laid upon stone ribs) .	129	31	22
Kenilworth (1300)	90	50	—
Swansea . .	88	30	—
Another . .	58	33	—
Spofforth . . .	76	36	—
Caerphilly .	70	—	35
Lumley . . .	90	—	—
Eltham (1386)	100	36	55
Durham Castle . . .	180	50	36
Castle Hall, Leicester	78	51	24
Dartington (1476) . .	70	40	44
Raby	90	36	—
Warwick . . .	62	35	25
Chester . .	99	45	—
Berkeley . .	51	32	—
Crosby Place	69	27	38
Goodrich .	65	28	—

HALLS IN ECCLESIASTICAL BUILDINGS.

In investigating the ruins of abbeys, some of
the halls may be traced with a certain degree of accuracy. That at Worcester is
perfect . . . . 120 38 —
The largest episcopal hall was at Norwich . 110 60 —
Others at Salisbury and Wells, which had
dividing arches; and Lincoln, which had
likewise an arcade of stone, supported by
pillars of Purbeck marble.

	L.	B.	H.
W. Wykeham had built (before 1400) the halls of New College, Oxford	78	45	30
Winton College .	63	33	—
Bishops Waltham	66	27	25

These were, doubtless, equalled or exceeded by the Convent halls, especially those of Glastonbury, Fountains, and Reading.

[I] page 298.—I have considered Chaucer and Lydgate as affording the most satisfactory evidence respecting castles, and offer no apology for quoting them frequently. The poets of Gothick times, in their minutely descriptive imagery, give us so distinct a picture of castles and their parts, as they existed in their own time, as to offer certain evidence of their being conversant in the art, principally in " *The Romaunt of the Rose*," and " *The Troy Boke.*"

And shapen was this herber roofe and all
As a prety parlour.

Chaucer.

Bothe the castle and the toure,
And eke the halle, and eberie bowre.

Id.

Aftyr mete, they went to pley,
Alle the folk as I you sey,
Some to chambre and some to bowere,
And some to the hie towre,
And some in the halle stode.

Metrical Romance, Ellis.

[K] page 301.—EXTRACTS FROM LELAND'S ITINERARY.

" Michael De la Pole, marchant of *Hulle*, came into such high favour with King Richard II. that he got many privileges for the towne. And in hys time, the toune was wonderfully augmented yn building, and was enclosyd with ditches, and the waul begun ; and in continuance endid, and made al of brike, as most part of the houses at that time was. In the waul be four principal gates of brike." He likewise enumerates twenty-five towers. " M. de la Pole buildid a goodlie house of brike, against the west end of St. Mary's Church, lyke a palace, with goodly orcharde and garden at large; also three houses besides, every on of which hath a tower of brik."—*Itin.* vol. i. p. 51. This was the first instance of so large an application of brick building in England.

Shirbourn, Dorset, " has four great towers of three loggyns (stories) in higth. The keep is full of vaultes. There be few pecies of work in England of the antiquity of this, that stondith so hole and so wel couched."—vol. ii.

Launceston, Cornwall, " the strongest but not the largest I ever saw in England."—vol. ii.

Bolton, Yorkshire, (in the time of Richard II.) " has four great strong towers of good loggins. It was in makyng eighteen yeres, and the charges of the building came by year to 1000 markes."—vol. viii.

Rockingham, Yorkshire. " One thing in the waullis of the castel is much to be notid, that ys, that they should be embatteled on both the sides. So that if the area of the castelle were won by coming in at either of the two greate gates, yet the keepers of the wauls might defend the castel. I markid that there is a strong tower in the area of the castel, and from it over the dungeon-dyke is a drawbridge to the dungeon tower."—vol. i.

Pontefract, Yorkshire, " A dongeon *(the keep)* of six semi-towers, 3 bigge and 3 smaul."

Wallingford, Berks. " Three dykes large and depe."

Brauncepeth. " Three towers of loggyng and three *ad ornamentum.*"

Shire Hutton, Yorkshire. " I markyd in the forefront of the first area of the castell of Shirehutton three great and high towers, of the which the Gate-house was the midle. In the seconde area ther be 5 or 6 towers, and the stately staire up to the haull is very magnificent, and so is the haul itselfe, and all the residew of the house, in so much, that I saw no house in the North so like a princely logginges. The castell was wel mainteined, by reson that the late Duke of

Norfolk lay there for ten yeares, and sins, the Duke of Rich-mond.   Built by Ralph Neville of Raby, first Erle of West-moreland, who hath builded three castells beside."—vol. i.

Wresil, Yorkshire.   " The house is the most proper be-yond Trent.   There are five towers, and one at each corner, and the gatehouse seemith newly made by Percie Erle of Worcestre."—vol. i.

Bolton, York (as above).   " One thing I much notid in the haulle of Bolton, how chimneys were conveyed by tun-nels made in the sides of the walles, betwyxt lights in the haull ; and by this means and by no louvers is the smoke of the hearth in the hall strangely conveyed."—vol. viii.

Wresil (as above). "The castelle is al of very fair and greate squarid stone bothe within and withoute, wherof (as sum hold opinion) much was brought owt of Fraunce.   One thing I liked exceedingly yn one of the towers, that was a study caullid paradyse, where was a clauset in the middle of 8 squares latised abowte : and at the top of every square was a deske ledgid to set bookes on, and cofers within them, and these seemed as yoined hard to the toppe of the clauset, and yet by pulling one or al would come downe breste high in rabbets, and serve for deskes to lay bookes on."

" The gardrobe in the castelle ys exceeding fair.   And so are the gardens within the mote, and the orchardes withoute. And in the orchardes were mountes *opere topiario,* writhen abowte with degrees like turninges of cokilshells to cum up to the top without pajn."—vol. i.

Belvoir, Rutland.   " The dungeon (keep) is a fair round towr, now turned to pleasure, as a place to walk yn, and to se all the country abowte, and railed about the round walle, and a garden platte in the midle."—vol. i.

Raby, Durham, " is the largest castel of loggyns in all the Northe country : all the chief towers of the 3 courts as in the hart of the castell.   The haul and al the houses of offices be large and stately, and in the haulle I saw an incre-dible great beam of a hart.   The great chamber was exceed-ing large, but now yt is fals rofid, and divided into 2 or 3 parts.

I saw ther a littel chamber wherin was in wyndowes of color-
id glasse al the petigre of the Nevilles, but it is now taken
down and glasid with clere glasse."—vol. i.

Devizes, Wilts.—" This castel was made in Henry firstes
dayes by one Roger Byshop of Salisburye. Such a pece of
castle werke so costly and strongly was never afore nor sence
set up by any bishope in England. The kepe or Dungeon
of it set upon an hille cast by hand is a pece of worke of an
incredible coste."—vol. vi.

Bolton, (as before). " Ther is a very fayr clokke at Bolton *cum motu solis et lunæ*, and other conclusions."—vol. vi.

Sudley, Gloucestershire. " One thing was to be notid in
this castle, that part of the windows of it were glased with
berall."—vol. iv. It may be remarked, that the nati·e beryl
is an opaque stone of a dark green colour. The " berall "
here mentioned was green glass, with a knob in the centre of
each pane, at this time very frequently used by glaziers.

Nottingham. " The base courte is metely large and
strong, and a stately bridge is there with pillers bering bestes
and giants over the ditche into the secund warde, the fronter
of which warde is exceeding stronge, with towers and port-
coleces. But the moste bewtifullest part and gallant building for lodgyng, is on the Northe side, wher Edwarde 4
began a sumptuous pece of stone work, of the which he
clenely finisched one excellent goodly tower of 3 hightes yn
buylding, and brought up the other part likewise from the
foundation with stone; and mervelus fair cumpacid windowes
to laying of the first soyle for chambers, and ther lefte.

" Then, King Richard his brother, as I hard ther, forced
up upon that werke another peace of one lofte of tymber,
making round windows also of tymber, to the proportion of
the aforesaid windowes in stone, a good foundation for the
new tymbre windows. So that surely this north part is an
exceeding pece of work." Leland does not frequently enter
so much into detail. Edward IV. intended to have converted this castle into a palace, and his brother Richard to finish
it, had his short reign allowed him so to do.

Warwick. " The magnificent and strong castle of Warwick being at the weste south weste end of the towne hard by
the right ripe of Avon, is sette upon a huge rock of stone,
and hath 3 goodly towers in the east front of it. Ther is a
fayre towre on the north syde of it, and in this part of the
castle K. Richard 3. pulled down a piece of the wall, and
began and half finisched a mighty towre or strength to shoote
out gunnes. This peice as he left it, so it remaineth un-
finisched. The Dungeon now in ruine standeth in the west
north west part of the castle. There is alsoe a towre in west
north west, and through it is a postern gate of yron. All
the principal lodgines of the castle, with the hall and chappell,
lye on the south syde of the castle, and the King (Henry 8th)
doth muche cost in makinge foundations in the rockes to
sustein that syde of the castle. For great pieces fell owt of
the rocke that susteined it." As Warwick castle is one of
the most perfect which is now seen, it is worthy observation
how exactly Leland has given an account almost of its present state; and from this singular instance which affords an
opportunity of judging, we may conclude that he was scrupulously accurate in his description of those which are dilapidated, or no more seen. The towers, all of them different,
but of peculiar architectural magnificence, deserved his
special notice.

Denbigh. "The castelle is a very large thing, and hath
many towres in it. But the body of the worke was never
finisched. The gate hous is a mervelous strong and great
peace of worke, but the *fastigia* (battlements) were never
finisched. If they had been, it might have beene countid
among the most memorable peaces of workys in England.
It has diverse wardes, and diverse portcolices. On the front
of the gate is set the image of Henry Lacy Erle of Lincoln,
in his stately long robes. Ther is another very high tower
and large, in the castelle, caulled the red towre."

Pembroke. " The castel standith hard by the waul (of
the town), and is very larg and strong, being double wardid.

In the utter ward I saw a chaumbre wher K. Henry the vij
was borne, in knowledge wherof a chymeney is new made,
with the armes and badges of K. Henry vij.   In the bottom
of the great strong round toure in the inner warde, is a mar-
vellus vaulte, called *the Hogan*.   The toppe of this towre is
gathered with a rose of stone almost *in conum*, the top wherof
is keverid with a flat mille stone."

Bristol. " In the castil be 2 courtes.   In the utter courte,
as in the northe west part of it, is a great dungeon towre,
made, as it is sayde, of stone browght owt of Cane in Nor-
mandye by the redde Erle of Glocester."

Scarborough, Yorkshire. " At the est end of the towne,
on the one poynt of the bosom of the se, where the harborow
for shippes is, stondith an exceeding goodly larg and stronge
castelle, on a stepe rocke having but one way by the stepe
slaty crag to cum to it.   And or ever a man can enter *aream
castelli*, ther be 2 towres, and betwixt eche of them a draw
bridge, having a stepe rok on eche side of them.   In the first
cowrte is the Arx and 3 towres in a row, and then yoinith a
waul to them, as an arm down from the first courte to the
point of the se cliffe, conteining in it 6 towres, where the
2^d is square and full of logging, and is caullid Queen's Towre
or Lodging.   Within the first area there is a great grene,
conteyning (to reckon down to the very shore) a xvi acres."

In a careful perusal of Leland's Itinerary, undismayed by
his obsolete language, we may discover, in the different English counties, sometimes even minute notices of manor-places
of great extent, the residence of those who built, and their successors who enjoyed them for a century at least.   We can hardly
suppose that, as such a period only had elapsed, Leland had
not the opportunity of surveying many of these palatial or
domestic castles in their pristine state.   His descriptions are
amusing, from their simple phraseology: " Wher Master
St. John dwellith, a right praty manor-place," and a " pleau-
saunt and gallant house."   Such was the dawn of improvement in the earlier style of our DOMESTIC ARCHITECTURE.

[L] page 308.—*Barrington* observes, that "the use of brick, so frequent with the Romans, was lost till the reign of Richard II." *Delapole's* brick edifices at Kingston-upon-Hull have been already adverted to. His son, the Earl of Suffolk, erected a palace in Southwark, afterwards called "The Mint." During the reigns of Henry V. and VI. Hurstmonceaux, in Sussex, was built by Sir Roger Fiennes in 1426. This particularly beautiful specimen, after the long possession of its noble owners, had been purchased by Mr. Hare Nayler. It was in no dilapidated state when he consigned it to Samuel Wyat, the architect, to dismantle it utterly. Ralph Lord Cromwell, treasurer to Henry VI. was the founder of two very remarkable structures of brick — Tattershall Castle in Lincolnshire, in 1440, and S. Winfield manor, Derbyshire, left incomplete at his decease. The first-mentioned is a very lofty single tower, rectangular, and flanked by four turrets. The macchicolations are of extraordinary depth, and the windows are well proportioned, with pointed heads. Gateways of brick, with window-frames of freestone, were not unusually attached both to abbeys and mansions, where all other parts of the building were of stone or flint. The practice of squaring flints, unknown to the Romans, appeared first in England in the fifteenth century. Parts of Arundel Castle, of that date, still retain curious specimens of this mode of mixing flints with indurated chalk, cut into squares, and alternated.

[M] page 313.—This tapestry appears to have been placed in Warwick castle before the year 1398. It was then so distinguished and valued a piece of furniture, that a special grant was made of it by Richard II. dated in that year, conveying "that suit of arras hangings which contained the history of the famous Guy Earl of Warwick, with the castle and other possessions, to Thomas Holland Duke of Kent;" and at the same time, a similar grant to John Holland Duke of Exeter, of Arundel castle, with its rich tapestry and furniture.—*Dugdale's Baronage*, vol. i. p. 237.—*Warton's His-*

tory of English Poetry, vol. i. p. 212. The great halls in
the royal palaces of Westminster and Eltham were hung
round with moveable tapestry. Indeed, it was at first so
costly and valuable, that it was usually transferred as often
as the owner changed his residence.

> The halle was hangyd round and circulare
> With clothe of gold, in richest manere.
>
> HAWES' *Palace of Pleasure.*

These suits of arras were of very great price, and their
subjects, as in the paintings which preceded them, were taken
from legendary tales, and sometimes from the Trojan war,
and allegorical representations. A more common sort was
called *verders* or *verdoys,* representing a forest of trees, to
which mottoes were appended. More anciently, they decorated the high table only, or the *hautpas,* and were called in
wills *dossers,* from having been placed at the back of the
lord upon state-days, but afterwards in privy chambers and
parlours. This verdoys or forest-work was thickly covered,
without any attempt at perspective, with representations of
large trees, and enlivened with rude figures of deer and wild
beasts. Such were first manufactured and imported to us
from Arras in Flanders, from which circumstance they received their name. In certain instances, strained cloth or canvass
was substituted, upon which similar subjects were delineated
in colours with resinous size, and the rooms were fitted up by
frames and hooks placed at proper distances in the walls.

As Warton observes, in a note too long to be reprinted,
but too curious not to be referred to (*Hist. Poet.* vol. ii.
p. 41. 8vo.) : " The stores of romance were not only perpetually repeated at their festivals, but were the constant object
of their eyes. The very walls of their apartments were clothed with romantic history. But tapestry of sacred events or
legends was exhibited in churches, and behind the high
altar." CHAUCER calls tapestry *radevore,* of which *Tyrwhitt*
gives an imperfect explanation. The lines are :—

> So that she worken and embrauden couthe,
> And weaven in stole, the radevore.
>
> *Legend of Good Women.*

[N] page 315.—Bridges were, in many instances, so necessarily connected with castles, as in fact to form a part of the fortress. They were, in some others, guarded by a gateway between towers connected with the town walls, and during sieges, capable of being applied to obstruction and defence. I have therefore considered them as military.

The two chapels upon the bridges of London and Bristol were handsome structures. The first mentioned, dedicated to Thomas à Becket, had a spacious and elegant interior. *W. Worcestre*, in his *Survey of Bristol*, describes the chapel on the bridge as very ornamentally built, and as having a lofty tower attached to it, which had its foundation upon one of the piers.

DISCOURSE VI.

WE must consider that the æra of the more ancient baronial keeps and castles, with the subsequent additions upon a large scale, and the improvement of their architecture, even to a certain degree of picturesque beauty, had passed away. We have yet one singular instance of their restoration.*

The fifteenth century now opens upon us. It exhibits vast mansions, in numerous instances,

---

* Appelby Castle, Cumberland, was chief of the five castles which, having been dismantled and almost laid in ruins by Cromwell, were nearly restored to their pristine grandeur by their owner, Anne Countess of Dorset, Pembroke, and Montgomery, who was the last heiress of the illustrious house of Clifford. The other four were Skipton, Pendragon, Brougham, and Brugh; and for many years of her widowhood she dedicated the greater part of her large jointures to the renewal of their original state. Two centuries of desertion and neglect have (Appelby excepted) once more reduced them to ruin.

of the noble and opulent, in which the characteristic style of the castles, immediately preceding, was not entirely abandoned, but superseded, and mixed up with a new and peculiar manner.

This kind of architecture wanted the sanction either of the ecclesiastic or military. From the lapse of years, the vicissitudes of property, but rather from the caprice of individual possessors by entire demolition or repairs, many of the more remarkable of these castellated houses are now sought for in vain.

We may experience a very imperfect satisfaction from ascertaining that, spacious and even splendid mansions have arisen and disappeared during the TUDOR age, of which no traces remain but the sod and the field, and no memorial but in the records of the times. This observation applies equally to the residences of the nobility, which may be termed " palaces," as to the great manerial houses built in emulation of them. Yet to be certain that they did *once* exist in all the perfection that the progress of architectural arrangement in their several periods would admit of, proves that great wealth always sought to be exhibited in a sumptuous display ; and that a love of all the distinction it can procure, was ever congenial with the human mind. It may be allowed too, that a large and magnificent residence was the most obvious and lasting evidence of it. In the

centuries which immediately preceded the sixteenth, a great number of small rooms, for the
reception of a multitudinous household, and
but very few calculated either for comfort or
convenience, were inclosed within these walls.
The chief provision was made, in a few of enormous size, for a noble display of hospitality.*

Much has been written accurately, and published, respecting the royal residences, in the
details of which the lovers of our national
antiquities will find competent information.
Of this gorgeous style, peculiar to the earlier
TUDOR ærà, a concise preliminary, with occasional remarks, will be all that lies within the
limits or intention of these Discourses. But
some recapitulation, (though I have very slightly adverted to that subject in particular,) becomes expedient, without entering into the
latitude of investigation and research.

The Tower of London was the first palace
of the Norman kings, but it was strictly military. William Rufus has the credit of founding
Westminster Hall. Henry I. built a palace at
Oxford, where in his royal state, in his new
hall, he kept his feast of Christmas in 1115; as
did Henry III. in 1229 and 1267, at Woodstock, in the vicinity. There Henry II. built
a house of retirement, concerning which many

* See the household books of the nobility, which have
been printed.

well-known legends are remembered. By
Henry III. the Palace of Westminster is said
to have been refounded; enlarged, and very
sumptuously, by Edward III.; indeed, from
the reign of Rufus to that of Richard II. who
finally completed the original buildings in the
state apartments, with the great hall and
Chapel of St. Stephen, until it had gained a
greater extent than any contemporary palace in
Europe.* Edward III. had likewise re-edified
and greatly extended Windsor Castle, as a
habitable fortification. He had too a suburban
palace at Kennington. The great halls at
Westminster, Eltham, Kenilworth, Dartington,
and Crosby, I have previously noticed.†

Several of these monarchs, in succession, seem
to have been content to have added to the baronial residences, which had devolved to them,
rather than to have raised new structures upon
their foundations; for they not only occupied
the palaces, already perfect, but rendered several of the castles which had devolved to them,
palatial. The court during the summer months,
was in a state of successive migration, so that
all of them were occasionally inhabited.

Henry IV. inherited John of Gaunt's Castle
of Kenilworth, and the Savoy, London, both of
which he had increased by much splendid
building. His victorious son had not the

* See Note [A] page 376.   † See Note [B] page 376.

power, during his French war, to add to them. By the exorbitant ransoms, which his commanders demanded of their prisoners, several of them were enabled to construct mansions of very great extent and expense, in different counties where they possessed an influence by their large revenues. Of these, Hampton Court, Herefordshire, by Sir Rowland Lenthal; and Ampthill, Bedfordshire, by Sir John Cornwal Lord Fanhope, are signal examples.

In the earlier part of the reign of Henry VI. Humphrey Duke of Gloucester, then Regent, built at Greenwich a palace of extraordinary beauty, elaborate both in design and finishing. From its superiority over others, it was denominated by the founder " Placentia or Plaisance."* Edward IV. finally completed and enlarged it, and it was the birth-place of Queen Elizabeth. Three Lords Treasurers, Cromwell, Say and Sele, and Boteler, expended large sums upon their grand residences: the first mentioned at Tatershal, Lincolnshire; and at Wingfield Manor, Derbyshire; the others at Sudley, Gloucestershire : and Hurstmonceaux, Sussex; all of which are now dilapidated or destroyed.†

---

* *Mon. Vetusta,* vol. ii. pl. 25. View of the palace. *Leland's Itin.* vol. vi. p. 110. The sites of castles and castellated houses are well pointed out in the *Magna Britannia,* by D. and S. Lysons, 4to. 1806–1822. † See p. 330.

By Edward IV. a tower and a large court of apartments were added to Nottingham Castle; and his brother Richard III. augmented Warwick, and Middleburg, in Yorkshire.

When the Tudor dynasty was completely established, Henry VII. upon the ruins of a former palace which he had repaired, and which was afterwards destroyed by fire, built another splendid palace upon its site, at Shene, in Surrey, which, when finished, he denominated " Richmond," in allusion to his former title. Not a vestige of this vast structure remains to be seen. It had many tall turrets, finished by pinnacles and gilded vanes. The large dimensions of the state apartments are given in the Survey, when offered for sale by the Parliamentary Commissioners, in 1649. Their chief peculiarity consisted in numerous bay-windows, of a capricious formation, with rectangular or semicircular projections, producing a picturesque effect; and octangular small towers, inclosing noel staircases, which were finished with mitred cupolas, fringed with rich crockets. These were not regular hemispheres, but had a globular or bulbous shape, with a general resemblance to the royal crown, as used in that day.*

---

* Alofte the toweres, and golden fane's goode
Did with the wynde make full swete armony.—CHAUCER.

View of Richmond Palace, *Vetusta Monumenta*, vol. ii. Survey in 1649, *Lysons' Environs*, vol. i. p. 441. Privy

The Tudor style thus introduced and confined to domestic architecture, deviated into
three distinct manners, or rather should be
discriminated.

I. The first, already treated upon.—II. The
variations under Henry VIII.—III. The Elizabethan style, as it admitted of Italian ornament, in the designs of John of Padua; and
probably in more instances, the French manner
of embellishing their palaces, which was described in several treatises, with which our
own architects became conversant at least, if
they had not actually visited France.

The zenith of gorgeous expense in the reign
of Henry VIII. will supply so many instances
of a more grand style of building, that I shall
offer no apology for describing briefly the re-

Purse Expenses of Henry VII. published in the *Excerpta
Historica, Bentley.* *Chapter-House Records* at Westminster,
discovered since 1808. Castles, royal palaces, buildings at
Windsor, &c. in the reigns of Edward IV. Henry VII. and
VIII. See entries in Henry the Eighth's privy purse expenses, published by *Sir H. Nicolas,* 8vo. 1830. *Parliamentary Survey* in the Augmentation Office.

" Such palaces as King Henry the Eighth erected after his
own devise, do represente another kind of patterne, which, as
they are supposed to excell all the rest that he found stand-
inge in this realme, so they are, and shall be, a perpetual pre-
cedent unto those that do come after to follow in their workes
and buildinges of importance. Certes, masonrie did never
better flourish in England than in his time."—*Harrison's
Description of England.*—See Note [C] page 378.

sult of an inquiry, as to those founded or completed by himself, or erected either by his officers of state, or his courtiers. As a proof of his taste for splendour and expense, no less than ten royal mansions, large enough to have contained his multitudinous retinue, rose at his command.

I. PALACES BUILT OR REPAIRED BY HENRY VIII.

1 Beaulieu, or Newhall, Essex.
2 Hunsdon, Herts, originally built by Sir J. Oldhall, *temp.* Edw. IV.
3 Ampthill, Bedford.
4 Nonsuch, Surrey.
5 York Place, Whitehall, Westminster.
6 Bridewell and Blackfriars, London, for the reception of the Emperor Charles V.
7 St. James's, Westminster.
8 Kimbolton, Huntingdonshire, the jointure of the divorced Queen Catherine of Aragon.
9 Sheriff Hutton, Yorkshire, given for the residence of Henry Duke of Richmond, the King's natural son.
10 King's Langley, Herts.

TEMPORARY PALACES, PAVILIONS, AND GALLERIES.

Le Champ de drap d'Or, a magnificent pavilion, erected between Guisnes and Ardres. He added a spacious gallery to the " Plaisance," at Greenwich, which was the scene of his frequent feasts and revelries.

At Hampton Court, after his possession from Cardinal Wolsey, he built the great hall, or, more probably, only finished it, but he left Nonsuch, in Surrey, in an imperfect state, to be rendered complete with foreign embellishments, by Henry Fitz-Alan Earl of Arundel.

Although the more ancient castles having so far suffered from sieges and dilapidations, were at this period considered as being incapable of repair and habitancy, their possessors, in many instances, after having retained the site and applied the materials, continued the original name, and the new buildings of this age were called Castles, as at Belvoir ,Raglan, and Thornbury. The quadrangular area was an innovation peculiar to the Tudor style, of which castles constructed for defence could not admit.

Haddon Hall, in Derbyshire, had an earlier origin, having been continued and increased till the Elizabethan æra, by its possessors, during the previous century. Its plan is consequently irregular; and it is chiefly to be remarked for the furniture and interior decoration of the apartments, which are extremely curious, and in a state of singular preservation.*

Lulworth Castle, in Dorsetshire, which was begun in 1588, and not finished before 1609. It is an exact cube of eighty feet, with a round tower at each angle, thirty feet in diameter, and rising sixteen feet above the walls, which are six feet thick.

* See Note [D] page 379.

Longford Castle, in Wiltshire, was finished in 1591. It has a triangular form, with a circular tower at each extreme angle, and a small staircase in each of the three corner towers. It has an open court in the centre. These imitations of castles were probably the design of the same forgotten architect.

Gosfield, Essex, of a castellated exterior, is antecedent to this age as to its foundation; but the two quadrangles were erected late in the fifteenth century.

Brereton Hall is one of the most remarkable of the Cheshire houses, entirely constructed with timber frame, among numerous specimens in that and the adjoining counties.

It is worthy of inquiry from whence this new manner was derived.

About the middle of the fifteenth century, Philip Duke of Burgundy, surnamed " The Good,"* introduced into the French provinces and the Netherlands, then under his command, a novel style of decorative construction, which prevailed during his own and his son's reign, of which there are some proud examples. The palace at Dijon, and the Château Fontaine le Henri, near Caen ; the Place de Justice, and the mansion called the Burghterode, at Rouen, have long engaged the admiration of the architectural professor. To enter into a farther

* 1419—1467.

detail is not to my present purpose. It is adverted to incidentally, as a conjecture has been offered, with incomplete analogy, because the TUDOR style is not exactly imitative of the BURGUNDIAN, thus designated.* Professor Wheley makes the following judicious remark in distinction. " It has a great community of character, though considerable differences of detail, when compared with our TUDOR architecture. It seems to be marked by a peculiar form of arch, the elliptical, or the flat-topped, as the *Tudor* is characterised by the four central arches."† The broad obtuse *Tudor* arch has a strong lateral pressure, and being sustained on slender columns, has a perpetual tendency to throw them out of the perpendicular.

Of this species of architecture,‡ no just idea can be formed, excepting by a discrimination of its leading points and constituent members

* " On the exterior, the building of the Palace of Dijon, the best specimen, is characterised by the surbased pointed arches of the doors. The arch is surmounted by an ogee label, which breaks into a few foliaged crockets, and spreads at the apex into a tall mural finial. Instead of battlements, the walls are surmounted by a pierced balustrade."

† *Essay, ut supra.*

‡ " Of the derivatives of the GOTHICK, which thus appeared after it had lost somewhat of its original purity, perhaps the most beautiful, and the least degenerate, is the TUDOR architecture. In some cases, indeed, this style pos-

—a task I shall attempt, though very far from claiming absolute accuracy.

A ground plan formed around a quadrangular area, and approached by a very lofty gateway tower, embattled and flanked by more lofty angular turrets, appears to have been the first innovation which was regularly in usage, in the considerable buildings now to be noticed. When of brick, the doorcases and the dressings of windows were of fine stone. The gateway was centrally placed. It was frequently embellished with vitrified bricks in squares, and circular cavities, in which were busts in *terra cotta,* as in Holbein's gateway at Whitehall, and at Hampton Court. Into the walls, likewise, were inserted various members of fantastic architecture, exhibiting supporters, cognizances, and escocheons of arms, moulded in baked clay with accuracy and skill. But still more elaborately wrought were the tall, clustered chimneys, with an intricacy and variety of pattern, beyond description, covering their shafts.

Several, particularly beautiful and curious, still remain at Thornbury, and East Barsham, in Norfolk. Indeed, more complete specimens

sesses so much boldness and breadth of parts, as to be scarcely inferior to any form of Gothick architecture."—*Essay, Wheley,* (published anonymously,) *ut supra.* It has been not unaptly denominated " The Architecture of 𝔒𝔩𝔡 𝔈𝔫𝔤𝔩𝔞𝔫𝔡 " in contra-distinction to that immediately succeeding it.

of this ingenious manufacture are no where found. This most useful expedient for rich and minute carving in stone, originated in Italy or France, from whence it was imported, and afterwards adopted by us. Torrigiano, who made the monument of King Henry VII. taught our own artists to model portraits in *terra cotta* (moulded brickwork); and several heads of Henry VIII. are still extant, larger than life. All of these, destroyed or remaining, were probably the works of the same artists. Primaticcio taught the French to cast models in plaster. A peculiarity in these spacious mansions which prevailed during the reigns of the Tudors, consisted in placing beside the great staircase, communicating with the hall, several small octangular or hexagonal towers, which contained others. These generally occur at the angles of the great court, and exceeding the roof in height, gave a very picturesque effect to the whole pile of building.

In counties where stone does not abound, an almost perfect substitute was found in brick; and with greater frequency and excellence in the eastern. Placing the bricks, when vitrified with change of colour,* in alternate squares

* In Norfolk and Suffolk, more particularly, are several singularly fine specimens, well recognised by the architectural antiquary, and which have been engraved by the Society. The mode above mentioned is remarkable at Layer Marney,

and lozenges, as well as in other forms, was not an uncommon practice.

Adverting to the interior parts, we find the halls equally spacious with many erected in former centuries. The halls of New Hall, Essex, Richmond, Hampton Court, and Christchurch, Oxford, may be selected as superior examples, not to enumerate others. Each of them was remarkable for its high-pitched roof, composed of timber frame, which was jointed with admirable contrivance, and supported by brackets and rafters, upon which the art of carving and originality of design were mutually displayed.* The boldness of projection and the beauty of unpainted oak or chesnut, upon a grand scale, never attained to greater excellence. At the upper extreme end of the hall, where was the elevation, anciently called "*Deys*," stood the high table for the superior guests; and at the side was the large semi-hexagonal bay-window,† branching from the

Essex. Escocheons, within quaterfoils of fanciful forms, were usually placed above the centre of the gateway, and between supporters.

* Painting in fresco on walls was in usage from the reign of Henry III. to that of Elizabeth; and even then in a much lower grade of art. It was superseded by tapestry, but still of inferior execution, though of extreme cost, previously to the time of Henry VIII.; but the estimation of it continued for a century afterwards.

† See Note [E] page 385.

floor to the ceiling, in which, partially inserted, were armorial bearings, cognizances, and rebus on the name, in stained glass. This upper compartment of the hall was paved with fictile tiles, like delft ware, in chequer work, most frequently of two colours only, describing scrolls, mottoes, and arms.

Ypaved with poyntyl, one poynt after·other.

P. PLOWMAN.

The windows were oblong, or else nearly square, and very wide, divided by a transom, which was sometimes crenellated, or worked into small battlements, and finished externally with labels. These were commonly of green opaque glass, " rich windows which excluded light," a circumstance of little consequence, as they opened to the quadrangle ; and if otherwise, a distant prospect had few charms for our ancestors.

In the middle of the hall was a raised hearth, upon which the fire was laid, with cleft wood, upon " andyrons ;" and the smoke was conveyed through the louvre or cupola rising from the roof. This custom was continued in college halls unto a late period.

In a baronial mansion, upon the largest improved scale, there were more spacious apartments than in former times, and those which admitted a greater degree of ornament, and of which the arras hangings were most considered.* Such were the withdrawing-room for my lord's guests when they quitted the hall; the presence-chamber, " hangyd with cloth of arras ;" parlours both for winter and summer; " the lady's bowre," or apartments for females; and the long gallery: nor must the kitchen, with its gigantic apparatus, be overlooked. Terminating gables between turrets, were characteristic of this style, and had lacings on the ridges with an ornament, which the masons called " hip-knobs." The stone for the dressings of doors and windows, in brick buildings, was brought from Caen, and cornices were placed beneath the eaves. In *Borde's Dietary of Health,* dedicated to T. Duke of Norfolk (1547), are given rules for planning and building a nobleman's house.†

In order to specify mansions which are most to our present purpose, and in which the foregoing description of the *Tudor architecture* was, or still remains conspicuously seen, the subjoined list will supply a satisfactory view, and in a succinct form. Farther particulars concerning them, may be referred to in the Appendix.

* See Note [F] page 366.

† *Exemplars of Tudor Architecture, by T. F. Hunt,* 4to. 1830. This very ingenious artist and author did not survive his publication long enough to reap the merited reward of fame or fortune.

II. BUILDINGS BY THE OFFICERS OF STATE AND OF THE COURT, TEMP. HENRY VIII.

1 THORNBURY	Edward Duke of Buckingham	High Constable of England	Gloucester	1511 —	The greater part in ruins.
2 RAGLAN	Charles Earl of Worcester	Lord Chamberlain	Monmouth	1520 —	In ruins.
3 KENINGHALL and FRAMLINGHAM	Thomas Duke of Norfolk	Lord High Treasurer	Norfolk, Suffolk.	1515—1530	Destroyed.
4 COWDRAY	William Earl of Southampton	Lord High Admiral	Sussex	1522—1540	Destroyed by fire.
5 GRIMSTHORPE	Charles Duke of Suffolk	Lord Steward of the Household	Lincolnshire	1515—1540	Taken down partly.
6 HAMPTON COURT	Cardinal Wolsey	Prime Minister	Middlesex	1525 —	Part perfect and part rebuilt.
7 HORSEHEATH	Sir Giles Allington	Master of the Ordnance	Cambridgeshire	1528 —	Taken down.
8 TODDINGTON	Sir Thomas Cheyney	Warden of the Cinque Ports	Bedfordshire	1530 —	Taken down.
9 THE VINE	William Lord Sandes	Lord Chamberlain	Hampshire	1530 —	Rebuilt.
10 HEVER CASTLE	Thomas Earl of Wiltshire	Lord Privy Seal	Kent	1520—1530	Restored in part.
11 WANSTED	Richard Lord Rich	Lord Chancellor	Essex	1540 —	Taken down.
12 CHEYNEYS	John Lord Russel	Lord Privy Seal	Bucks	1540 —	Dilapidated.
13 HILL HALL	Sir Thomas Smyth	Secretary of State	Essex	1546 —	In part.
14 BASING	Sir W. Powlet	Lord Treasurer	Hants	1540 —	Destroyed.

I have observed, for the sake of more accurate definition, that the *Tudor architecture* exhibited three distinct styles of ornamental arrangement in the several æras of Henry VII, his magnificent son, Edward VI, and Queen Elizabeth; and of these some explanation will not be deemed irrelevant in the course of this inquiry.

A parallel may be drawn between the styles of domestic buildings during the reigns of the two contemporary monarchs, Henry VIII. and Francis I. of France,* analogous as to a general description, but by no means strictly accordant in every point. As far as the distribution of the apartments, they were not dissimilar.

In the exterior of the French Châteaux, a perpetual repetition was presented of towers and turrets, consisting of heavy parts, not connected by any regular design, detached from each other by fortified walls, and crowned by immense roofs, either obtusely conical, or spread out at length, as if under a pavilion, which contained several distinct floors, occupying at least one-third part of the total elevation. The grand roof was still higher in the general proportion, as the ridge was finished by an open

* Francis I. rebuilt the old palace of the Louvre, from the design of Pierre Lescot, finished in 1540, which differed widely from it.—*Legrand, Déscription de Paris et de ses Edifices,* 8vo. 1808.

balustrade of carved work, extending for the whole length, which was considered as a distinguishing mark of seignory. Windows of a peculiar construction (called *grenier* and *dormier**) rose immediately from the external wall, and were continued almost to the summit, which were rendered very ornamental. The windows themselves were of an oblong form, with transoms, and the surfaces of the superstructure partook of all the carved varieties of the front. They terminated in pediments between two lofty finials. Of this manner, there are, among others, two prominent examples, which have been accurately engraved † — the Château de Melan, and that of Josselin, both of them in Britany.

Holbein‡ was established in England under the royal patronage, and had gained sufficient influence for a partial introduction of the mixed style —*Gothick*, with a certain adoption of *Roman* architecture, as it began to revive in

* By these, light was communicated to the granaries and dormitories, which occupied the roof. These could not be reconciled to any plan of Grecian or Roman architecture. Such was the first Louvre, when Pierre Lescot built the present grand court, upon his own model.

† By *Vaucelles*.

‡ When the Italian members of ornament took place of those peculiar to the latest Gothick, upon their introduction, partially only, as in the reign of Henry VIII, they were noticed by Hall, in his Chronicle, as " *anticke worke of Romayne figures.*"

Italy. The grand portal of Wilton house, (now removed into the park,) and that already mentioned at Whitehall palace, gave an unquestionable proof of his skill in ornamental design, as it was first applied, in his time, to decorate buildings of a superior order. The first transition from what may be termed " the expiring Gothick" in its last modification, took place in the short reign of Edward VI, and, under the direction of an architect known by the name of John of Padua, obtained in a few very memorable instances. Of this eminent person the real history is obscure; but it is certain that he enjoyed the patronage of the Protector Somerset, and others of the Court, and that several very sumptuous edifices were constructed by him.* From his designs were erected the palaces of Somerset House, in the Strand, and Sion House, Middlesex, with Longleat, for Sir John Thynne, in Wiltshire.

The palace called Somerset House was a proof of the ambitious magnificence of the Protector-Duke, from which he was led to the block when the walls only were finished. To found this immense pile, he destroyed the cloister of St. Paul's cathedral, and the palaces of the bishops of Worcester, Lichfield, and Llandaff, and in order to apply their materials to that purpose. It was built, but not com-

* See Note [G] page 388.

pletely, soon after the year 1549; and, with the addition made by Inigo Jones for the reception of Queen Henrietta, was entirely taken down, and the site is now occupied by a celebrated modern edifice.

The honour of having introduced the Roman architecture into England, in any large building, must be attributed to John of Padua, but without doubt, with all the deficiency of a first introduction, which was subsequently perfected by the superior genius of Inigo Jones.

The left bank of the Thames had a splendid display of palaces, which were situate between the Temple and Westminster, in magnificent succession, and had an immediate communication with the river.*

Sion House, upon the site of the nunnery, had been finished in its ground-plan only, when its founder was beheaded. Longleat was nearly completed, and remains one of the grandest structures of the kind in England.

Mr. Wilkins, the Cambridge architect, has attributed the design of the two beautiful gateways in Caius College to John of Padua: but

---

* These were, Essex House, Arundel House, Durham, Salisbury, and Worcester Houses, Somerset House, abovementioned, Northampton, now Northumberland House, and York House, now Whitehall, the original proprietorship of which may be traced by the names of the modern streets built upon their sites. Hollar has drawn or engraved most of them, as they stood in his day.

his pretensions are disputed by another foreigner, Theodore Haave of Cleves, whose portrait is preserved in the library, painted by himself.

The gateway called the " Porta Honoris,"* nearly resembles, in its columns and ornaments, the tombs of the nobility erected in that age, with various members of Roman architecture upon a small scale. It was intended to exhibit the new manner, and excited great admiration.

Besides these, the great additions made to Sudley Castle, Gloucestershire, by the Lord-Admiral Seymour, and Catlage, Cambridgeshire, by Edward Lord North, were remarkable, as having been built in the reign of Edward VI, but which are both now dismantled and destroyed.

It is essential to the design of my inquiry, to notice the former existence of those grand edifices, which no longer remain to us, no less than such as are, generally speaking, still perfect, or have been retained in part. Even these mansions are falling away apace. In every quarter of a century a class must disappear, by the joint operation of repair and decay. Most of their remains have been removed to raise or to be incorporated with other buildings.

* Engraved and described in the third volume of the *Vetusta Monumenta*.

We now reach the third and last æra of the Tudor Gothick, with its specific varieties, as peculiar to the reign of Queen Elizabeth, with which this investigation will terminate.

Domestic architecture had now assumed a more scientific character. No building of consequence was undertaken without a plan previously regulated.* Early in the reign of this queen, we had the treatises of Lomazzo and Philibert de Lorme translated into English, and the new system was sedulously adopted by the best architects of our own nation, when they were employed to construct palaces for the nobility.†

Any attempt to authenticate the works of several principal architects, at the close of the fifteenth and the commencement of the sixteenth century, would be attended with partial success; several, who were sufficiently meritorious, are recorded, but without a specification of their individual works. Yet the names of the following professors of architecture, whose works, many dilapidated and some destroyed, have been, in rare instances, indubitably ascertained, have been rescued from the oblivion which conceals those of the immediately preceding and darker age. The more eminent

* See Note [H] page 388.

† *Du Cerceau, Les plus excellens bâtimens de France*, 1607, folio, with minute engravings of thirty houses, built in the sixteenth century.

of these will appear in the following series, which is chronologically arranged, as nearly as possible.

I. ROBERT ADAMS, Surveyor of the Works to Queen Elizabeth.*

II. JOHN SHUTE. I cannot authenticate any of his buildings, but he is known to have written on the subject, and has styled himself " paynter and architecte."†

III. BERNARD ADAMS.

IV. LAURENCE BRADSHAW.

V. JOHN THORP was the most celebrated architect of his day, and was consequently selected to design and build the magnificent palace of the Lord Treasurer, at Burleigh in Lincolnshire, and another for the Lord Buckhurst, at Buckhurst, Sussex, now taken down. A very curious MS. book of his designs, and which had belonged to him, is still existing, and preserved in the best private library of architecture in England.‡ This affords evidence that there were few celebrated houses then erecting, in which Thorp was not engaged.

VI. GERARD CHRISTMAS was associated with Bernard Jansen in building Northampton, afterwards called Suffolk, and now Northumberland House, not strictly within the reign of

* Buried in the old church of Greenwich. Inscription :—
" R. A. operationum regiarum supervisori, architecturæ peritissimo. Ob. 1595."

† See Note [I] page 390   ‡ See Note [K] p. 390.

Elizabeth, in which both of them had gained some professional fame. Christmas inserted his cypher in the street front, C. Æ. (*Christmas ædificavit.*)

VII. BERNARD JANSEN. He was the architect who probably designed, and was the first employed by T. Howard, Earl of Suffolk, and Lord High Treasurer, in the very large and sumptuous mansion called Audley Inn, Essex.

VIII. MOSES GLOVER was associated with Gerard Christmas and the last-mentioned, in completing Northumberland House, and probably Sion House, Middlesex, for Henry Earl of Northumberland, who had expended 9000*l.* in that great work.

IX. ROBERT SMITHSON, and his son, HUNTINGDON SMITHSON,* were engaged in that most beautiful structure, Wollaton House in Nottinghamshire, and likewise at Bolsover, Derbyshire. Thorp was at least consulted, as there are designs for Wollaton among his MSS. above noticed.

X. THOMAS HOLTE. Hearne discovered that he was a native of York. He designed and built the Public Schools and the college quadrangles of Merton and Wadham in Oxford. He first introduced columns of the five clas-

---

* His epitaph is in Wollaton Church. He is said to have died in 1614, aged 79, and is styled " Architector or Surveyor unto the most worthy house of Wollaton, with divers others of great account." — Epitaph in Bolsover Church : " Huntingdon Smithson, Architect, Ob. 1648."

sical orders, and applied them, in a series from
the base to the summit, in the west side of the
tower of the Schools. This idea was evidently
borrowed from Philibert de Lorme, in the
Château d'Anet, near Paris, destroyed at the
revolution. It was at best but a conceit, and
from being incongruous with other parts, did
not occur often in this country.

Excepting from the preservation of Thorp's
MS. which specifies so many buildings in which
himself had been concerned, we must rest content with the proof of a single edifice having
been designed or finished by several of the
architects here enumerated, of whom information has been incidentally collected. It must
be observed, too, that the same individual architects lived and flourished in the next century.
Many of their grandest works were not completed before the middle of the reign of James
the First; so that the last TUDOR style may be
said to have been practised to the days of Inigo
Jones, in whose early works it may be traced.

This fashion of building enormous houses
was extended to that period, and even to that
of the Civil War. Audley Inn, Hatfield, Charlton, Wilts, and particularly Wollaton, are those
in which the best architecture of that age may
be seen. Others of the nobility, deserting their
baronial residences, indulged themselves in a
rivalship in point of extent and grandeur of

their country-houses, which was of course followed by opulent merchants, the founders of
new families. Sir Baptist Hicks, the king's
mercer, (afterwards ennobled,) built Campden
House, Gloucestershire, which was scarcely inferior to Hatfield, which was afterwards burned
down.   There is scarcely a county in England
which cannot boast of having once contained
similar edifices; a very few are still inhabited;
others may be traced by their ruins, or remembered by the oldest villagers, who can confirm
the tradition ;* and the sites, at least, of others
are pointed out by descriptions, as having
existed within the memory of man.

A new æra of domestic architecture now.
presents itself to us, not indeed absolutely dissimilar to that immediately preceding, but in
a short process of time introducing new designs
and ornamental features : it has therefore gained, from modern definition, to be termed the
TUDOR style.   This, as it prevailed for more
than a hundred and twenty years, including
the Elizabethan peculiarities, will require historical investigation, with comparative criticism.   Pursuing that investigation from the
middle of the fifteenth to the close of the sixteenth century, those extensive, and otherwise
remarkable structures, only require notice as
they were the work either of the sovereigns

* See Note [L] page 391.

themselves, or, in certain instances, of the most wealthy nobility.

This new manner obtained, at first, a gradual preference only, and was intermixed ; but it afterwards became complete, and was characteristic of itself. There was a transition from rude and massive strength to light and comparative convenience.

I must recapitulate, in order to afford my readers a nearer view of that kind of domestic architecture, when, by its introduction, that which is strictly military was superseded, by offering a chronological classification of the several reigns in which there is a certain evidence that these mansions were erected.*

Capital Mansions begun or built in the reign of Henry VIII.

Cothele, Cornwall	. 1500.	Perfect.
Place-house in Fowey, ditto	. 1510.	Considerable remains.
Hengrave, Suffolk	. 1534.	In perfect repair.
Barsham Hall, Norfolk	. 1515.	In ruins.
West Stow Hall, ditto	. 1510.	Reduced.
Gifford's Hall, ditto	. 1500.	Perfect.
Harlaxton, Lincolnshire	. 15—.	Perfect.
Penshurst, Kent	. 1520.	Perfect.
Oxburgh, Norfolk	. ——	Perfect.
Mount Edgecumbe, Cornwall	——	Perfect.
Belvoir Castle, rebuilt	. 1525.	Perfect.
Westwood, Worcestershire	. ——	Perfect.
Westonhanger, Kent.		
Sutton, Surrey	. ——	Perfect.
West Wickham, Kent	. 1510.	Repaired.

This list, if all now dilapidated or entirely taken down were enumerated, might be extended to several pages.

During the reign of Henry VIII, and in those which immediately followed it, the courtiers and opulent gentlemen vied with each other in the vast expenditure which they employed in erecting most spacious houses, in the several provinces which they inhabited. And when any memorable change took place in the construction or architectural ornament of any considerable mansion-house, it was readily imitated or adopted by others. All novelties in domestic architecture, as in personal fashions, emanated from the court, especially if the sovereign happened to be popular, and were progressively disseminated through the higher or more opulent ranks. And hence originated much of the extraneous and puerile ornament,* which was particularly displayed in large chimneypieces, so frequent in mansion-houses of consequence. Leaving the historical inquiry into the subject, as far as I have endeavoured to render it more accurately known,—the several

---

* The shell-roofed niche, grotesque pilasters, with caryatides, &c. columns having the lower part covered with carved foliage, and the upper parts fluted, with a jumbled mixture of cherubim, birds, and lions' heads, armorial bearings, and mythological hieroglyphics, composed the designs of various objects of composition and false decoration, which prevailed during the long reign of Elizabeth, and continued in the early part of that of her successor."—*Britton's Arch. Antiq.* vol. ii. 101. Collectively speaking, there was an intricacy of design which appeared to defy explanation.

component parts and discriminating features peculiar to the mansions which were the last erected after the Tudor manner, with more frequent use of the members borrowed from France and Italy, require a distinct examination.

With respect to the last æra, which bears an analogy only, not an exact resemblance, to the two which preceded it, a more minute description may not be irrelevant.

Next to the hall,* the apartment of the greatest importance was the long gallery, which was the frequent resort of the inmates, as an ambulatory, so necessary in this climate; and for social intercourse, which admitted the ladies.† It was sometimes lined with wainscot of oak pannel, wrought within the squares or stiles, with carved tablets, resembling a scroll, and well known as most common in the time of Henry VIII. The cornices were rudely cast, in plaster, to represent armorial cognizances, with festoons or vignettes of fruit and flowers. Beside these, were numerous escocheons affixed, which the pride of ancestry delighted, everywhere, to contemplate.

* See Note [M] page 392.

† In the more ancient castles there were no galleries, but the "alures," or walks upon the walls within the battlements, which were frequented by the ladies for air and exercise. About the Tudor age, when castellated houses were common, long galleries were first introduced, and the halls reserved for feasting or assembling at meals.

In the windows at either end of these long rooms, occupying generally the extent of one side of the quadrangle, and next under the roof, a display was made of arms and quarterings collectively, in blazonry of the richest colours, in brilliant glass.

The galleries of this later date exceeded, in fact, many that had been previously built, especially in point of length.* Those of Audley Inn and Hatfield were the most remarkable. Such portraits as were the works of superior artists were most highly valued, and deposited as furniture of the large dining-rooms, more often than in galleries. The painters of eminence, in that age, were rare, and their price proportionate. Among other embellishments of the " great chamber of state," was a most sumptuous chimney-piece composed of alabaster or marble, richly carved and gilt. It was usually of very large dimensions, widely spread, and reaching from the floor to the ceiling. There were sometimes statues placed within columns and niches, which represented some the cardinal virtues, or grotesque *termini*, in the Roman manner, then lately introduced into this country. The whole was painted with gaudy colours; and the armorial bearings of the family, in one large escocheon, or the quarterings dispersed into many others, were

* See Note [N] page 392.

an indispensable decoration. In certain instances, the chimney-piece was of carved freestone, left plain. The almost perfect resemblance of these to the superb monuments, which, in that age, were dedicated to the memory of the dead, leave no doubt that the original idea had the same analogy. Of this opinion one most splendid instance will suffice —that of the mausoleum of Robert Dudley Earl of Leicester, in the Beauchamp chapel, Warwick, and the chimney-piece preserved in the gatehouse of Kenilworth Castle.

I have already adverted to the wide cornices usually inclosing the frieze, which encompassed the room, and sometimes no small part of the ceiling. They were cumbrously wrought in plaster-work, and exhibited very grotesque forms and figures, which afterwards, under the influence of Inigo Jones, yielded to an improved style of ornament.* A peculiarity in the wainscoting was, that the pannels were carved in the form of scrolls, (a name given to distinguish that kind,) and sometimes enriched with raised letters, composing cyphers, mottoes, or sentences. Where the walls were whitelimed only, poesies and moral proverbs were inscribed upon fantastic labels, rudely painted.

Externally considered, the fabric, both from its great extent and height, was very command-

* See Note [O] page 393.

ing. Each floor or stage included lofty apartments. Very capricious shapes were adopted,
chiefly of the new model, borrowed from the
French or Italian school, and applied as parapets above the upper cornice. In some instances, which shall be noticed in the Appendix, the interstices of the balustrade were filled
up by many large capital letters, carved in
stone, allusive to the founder's or the architect's name, and date of the building.*

The chimneys were likewise disposed in somewhat of a more classical taste, with members
and ornaments, in the Roman manner, grouped
several together, with a rich entablature, as at
Burleigh.†

Porticoes, or rather inclosed porches, and
open corridors, were introduced into the fronts,
either separately or conjoined, particularly at
Audley Inn, Burleigh, and Charlton, Wilts. Both
the arches and piers admitted a considerable
degree of ornament, not inferior in point of profuse decoration to other prominent members of
the whole structure. After the French and
Italian fashion, architecture became allied to

* See Note [P] page 393.

† Not only Queen Elizabeth's celebrated minister, Lord
Burleigh, expended his great wealth upon this, but likewise
Theobald's, and Cecil-house, London. His son Lord Salisbury, at Hatfield, whose elder brother, Thomas Earl of Exeter, built Wimbledon and enlarged Cecil House, Strand. All
these were large and sumptuous mansions.

gardening, in the immediate environs of great houses. The walls were extensive, and formed of hewn stone, and the flights of steps often repeated and finished by balustrades. In the perspective view, where the ground rose with sudden elevation, they appeared to have formed a constituent and important part of the general plan, and to have greatly added to a magnificent effect.* Wimbledon, when in its perfect state, presented a superior example.

Of those I have mentioned in the course of this inquiry, in not a few instances " the substance of these fabrics has passed away, but their very shadows are acceptable to posterity." The graphic art, even in its early imperfect state, has been employed to transmit to us the image of the vast structures which were the ambition of the Tudor age, so that they may be clearly revived in our imagination, and more forcibly when we visit their sites. In modern views but a limited satisfaction is given to the investigating antiquary, for landscape usurps the scene, and truth of delineation is made subordinate to the picturesque idea. Candour must allow, that the restorations applied to these ancient houses, when rendered subservient to modern accommodation, adopt a very equivocal character with reference to any system of architecture.

* See Note [Q] page 393.

Within the last very few years, three artists of singularly distinguished merit have been withdrawn from us, from whose delineations the architectural antiquary has derived a satisfaction, as great as could have been communicated by exquisite art and consummate feeling of the subjects which they have elucidated.* In the present age, although fertile in genius of the most promising cultivation, we may hope that equal taste and ability may supply their loss; but those who can appreciate such merit, will indulge no sanguine expectation of immediate success in the same degree. But this observation refers only to the graphic representation of the different styles of Gothic architecture.

What may be specifically termed MUNICIPAL ARCHITECTURE, is the original formation of cities during the particular periods which have been already noticed in due course. A singular uniformity and correspondence pervaded all the ancient English cities. On the continent, more especially in those of France, Germany, and the Low Countries, the general plan will

* The works of WILD, PUGIN, and HUNT, will be long held in high estimation. They are now terminated. The first mentioned, whose perseverance I have often witnessed as his attached friend, has acquired his meed of fame by ceaseless exertion to acquire fidelity of representation, and by much too great a sacrifice—the loss of sight. The others have sunk into their graves in the middle period of life. See Note [R] page 394.

be found scarcely to have varied from our own; and, as if by convention, they were the same everywhere. During the middle centuries, almost all the cities and great towns offered nearly a similar appearance to the exterior view. Encompassed with lofty turreted walls, having large gateways and narrow streets, spacious houses of carved frame woodwork, many small and one or two large and magnificent churches, and townhouses—these will complete the description of the greater part of our old towns; and yet in local features, each may be proved to have borne a character distinctly from each other. It is from this consideration, that such remarkable objects being pointed out by intelligent topographers, will increase the interest we take concerning any one of them in particular. With very few exceptions, they are laid out in four chief quadrivial streets, at right angles, which led to the four gates; and in the centre of the intersection stood a market, or high cross, of lofty and elaborate masonry, with the statues of such kings as had been their patrons. Very remarkable ones were then seen at Coventry, Winchester, and Bristol. The quarters were subdivided into close streets, lanes, angiports communicating with the postern-gates; and all of them very narrow and incommodious.

But not till the beginning of the last century

had any of these yielded to modern improvement. Nothing is now known of the former sites, excepting from old plans and charts, and topographical investigations.

This kind of civil architecture may be considered in the present age rather as presenting objects picturesque and curious in themselves, than of study and imitation ; and may be classed rather with those which belong to the Elizabethan æra, than that of the earlier Tudors, though doubtless there were many which were contemporary with them. I speak of the last style of them, for we know that a similar construction in large towns prevailed as early as the days of Edward III, but with much less ornament externally.

This particular mode of building was likewise frequent in those counties where timber was more abundant than stone.

Wealthy burgesses affected an ornamental display in their houses, especially as to expensive carvings, which is evident from what little is still spared to us by subsequent improvement and innovation. Enough is yet left to delight every true admirer of the picturesque. On the continent, with certain variation from the English mode, the same manner of building pervades most of their large towns, and in a much better state of preservation than with us, especially in those of Germany, the Netherlands, and France, where timber enters largely into the construction of the outer walls. By these are formed the striking street scenery of Antwerp, Brussels, Louvaine, Nurembourg, Ulm, and Rouen, not to multiply instances. In England, at Chester, Shrewsbury, and Coventry, and within a few years past, at Bristol,* they prevailed universally.

Specimens in England exhibit frequently uniform and consistent embellishment, which was not void of elegance and elaborate finishing.† This manner was certainly much better suited to the painter's eye than to comfortable habitation, for the houses were lofty enough to admit of many stories and subdivisions, and being generally placed in narrow streets, were full of low and gloomy apartments, overhanging each other, notwithstanding that they had fronts nearly composed of glass, with the projecting windows and the interstices filled for nearly the whole space. Admirable contrivances were used in framing the roof, and the gables and barge boards exhibited singularly beautiful specimens of the art of carpentry. More particularly in imitation of vegetable or other forms, hitherto almost confined to stone, great skill, and sometimes even taste were manifested, in exuberance of fancy and good execution. Such occurred

* See Note [S] page 395.
† *Pugin's Ornamental Gables*, 4to. 1831.

more frequently in manor-houses in the counties of Chester, Salop, and Stafford.

I must now hasten to finish my observations.
A farther recapitulation is unnecessary to the
plan of these Discourses, and would inevitably
be tedious.

Extending the inquiry, in a limited degree,
beyond the term prescribed by my original intention, the superb structures which arose during the reign of James I. or were completed in
it, assumed a distinctive character from the
TUDOR style, in a degree of discrimination far
beyond what has been generally considered.

J. Thorp I have already quoted as the most
celebrated architect, concerning whom we have
equal evidence, and, more than all, his imitations of De Lorme and the French school,
which he had introduced with so great success,
became the prevailing genius of our national
architecture, where means of practising it were
afforded.

By these the last efforts of the TUDOR manner were superseded, and no very sumptuous
building, which was then being erected, either
in the elevation or distribution of apartments,
partook largely in designs which had so recently preceded it. The distinction is decided.

Inigo Jones, in the early career of his architectural fame, and before he had seen and so
happily studied the works of Palladio in Italy,

adopted the best examples of the domestic architecture then prevalent in this country. Many are the mansions which in this and in the latter periods of his life have been attributed to him without proof of any kind. Walpole has noticed several ; some with certainty, others in doubt ; but he observes " that Jones seems to have enticed the age, by degrees, into good taste." His works were, with great probability, not frequent, but upon the largest scale of magnificence, and he is justly denominated " the father of classical architecture in England."*

The castles of the middle ages, and the vast mansions peculiar to the Tudor reigns, have been alike involved in one common ruin ; and in the present day there are solitary remains only in any degree of their former perfection. Yet there are enough to supply the inquiring

* INIGO JONES was born in 1572, and died in 1652, at the age of seventy-nine years. His first public work, as known, was when he was thirty-three years old. He resided in Italy for several years before 1606. In his second visit to Rome, in 1612, he does not appear to have remained there more than two years. He purchased when there, the edition of Palladio's architecture, published in 1613, the margins of which he filled with notes and sketches. This invaluable book was bequeathed to Worcester College, Oxford, by the well-known amateur, Dr. G. Clarke. See *Walpole's Anecdotes*, vol. ii. pp. 330 to 355, last edition. In the Duke of Devonshire's collection are other MSS. which were procured by Lord Burlington.

antiquary with definite ideas respecting their original history, plan, and specific design.

The leading causes of their destruction are supplied by history in the earlier periods ; nor are many others which present themselves upon due inquiry, difficult to be accounted for, independently of the ravages of war or gradual decay.

No period was more fatal to the fortresses of that time, than the spoliation during the civil war in the reign of Charles I, if, indeed, the general demolition of them, by the orders of Cromwell, when Protector, be excepted.

Most of the battles had been decided in the field. When his predatory army had gained either a castle or fortified mansion-house, after a siege and celebrated defence, it was usual with them to burn it down in revenge, or to dismantle it totally, and sell the lead and timber as plunder for the soldiers. It is memorable that such castles and large country houses, which had resisted him most, were doomed by Cromwell to be laid level with the ground.

After the restoration, the introduction of the French fashion in architecture prevailed, to the destruction of many a magnificent *Tudor* mansion, or of such parts as then remained. The Dutch taste, under William III, completed the same effect.

Subsequently many an ancient patrimonial house has suffered a gradual, but certain decay, or, at least, been

" Left untended to a dull repose."*

More than twenty years ago, I published " Observations on English Architecture," but upon due consideration, instead of a second edition, I determined upon offering a series of Discourses, chronologically placed, in which I should attempt a condensation of critical opinions and historical facts, either original, or acquired from other authors, during the interval of that publication.

I trust that no negligence of investigation will be apparent, nor conspicuous error be frequently discovered. Many instances in proof of any style or peculiarity of architecture, which may seem to those who have pursued the same path with equal interest, to bear a stronger relation, may either be unknown to me, or considered as of inferior importance.

The progress of literary curiosity has been directed, of late years, to the acquirement of

* Resemblances of a great number of these seats of the gentry in the several English counties, were engraved with a certain degree of truth and effect by *Burghers* and *Kip.* By the latter, *Britannia Illustrata,* 80 plates, fol. 1714 ; *Atkyns' History of Gloucestershire,* fol. 1711 ; *Plot's Staffordshire,* and many single plates ; so that though substance be sunk in oblivion, the shadow still presents itself to us.

more systematic knowledge concerning our national architecture in the past centuries. This has been effectually promoted by works of acknowledged merit, and the skill of the graphic artist has been employed with deserved success, both in point of number and accuracy.

New facilities have been by these means opened to the student, and not without increased gratification to the amateur. To enlarge the sphere of useful information has been the main object of this treatise.

It may not be a merely fanciful analogy, if the Grecian and Gothick styles were allowed to admit of a comparison; as the Doric with the Norman, the Ionic or Corinthian with the pure and decorated Gothick, and the Composite with the Florid and subsequent varieties introduced in the Tudor age. Resemblance is out of the question; but the collation of them, as far as their succeeding each other in a like gradation, is, at least, a singular coincidence in the history of art.

ANNOTATIONS ON TUDOR ARCHITECTURE,
ILLUSTRATIVE OF THE SIXTH DISCOURSE.

[A] page 336.—See a very curious and accurate plan of all the buildings of which the ancient palace of Westminster was composed, from actual plans which were continued dur_ing fifty years, by the late W. Capon, (*Monumenta Vetusta*, vol. v.) with notes and remarks.

[B] page 336.—The hall of the palace at *Westminster* was certainly rebuilt by Richard II. on the foundations of that of William Rufus, and perhaps of a still earlier; for a great hall was the necessary appendage of an ancient palace. It was completed in 1397. The construction of the roof, by which its extraordinary force and pressure on the side-walls is effectually lessened and counteracted, is admirable, and proves that the architect possessed a very superior mind. The roof, of chesnut timber, exhibits both beauty and skill in scientific carpentry.

Eltham Hall was erected earlier in his reign, about 1385. It still remains, as a barn, and has a peculiarity, that the windows are placed in couples.

The hall in *Kenilworth* Castle has only one side remaining. It was finished in 1397, two years before the death of John of Gaunt, who had been long engaged in enlarging that castle.— *Dugdale's Warwickshire.*

Dartington, much inferior to the others. See *Lysons' Magna Britannia, Devonshire.* Built by J. Holland, Duke of Exeter, about the same period.

There is an indisputable evidence concerning an architect of celebrity in the reign of Richard II. *Rot. Pat.* 17 Ric. II. 1394. " Pro Nicolao Walton, Magistro Carpentario et Depositore operum Regis, quoad artem Carpentarii, quamdiu se bene gesserit, pensionem," &c.—*Rymer's Fœdera.*

Dimensions.—	L.	B.	H.
Westminster	228	66	—
Eltham	100	30	55
Dartington	70	40	44

Kenilworth, very spacious, but the exact measurement unknown.

John of Gaunt obtained a warrant from Richard II. in 1392, directed to *Robert de Skillington*, Master-mason and supervisor of his buildings at Kenilworth, to impress twenty masons, carpenters, &c.—*Dugdale ut sup.* Henry VII. is styled by *Harrison*, (in his *Description of England*, p. 330,) " the onlie phoenix of his time for fine and curious masonrie ;" and by *Leland* (Cygn. Cantat. *in notulis*) " unicum in architecturâ hujus sæculi lumen." *Holinshed* remarks, that his buildings were " most goodlie, and after the newest caste, all of pleasure." To the palace of Eltham he made very considerable additions. The large sums which he applied for these purposes prove that his sepulchral chapel at Westminster was not the only object of his expenditure. He paid for the repair of the very ancient palace of Woodstock 894*l.* in the year 1494, and sumptuously enlarged the castle of Ludlow, for the residence and court of his son, Prince Arthur.

Speed (*Hist. of Britaine*, p. 995.) observes concerning Henry VII.—" Of his buildinge was Richmond palace, and that most beautiful peice, the chappell at Westminster ; which formes of most curious and exquisite buildinge, he and Bishope Fox first, as is reported, learned in France, and brought with them into England."

Gothick architecture, of the new style, was effectually advanced by that monarch, who, from the enormous wealth that he had amassed, left the ecclesiastical buildings to be completed by his executors. In the early part of his son's reign, the chapels of King's College, and of Westminster and Windsor, were entirely finished.

HECTOR ASHELEY, a famous master-mason, was retained in the service of both monarchs. He is very frequently mentioned in the Privy Purse Expenses of both those monarchs. Sir RICHARD LEA is noticed as a favourite architect of Henry VIII. and it is therefore conjectured that he was employed about his palaces; but from all remaining evidence it appears that he, with greater probability, excelled as an engineer as military architect. He was certainly so employed by his royal master, as Jerome da Trevigi had previously been. Walpole specifies no work which he completed as a civil architect.—*Anecdotes of Painting*, last edit. vol. i. p. 219. note.

[C] page 339.—The survey taken by order of Parliament in 1649, affords a very minute description of Richmond Palace as it then stood, with satisfactory information as to plan and distribution of the chief apartments in such buildings, and elucidates our present investigation. " The great hall was a hundred feet in length, and forty in breadth; it is described as having a skreen at the lower end, over which, says the Survey, is 'a fayr footpace in the higher end thereof; the pavement is square tile; and it is very well lighted and seeled. At the north end is a turret or clock-case covered with lead, which is a special ornament to the building.' The privy lodgings are described as a free-stone building, three stories high, with fourteen turrets covered with lead, ' a very graceful ornament to the whole house, and perspicuous to the country round about.' An octagon building is mentioned, called the ' canted *(angular)* tower,' with a staircase of a hundred and twenty-four steps. The chapel was ninety-six feet long, and forty broad, with ' cathedral seats and pews.' Adjoining the privy garden was an open gallery, two hundred feet long, over which was a close gallery of the same length." —*Lysons' Environs*, vol. i. p. 441.

Floors of coloured brick, glazed, or sometimes enamelled with figures and armorial bearings, were invented and used as early as the reign of Edward III, and were common for two centuries after.

Ʈɧe flore anð bencɧ ɯaʒ pabyð faire anð ʒmootɧe
Ꮤitɧ ʒtone'ʒ ʒquare, of manie ðiberʒ ɧeɯe
Ꮪo ɯol joyneð, tɧat for to ʒay tɧe ʒotɧe
Ꭿl ʒemeð one, tɧat none tɧe otɧer kneɯe.

CHAUCER.

[D] page 341.—Farther observations on the palaces and buildings erected in the reign of Henry VIII.:

New Hall was begun before 1524. It had two large quadrangles, a hall 96 feet by 50, and 40 feet high. There was a particularly magnificent gateway, with the royal arms, and this description:—

ɧenricuʒ rex octabuʒ, rex inclytuʒ armiʒ,
Ꮇagnanimuʒ ʒtruxit ɧoc opuʒ egregium.

Nonsuch. Left incomplete by Henry VIII. and finished by Henry FitzAlan Earl of Arundel. There were two quadrangles, two very sumptuous gateways, and two octangular towers, five stories high, at the east and west corners. From a print by *Hoefnagle,* in Queen Elizabeth's time, it appears that the walls were covered by bas-reliefs in plaster, and that there were statues so composed, the earliest introduction of them as ornaments into England. In the Parliamentary Survey in the Augmentation Office, the materials of the house were valued at 7020*l.* *Camden* says, " It is built with so much splendour and elegance, that it stands a monument of art, and you would think the whole science of architecture exhausted in this building. It has such a profusion of animated statues and finished pieces of art, rivalling the monuments of ancient Rome itself, that it justly has and maintained its name from thence."

Hæc, quia non habent similem, laudare Britanni
Sæpe solent, *nullique parem* cognomine dicunt.

LELAND.

See *Hentzner's Travels, edit. Walpole,* and *Lysons' Environs,* vol. i. p. 151.

Charles II. gave this palace to the Duchess of Cleveland, who pulled it down, and dispersed the materials.

York Place, Whitehall, was originally the palace of the Archbishops of York, and was called by Wolsey York Place. It was exchanged by him with the King for Hampton Court, in 1526.

Hunsdon. Originally built by Sir W. Oldhall, in the reign of Edward IV. upon a large scale. Refitted for the royal children. Remains, but much reduced.

Le Champ de Drap d'Or. Holinshed, who gives a minute description of the architectural preparations of this splendid interview, says that it was a palace, " the which was a quadrant, and everie quadrant of the same palace was three hundred and twentie-eight foot long of assise, which was in compasse thirteen hundred and twelve foot about. This palace was set on stages by great cunning and sumptuous work." The description of the interior is too curious to be omitted. " The chambres were covered with cloth of silke, of the most fair and quicke invention that before time was seene. For the grownde was white, engrailed and battened with riche clothes of silkes, knit and fret with cuts and braids and sundrie new casts, that the same clothes of silke shewed like bullions of fine burnished gold ; and the roses in lozenges that in the same roofe were in kindlie course, furnished so to man's sight, that no living creature might but joy in the beholding thereof. Beside rich and marvellous clothe of arras, wrought of golde and silke, compassed of manie auncient storyes." *

At Greenwich, in the tilt-yard, Henry VIII. erected a large temporary palace, with halls and galleries, for the reception of the French Ambassador (see *Holinshed*); and in the *Cotton MSS. Brit. Mus.* is a plan of a very magnificent gallery which he designed to build, not improbably that above mentioned. For the Commissioners for the French match, Queen Elizabeth caused another to be erected within

---

* *Holinshed's Chron.* vol. iii. p. 647, copied from *Hall*, p. 605. In the royal collection at Windsor Castle, is a most curious and well painted picture of this gorgeous building, of which there is an engraving and account by Sir Joseph Ayloffe in the *Archæologia.*

the palace at Westminster, by Thomas Grave, Surveyor of the Works.—*Holinshed.*

Raglan was built by William Herbert, Lord of Chepstow and Earl of Huntingdon. It descended to Sir Charles Somerset, created Earl of Worcester, who made great additions in the reigns of Henry VII. and VIII, which were continued to the reign of Charles I. by the celebrated loyalist, the Marquess of Worcester. It was quadrangular, with a large hall, and similar apartments. The Marquess maintained it against a memorable siege. See *Pugin's* work as above.

Kenninghall, Framlingham Castle, and *Mount Surrey,* said to have been built upon an Italian, but, more probably, upon a French plan, were all of them the work of Thomas Howard third Duke of Norfolk, Lord Treasurer, and his more celebrated son.

Kenninghall " was a most noble structure, built in the form of an H, as a conceit denoting the name of the founder. It had two most spacious and stately fronts towards the east and west, seated upon rising ground in the centre of a large park. It was entirely taken down in 1650, and the materials sold. In the neighbouring village, many of the ornamental moulded bricks are seen inserted into walls."—*Blomefield's Norfolk.*

Framlingham. The castle was accommodated to all the purposes of a splendid dwelling-house. It was remarkable for moulded brick chimneys, more numerous and equally ornamented with those at East Barsham and Thornbury.

Mount Surrey. A country-house of an elegant design, built by H. Earl of Surrey, upon the site of St. Leonard's Priory (in 1542), near Norwich. It was pillaged and demolished in Kett's insurrection, 1549.

Cowdray. William Fitz-William Earl of Southampton, and Lord High Admiral, founded this noble mansion, and left it incomplete, in 1543 ; and it was not entirely finished before the visit of Queen Elizabeth to Anthony Browne, second Viscount Montagu, in 1591. In magnitude, and the ornamental architecture peculiar to that age, Cowdray was

not inferior to the many noblemen's residences, then about to
be erected in England, which, as it has been observed, " were
the works of tranquil times, at liberty to sacrifice strength to
convenience, and security to sunshine." The house with its
appendages, covered the space of an acre. The area of the
quadrangle was 107 by 122 feet, which was opened by a lofty
central gateway, finished by four light turrets, &c. Architecture of characteristic solidity and plainness prevailed externally, whilst the space, proportion, and great number of
the apartments, and their singularly curious embellishments
and furniture, gave to Cowdray a preference above most of
the provincial palaces erected by the courtiers of Henry VIII.
and his immediate successors. This venerable pile had been
preserved 'both in its form and furniture during two centuries by its noble owners; and the most genuine and valuable
series of early portraits, which had afforded a peculiar gratification to the virtuoso and antiquary, were, by the conflagration of a few hours on September 24th, 1793, reduced to a
ruin and ashes.—*Dallaway's W. Sussex*, vol. i. p. 246, in
which are views of Cowdray in its original and present state.

Thornbury. *Leland* describes Thornbury much at large,
Itin. vol. vii. fol. 75. Upon the site of an ancient castle,
built by the Audleys and Staffords, the most unfortunate of
that ill-starred race, Edward the last Duke of Buckingham,
soon after his possession of it, designed to erect a castellated
palace, of peculiar sumptuosity and architectural beauty.
Those in the survey taken in 1582, which are styled the
New Buildings, were begun in 1511, as we learn from the inscription upon labels upon the great unfinished gateway. An
octangular corner tower, flanking the southern front, is still
perfect, but open to the air. The western unfinished front
extends 207 feet, containing parts, to the first story, of four
large and two small towers. A more complete example of
the plan and arrangement incidental to the first style of
the Tudor architecture is not *now* to be seen; particularly in
the bay windows of the great apartments, and the chimneys of

moulded brick, excepting which last mentioned, the whole is of free-stone. It is graphically described in *Lysons' Gloucestershire Etchings*, *Britton's Architect. Ant.* and with more accuracy and science by *A. Pugin, Examples of Gothic Architecture*, 1832, 4to.

Grimsthorpe was more remarkable for extent than for architecture. The great hall was ornamented with the first Gobelin tapestry brought into England, by Charles Brandon Duke of Suffolk, and was part of the dower of his wife the Queen Dowager of France. About that time the east, west, and north fronts were erected, which have embattled turrets at the angles. The south front was rebuilt from a plan of Sir John Vanbrugh for the first Duke of Ancaster.

Hampton Court, after it had been chiefly built by Cardinal Wolsey, and enlarged with the hall and other apartments by Henry VIII. consisted of no less than five spacious quadrangles. These were reduced to three ; and upon the site of those taken down, was erected the " Fountain Court," by King William III, in which are the state apartments. Sir Christopher Wren was the architect. The garden front has an air of grandeur from its great length and height, which loses much of its effect, from the perpetual perforation of windows.

Horseheath. This mansion was taken down in 1665, by William Lord Allington, when a most splendid mansion was built, at the expense of 70,000*l.*, likewise taken down in 1777, and sold for its materials.

Toddington. The largest private house in England was built here by Paulinus le Peyvre, who was steward of the household to Henry III, at an enormous cost in that day, which is described by M. Paris. Sir Thomas Cheyney and his successors built another before 1580, where Queen Elizabeth was received, now dilapidated. It occupied four sides of a quadrangle, with a turret at each corner. North and south fronts 210 feet in length. Taken down in 1745.

The Vine. Rebuilt and modernised.

Wansted. Originally erected by R. Lord Rich, and greatly enlarged by R. Dudley Earl of Leicester. Rebuilt by
Lord Tylney. Sold for materials, 1826.

Cheynies. Part standing, but dilapidated.

Hill Hall. Begun in 1548 ; since completed ; and altered
by subsequent possessors.

Hever Castle exhibits interesting and venerable remains.
The quadrangle and hall are perfect, and are in the early
Tudor style of building.

Basing House. The siege and blockade of this grand
mansion, the outworks of which extended over fourteen acres,
was one of the most eventful facts which occurred during the
civil war. The ruins are particularly interesting to the antiquarian visitant. The plan nearly resembled that of Raglan,
with which it was contemporary, and its fate similar.

Watton Wood Hall (Herts). The original manor-house
was erected by Sir Philip Boteler. It was a noble quadrangular building of brick, with a gateway flanked by two
round towers, and a gallery of remarkable length. Burned
down in 1772.

Layer Marney. Built by Sir Henry Marney. The gateway and front are much neglected, but not in ruins. These
castellated mansions were usually constructed with chequer-
ed compartments of flint, or with lines, diagonally placed, of
dark-coloured glazed bricks. The mullions of the windows
are columns, with capitals imperfectly copied from the Corinthian.

Haddon Hall, Derbyshire. Founded by Sir R. Vernon
1452, and completed by Sir John Manners, in the high
Elizabethan style.

" The gallery is 110 feet long and seventeen wide, occupying the south side of the principal court. The wainscoting
is enriched with Corinthian pilasters, supporting arches, between which are shields of the arms and quarterings of Vernon and Manners. The frieze is ornamented with boars'
heads (the crest of Vernon), roses, and thistles, in plaster.
The great bedchamber, fitted up at the same time, has a deep

cornice, with boars' heads and peacocks, with a rude bas-relief of Orpheus charming the beasts, over the fire-place."— *Lysons' Magna Britannia, Derbyshire.*

Many of the rooms are lined with ancient arras, of most grotesque figures, or simple forest work, which represented trees bearing labels and mottoes. This oldest kind of tapestry was called " Verdoys," from the prevalence of green colour, and when they admitted subjects, they were representations of forest sports.

> On the wals old pourtraiture
> Of horsmen, hawkes, and houndis
> And harte' dire al full of woundis.

Chaucer's Dreme.

This kind of tapestry was called " Parke work"—figures and landscape, and was of woollen only. In the progress of luxury—in Cardinal Wolsey's sumptuous apartments, the gorgeous materials were of cloth of gold and silver. See various inventories.

[E] page 346.—A bay, in architectural acceptation, is a quadrangular space, over which a pair of diagonal ribs extend, which rest upon four angles. The same term is also used for the horizontal space comprised between two principal beams. A bay-window, in common acceptation, means simply a projecting window between two buttresses, and which is frequently placed at the end of a building. The use to which bay-windows were applied in great halls, during the fifteenth and the next century, appears from a MS. in the *College of Arms*, relating to a feast given in the hall of Richmond palace. " Against that his Grace had supped, the hall was addressed and goodlie beseene, and a rich cupboard set thereupon in a bay-window of nine or ten stages and haunces of hight, furnissed and fullfilled with golde, sylver, and parcele gilt." Bay-windows were generally composed of five parts of an octagon; but of a half circle between two angles, at Thornbury and Windsor.

Chaucer, in his descriptive poem of the " Assemblie of

Ladies," gives us an idea, not generally received, of the accommodation and comfort in the domestic architecture of his own age.

> The chambers and parlers of a sorte, *(in succession)*
> With bay windowes, goodlie as may be thought;
> As for daunsing and otherwise disporte.
> The galleries right wel ywrought,
> That wel I wot, if ye were thider brought,
> And toke good hede therof, in every wise
> Ye would it thinke a very paradise.
>
> CHAUCER.

[F] page 348.—Of the introduction of the manufacture of tapestry in this kingdom, we have satisfactory evidence. It was certainly previous to the year 1344, when there was a writ issued (17 Edw. Tertii, m. 41) — " De inquirendo de mysterâ Tapiciorum London." Henry VIII. gave a patent to John Mustian to be his arras-maker; and in the same reign, a private gentleman, named Sheldon, established at Barcheston, in Warwickshire, a manufactory in which some small pieces were made, consisting of maps of counties, some of which are still preserved.—*Walpole's Anecdotes*, vol. ii. p. 49. edit. *Dallaway.* In the same work is a full account of the manufactory at Mortlake, of Sir F. Crane, conducted by F. Cleyne, in the reigns and under the especial patronage of Kings James and Charles I. But there are documents to prove that needle-work, and even tapestry, was practised by the females of almost every nobleman's house, and likewise in those of the next lower rank, as the household books and wills afford sufficient instances.—*Testamenta Vetusta, Nicolas.* —*Ellis's Orig. Letters*, vol. ii. p. 15 n. Upon the Continent, it is well known that both Raffaelle and Giulio Romano were most extensively engaged in painting cartoons, to be wrought in tapestry; and that the princes of Europe were most ambitious of such splendid decoration of their state apartments, and were magnificent in their remuneration of these artists. The enumeration of the tapestries procured by Francis I. for his palaces, by Felibien, (tom. ii. p. 190.

12mo. 1725,) would exceed belief, both with respect to quantity and value, were not that author of good authority. To give some idea of the quantity, he says, that the story of Psyche, by Raffaelle, consisted of twenty-six pieces and one hundred and six yards. A volume would not suffice to collect all the details concerning tapestry of equal excellence, in the palaces of different princes and high ecclesiastics.

The first Gobelin tapestry was brought into England by Charles Brandon Duke of Suffolk, to ornament the noble mansion which he built at Grimsthorp in Lincolnshire. It was a part of the dower of his royal bride, Mary Queen of France, the younger sister of Henry VIII. This splendid appendage soon excited a similar taste in that sovereign and his favourite, Cardinal Wolsey. Our admiration is excited both in point of quantity and fine quality. Their several palaces, according to the accurate inventories preserved in the British Museum, were furnished in a profusion scarcely credible, both as to the number and the cost of the pieces, in multifarious subjects, wrought with silk and threads of gold and silver. In the fabrication of such gorgeous pieces, the most costly materials were used, as from the wardrobe accounts both of the King and the Cardinal is sufficiently apparent. *MSS. Harl. Brit. Mus.* No. 1419, *Survey of the Wardrobe,*1547.—In the palace of Hampton Court, probably placed there by Wolsey, were eighty-three complete suits. *Inventory of Cardinal Wolsey's Household Stuff at York Place and Hampton Court, MSS. Harl.* No. 599.—Lord Orford says, that at the sale of the effects of Charles I. the suites above-mentioned were purchased for Oliver Cromwell. " One set of hangings relating to the story of Abraham, in eight parts, at Hampton Court, was valued in the inventory at 8260*l.* ; and another in ten parts, the history of Julius Cæsar was appraised at 5019*l.*" The velvet bedchamber at Cowdray, fitted up for the reception of Queen Elizabeth in 1591, and in which she lay during the week she spent there, was hung with tapestry taken from some of Raffaelle's cartoons. Destroyed by fire.

It is curious to reflect, that of works, the component parts and workmanship of which were so extremely sumptuous, any complete vestige will be now found to be preserved in detached parts or fragments only, in the houses of the nobility, either on account of the decay of the material, or the entire change of fashion.

[G] page 352.—He was architect to Henry VIII. at the end of his reign, when his palaces were finished, so that he could not have been extensively employed. In *Rymer's Fœdera*, t. xv. p. 34, there is a grant of a pension to John of Padua for his services and inventions in architecture and music, dated 1544; and Mr. Walpole says, (*Anecdotes of Painting*, vol. i. p. 216,) that he was styled in another document " Devizor of his Majesty's Buildings." What his real name was,—how educated,—and what were his works previously to his arrival in England, no research has hitherto discovered, with any satisfaction. That he was continued in his appointments during the next reign, is certain. The pension was two shillings a-day, which, now so small, was, when granted, by no means an inconsiderable sum, and, besides other emoluments, was given merely to retain him in the court as a servant of the king.

[H] page 355.—The earliest publication in England relating to practical architecture, appears to have been " The first and chiefe grounds of Architecture used in all the ancient and famous monyments, with a farther and more ample discourse uppon the same than has hitherto been set forthe by any other. By John Shute, paynter and architecte. Printed by John Marshe. fol. 1563." *Walpole* mentions this work (last edition), and adds that the author was sent in 1550 to study in Italy, by John Dudley Duke of Northumberland, with the intention, probably, of employing him, on his return, upon some magnificent palace.

In the *Cabala* is a letter from Lord Burleigh, then engaged in erecting the sumptuous palace called by his name,

to his agent at Paris. "The book I most desired is made by
the same author, and is entitled, 'Novels institutions per
bien bâster et à petits frais, par *Philibert de Lorme*,' Paris,
1576." A proof that the great statesman was studying the
subject. In the *Dietarie of Health*, by *Andrew Borde*,
printed in 1542, are rules for planning and building a nobleman's house, which he supposes to be quadrangular.

Of Roman architecture, the earliest treatise which appear-
ed in England, is " A tracte containinge the artes of curious
paintinge, carvinge, and buildinge, written first in Italian, by
John Paul Lomatius, painter of Milan, and Englished by
Richard Haydock, Student of Physic, of Newe College,
Oxford. fol. 1598."

We have a sufficient proof that several English students
in architecture of this period visited Italy for acquirement
of knowledge and practice in the new system, and that
they had become sufficiently versed in the Italian language
to publish translations from it: *Shute*, as above mentioned,
and *Robert Adams*, " Ubaldine's account of the defeat of the
Spanish Armada, from Italian into Latin, 4to. 1589 ;" and
Haydock's translation of *Lomazzo*. In the next reign (1611)
we have " The first book of Architecture made by Sebastian
Serly (Serlio), entreating of geometrie, &c. by *Robert Peake;*
translated out of Italian into Dutch, and out of Dutch into
English." It is a small folio, black letter, with wood-cuts.

But a singular curiosity has been brought to light, which
was lately in the custody of Mr. Colnaghi, sen. (Printseller.)
It is a series of views and perspectives of the City of London,
its ancient buildings, with St. Paul's Cathedral, the Tower,
&c. upon the north-west shore, for a considerable extent.
Others are taken from the roof of the Mint (formerly Suffolk
House) in Southwark, overlooking that side of the river. Of
the royal palaces at Westminster, St. James, Plaisance at
Greenwich, Hampton Court, and Oatlands; there are distinct
elevations and parts, in many delineations of each. It is of
the largest imperial folio size, several of the views being so
long as to require to be folded. They were certainly taken

from the spots mentioned, which are represented with scrupulous accuracy, and give a true idea of London in 1558. The artist's name affixed is ANTONIO VAN WYNERGARD, and the drawings are tricked with a pen, heightened with blue.

[I] page 356.—JOHN SHUTE did not confine his translations to architectural subjects. In 1562 he published " Two very notable Commentaries, the one of the original of the Turkes, and the other of the warres of George Scanderbeg, translated from the Italian. 8vo. b. l."

[K] page 356.—The folio MS. of plans and architectural delineations, were the private memoranda of John Thorpe. How they came into the possession of the late Earl of Warwick is not known. At the sale of his brother the Hon. Charles Greville, they were purchased by Sir John Soane, by whose liberality an unrestrained permission of inspection was given to the present author, of which he availed himself in his edition of *Walpole's Anecdotes*, to which the reader is referred. *Vol.* i. *supplement*, p. 329.

There are forty-one plans and elevations, some of them with names specified in ink, and others of the same hand in pencil; but sufficient to ascertain almost all. Those most known or worthy remark are enumerated, including those which he built entirely, added to, or altered. Buckhurst; Copthall, Essex; Burleigh; Holland House; Wimbledon; Two Courts at Audley End; Ampthill; and Holdenby.

[L] page 359.

PALATIAL HOUSES OF THE NOBILITY,

IN THE REIGNS OF ELIZABETH AND JAMES.

	Names.	Date.	County.	Founder.	Architect.	Pres. State.
1	Burleigh	1577	North-amp.	W. Lord Bur-leigh	J. Thorp	Perfect.
2	Kenilworth	1575	War-wick	R. Earl of Lei-cester	—	Ruins.
3	Hunsdon	—	—	H. Ld. Hunsdon	—	Taken down.
4	Stoke Pogeis	1580	——	Earl of Hun-tingdon	—	Do.
5	Gorhambury	1565	Herts	Sir N. Bacon	—	Do.
6	Buckhurst	1560	Sussex	Lord Treasurer Buckhurst	—	Do.
7	Knowle	1579	Kent	The same.	—	Perfect.
8	Basing-house	1560	Hants	Marq. of Win-chester	—	Destroyed.
9	Catledge	1560	Cam-bridg.	Lord North	—	Taken down.
10	Wanstead	1576	Essex	Earl of Leicester	—	Do.
11	Wimbledon	1588	Surrey	Sir T. Cecil.		
12	Penshurst	1570	Kent	Sir H. Sydney	—	Perfect.
13	Hatfield	1611	Herts	R. Earl of Salis-bury	—	Do.
14	Westwood	1590	Wor-cest.	Sir J. Packing-ton	—	Do.
15	Hardwick	1597	Derby	Countess of Derby	—	Ruins.
16	Audley Inn	1610	Essex	Earl of Suffolk	—	Partly perfect.
17	Holdenby	1580	North-amp.	Sir Christopher Hatton	—	Destroyed.
18	Osterley*	1577	Middx.	Sir T. Gresham	—	Rebuilt.

It may be worth inquiry at how remote a period mansions, which were not military, but simply for domestic residence, were common in England. The most ancient and singular instance of a magnificent private house, was that (previously

---

* A curious anecdote relating to Osterley is given by *Fuller*, in his *Worthies of Middlesex*. " Queen Elizabeth, when visiting Osterley, observed to that magnificent merchant, that the court had better been divided by a wall. He collected so many artificers, that before the Queen had arisen the next morning, a wall was actually erected."

These mansions are not enumerated exclusively, but as supplying general information.

mentioned) built by Pauline le Peyvre, a favourite of Henry the Third, at Toddington, in Bedfordshire, the very site of which cannot now be ascertained.

Matthew Paris describes it minutely, p. 821. " Adeo, palatio, capellâ, thalamis et aliis domibus lapideis et plumbo co-opertis, pomeriis et vivariis communicavit, ut intuentibus admirationem parturient. Operarii namque pluribus annis edificiorum suorum, qualibet septimanâ, centum solidos, et plures x marcas recipisse asseruntur." This was a very rare and magnificent specimen of domestic architecture, when castles were so frequent and necessary.—At Little Billing, Northamptonshire, and Appleton, Berkshire, are large houses nearly as ancient.

[M] page 362.—DIMENSIONS OF HALLS OF THE TUDOR ARCHITECTURE.

	L.	B.	H.
Richmond Palace, .	100	40	— feet.
New Hall, Essex, . .	96	50	40
Christ Church, Oxford, . .	114	40	50
Hampton Court Palace, .	108	40	45
Trinity College, Cambridge,	100	40	50
Longleat, Wilts, ...	62	30	34
Sion House, Middlesex, . .	66	31	34

[N] page 363.—DIMENSION OF GALLERIES.

	L.	B.	H.
Richmond Palace . .	f. 200	above an open gallery of the same length.	
Haddon Hall, Derbyshire,	110	17	17 feet.
Harlaxton, Lincolnshire,	100	14	11
Hardwick, Derbyshire,	170	26	—
Theobalds, ...	123	21	—
Longleat, ...	160	—	—
Parham, Sussex, . . .	158	—	—
Audley Inn, . . .	226	34	22
Hatfield, . . .	162	19	16

Numerous instances both of halls and galleries might be adduced, but these are sufficient to prove their magnitude in the lower age.

[O] page 364.—See *Walpole's Anecdotes*, vol. ii. p. 4, last edition.

[P] page 365.—These inscriptions are composed of letters enclosed within the balustrade, as if within lines, so large as to be visible from the ground, being thorough-lighted.

1. At *Wollaton Hall.* " En has FRANCISCI WILLOUGH-BÆI ædes rarâ arte extructas, Willoughbæis relictas—incho-atæ 1580—1588."

2. At *Castle Ashby.* " Nisi Dominus ædificaverit domum in vanum laboraverunt qui ædificant eam."

3. At *Hardwick Hall*, Derby, the letters E. S. for Elizabeth Countess of Shrewsbury.

4. The letters H. N. were originally in the balustrade of what is now called Northumberland House, when first built by Henry Howard Earl of Northampton. Both these last-mentioned were frequently repeated.

[Q] page 366.—Of the imposing grandeur of an approach produced by terraces connected by broad or double flights of steps, with balustrades, we have no finer example than Sir Edward Cecil's palace at Wimbledon, in Surrey, when it was entire, as appears from a rare print by Winstanley, which has been copied in *Lysons' Environs*, vol. i. p. 524.

A few extracts from the Parliamentary Survey, in 1649, may communicate some idea of its great extent.

" The scite of this manor-house being placed on the side slipp of a rising grownde, renders it to stand of that height, that betwixt the basis of the brick wall of the lower court and the hall-door of the sayd manor-house, there are five several ascents consisting of threescore and ten stepps, which are distinguished in a very graceful manner. The platforms were composed of Flanders brick, and the stepps of freestone very well wrought. On the ground floor was a room called the stone gallery, 108 foot long, pillared and arched with gray marble." The hall was curiously fitted up. " The ceiling was of fret or parge-work, in the very middle whereof was fixed one well-wrought landskip, and round the same, in convenient distances, seven other pictures in frames as ornaments to the whole roome ; the floor was of black and white marble."

[R] page 367.—It is no more than justice to particularise their several publications, and to recommend them to every true lover of the Gothick style. None will more satisfactorily promote an acquaintance with subjects of which we should be unwilling to be ignorant, but unable, from circumstances, personally to inspect.

Twelve Perspective Views of the Cathedral of Canterbury, by *Charles Wild,* fol. 1807 : the same, of *York,* 1809 : of *Lichfield,* 1813 : and of *Chester,* 1813. These are etchings, shaded and coloured.

In folio, of a larger size, and with highly-finished engravings, *Illustrations of the Cathedral Church of Lincoln,* 1819 : the same of *Worcester,* 1823.

Specimens of Gothick, (edited by *E. I. Willson,*) by *Augustus Pugin,* Architect, 4to.

Examples of Gothick Architecture, selected from various Gothick edifices in England.

Pugin and Le Keux's Specimens of the Architectural Antiquities of Normandy, 4to. 1828.

Pugin's Gothick Ornaments, from various buildings in England & France, drawn on stone by *J. D. Harding,* 1831, 4to.

Pugin's Ornamental Gables, selected from ancient Examples in England, 4to. 1831.

Gothick Examples, a second Series, 1831, 4to. Two Parts only published at his death, 1832. (Castles only.)

Exemplars of Tudor Architecture, with illustrative details from Ancient Edifices, by *T. F. Hunt,* Architect, 4to. 1830.

Twelve Etched Outlines from Architectural Sketches made in Belgium, Germany, and France, by *Charles Wild,* sm. fol. 1833.

[S] page 370.—Etchings of superior merit and picturesque effect have been published of the old houses in Chester, by Cuitt, and of those in Bristol, by Skelton. The latter were taken from drawings by O'Neal, a very clever deceased artist, who was patronised during several years' residence in Bristol, by G. W. Braikenridge, Esq. my highly-esteemed friend. He is well known for his singular liberality to artists, and has collected graphic illustrations of his native city, to the amount of fifteen hundred separate drawings. He has thus preserved the memory of numerous Elizabethan houses, and other more ancient buildings, the very site of which would now be sought for in vain.

So numerous, and in many instances so excellent, are the engraved specimens now before the public, not only of the elementary parts or members of Gothick architecture, but of elevations, perspective interiors and sections, that I have declined to insert any embellishment whatsoever.

Many of those published are referred to in the course of these inquiries.

My sole view has been to compile a treatise, in which usefulness to the student or amateur, and acquirement by a moderate expense, should be the characteristics.

COLLECTIONS

FOR

AN HISTORICAL ACCOUNT

OF

𝕸𝖆𝖘𝖙𝖊𝖗 𝖆𝖓𝖉 𝕱𝖗𝖊𝖊 𝕸𝖆𝖘𝖔𝖓𝖘.

NULLIUS ADDICTUS JURARE IN VERBA MAGISTRI.

Hor. Epist. i. v. 14.

COLLECTIONS

FOR

AN HISTORICAL ACCOUNT OF

𝕸𝖆𝖘𝖙𝖊𝖗 𝖆𝖓𝖉 𝕱𝖗𝖊𝖊 𝕸𝖆𝖘𝖔𝖓𝖘.

Cough, and cry hem ! if anybody come—
A mystery—a mystery !

Othello.

I APPROACH this investigation with much diffidence, confining it entirely to historical facts : and it would have given me satisfaction if I had gained more than to be referred to a modern work of high estimation.* The mysteries of the masonic oracle are there darkly shadowed forth, and hid from my comprehension. A very superficial view is given of the history which was the sole object of my research. A justly-esteemed modern author† has sensibly observed — " that the curious subject of FREE-MASONRY has unfortunately been

---

* *Preston's Illustrations of Free Masonry,* (*Oliver's* edit.) In this work, which condescends to comparatively modern history, mention is made of certain Free Masons who have conducted celebrated buildings — instances by no means confirmed by chronological facts.

† *Hallam on the Middle Ages,* vol. iii. p. 435 note, 8vo.

treated of only by panegyrists or calumniators, both equally mendacious. I do not wish to pry into the mysteries of the craft, but it would be interesting to know more of their history during the period in which they were literally ARCHITECTS."

Concerning the extremely remote origin of these fraternities, I shall waive any inquiry, by excluding legendary tradition, or conjecture formed upon it, confining my research to evidence alone, which will be succinctly given.

That the sumptuous temples in which Ancient Greece abounded, were the works of architects in combination with a fraternity of masons, (κοινωνια,) no reasonable doubt can be entertained.* That with the Romans, such fraternities, (Collegia,) including the (Fabri) workmen who were employed in any kind of construction, were subject to the laws of Numa Pompilius, is an apparent fact. Need the modern Freemasons require a better authenticated antiquity, and not prefer a Roman origin to the mystified traditions of Jachin and Boaz? †

---

* To mention the more celebrated architects, with their known works : — to Ctesiphon and Metagenes the temple of Diana, at Ephesus, is ascribed ; Rhæcus of Samos, built the temple of Juno in that island, and Ictinus and Callicrates that of the Parthenon at Athens. This may be a sufficient selection from many others of scarcely an inferior fame.

† JACHIN and BOAZ were columns of a composed metal, in the first temple of Jerusalem, the architect of which was

To particularise even a few of the architects during the progress of the Roman empire, and the stupendous edifices which were designed and completed by them, is beyond the scope of this attempt.

The first notice that occurs of an associated body of artificers, ROMANS, who had established themselves in Britain, is a votive inscription, in which the College of Masons dedicate a temple to Neptune and Minerva, and the safety of the family of Claudius Cæsar.*　It was discovered at Chichester in 1725, in a fragmented state, and having been pieced together, is now preserved at Goodwood, near that city, the seat of the Duke of Richmond.　Pliny, the author

HIRAM.　The translation of Jakin is "*firm*," and of Boaz, " *in its strength*," so denominated by Solomon.　See *Kings*, c. vii. v. 15 ; and *Jeremiah*, c. xv. repeated in the xviii[th]. These columns, exclusively of their capitals, were eighteen cubits high and twelve in girth, and, like those now seen in Egyptian temples, extremely unsymmetrical.　HIRAM invented, or rather adopted, the capital with the lily.　The Corinthian acanthus was not invented, but altered by Callimachus, who devised the variation only from the lily of Hiram.—*Gabb's Finis Pyramidis*, 8vo.

* See *History of Western Sussex*, vol. i. p. 3, 4to. 1815. " The learned antiquary, Roger Gale, who has printed a memoir concerning this inscribed stone in the *Philosophical Transactions*, has decided, from internal evidence, that it is the earliest memorial of the Romans hitherto discovered in any part of Great Britain."　It is therefore the first proof of *associated* artificers established in this country.

of the well-known epistles, when pro-consul of Asia Minor, in one which he addressed to the Emperor Trajan, informs him of a most destructive fire at Nicomedia, and requests him to establish a COLLEGIUM FABRORUM for the rebuilding of the city.*

The title of ARCHITECTUS AUGUSTORUM was borne by Q. Cissonius, during the reigns of Severus and M. Antoninus.†

Previously to the foundation of Constantinople, " the magistrates of the most distant provinces were directed, by a royal edict, to institute schools, to appoint professors, and by the hopes of rewards and privileges to engage in the study and practice of architecture, a sufficient number of ingenious youths, who had received a liberal education."‡ A similar mandate was

---

* *Plinii Epistolæ, cum annotationibus Gesneri,* lib. x. Epist. xlii. 8vo. PLINIUS TRAJANO IMP. " Tu Domine despice, an instituendum putes, Collegium Fabrorum, duntaxat hominum CL. (150); ego attendam ne quis nisi FABER recipiatur, neve jure concesso, *in aliud utatur.* Nec erit difficile custodire tam paucos." The emperor refuses, and alleges as a reason — " sed meminerimus provinciam istam et præcipue eas civitates, ab *ejusmodi factionibus esse vexatas.*" The jealousy entertained by all arbitrary governments against confraternities, whose consultations are held under the seal of impenetrable secrecy, or the penalty annexed to the breach of it, was early displayed by Trajan, who rejects the proposal, under the apprehension of perpetual danger.

† A sepulchral inscription found at Naples. — *Gruteri,* p. 587, insc. 4.

‡ *Gibbon's Roman Empire,* vol. iii. p. 19, 8vo.

issued by the Emperor Theodosius.* Such were
the apparent origin of a scientific institution
among the Romans; but as the foregoing remarks are merely preliminary, or incidental, I
hasten to the Gothick field, from whence a
view may present itself, not only of masonic
establishments, but of many eminent master-
masons whose names and works have been
obscurely noticed, or without chronological
classification. In giving this series, the leading purpose of inquiry will be, to ascertain
those who were employed in our own country.

There is a certain document which proves,
that in the eighth century, Charlemagne had
invited artificers† from every country of Europe in which they were established, to erect
his magnificent church at Aix la Chapelle. His
æra may be therefore fixed upon as that least
liable to contradiction or doubt, as that of the
best authority of such a body on the Continent.

After the Norman conquest, the prelates
Lanfranc and Gundulph‡ brought over to England not only the style of architecture which
was peculiar to their own native province, but
the artificers themselves. These had been

* *Codex Theodosianus,* l. xiii. tit. 4. leg. 1. *Procopius* de
Edificiis. *D'Agincourt's History of Architecture,* imp. fol.

† " Brevi ab eo fabricata, ex omnibus Cismarinis regioni-
bus, *magistris* et *opificibus* advocatis."—*St. Gaul. Legend.*
l. i. c. 32. ‡ See pp. 33 and 34.

chiefly employed in building the two great churches at Caen, and that likewise of vast dimensions, attached to the Abbey of Bec.* Gundulph was no less eminent for his military architecture, and his designs were executed by the same hands.

The first master-mason whose works are extant in England, and his name authenticated, is William of Sens,† who was assisted and succeeded by William the Englishman in the completion of the choir of Canterbury cathedral, in the year 1179, as already noticed.

At the commencement of the next century, we may consider the fraternity to have been consolidated in this kingdom, as it had been for some years previously both in Germany and France. Beside the abbey church of Westminster, there were not a few sumptuous and extensive ecclesiastical structures, which, at

* P. 274.

† " Willelmus Senonensis in ligno et lapide artifex subtilissimus, ad lapides formandos, tornemata valde ingeniose, formas quoque ad lapides formandos, his qui convenerant sculptoribus, tradidit."—*Chron. Gervasii, X. Script.* Gervase is the most ancient of the monkish writers who has given an account strictly architectural. In others, there is a frequent obscurity in the expressions and terms used, and a substitution of one for the other in their description of any great building. We must not, however, allow the claim of the masons of Cologne and Strasburgh to supersede the French and Italian establishments, with respect to more than priority. They are enumerated in pp. 87 and 115.

that time, were making a contemporary progress.* Authors maintain distinct opinions as
to the priority of the German schools, from
whence it is contended that the master-masons,
with their *confrères,* or operatives, have emigrated into France and Italy.† Certain it is,

* See the architectural scale of cathedrals, p. 218 to 244,
from which it is evident that the founders were eager to employ these scientific men upon their arrival in England in a
sufficient number. The only persons connected with the
building of Salisbury and Westminster were Elias de Berham and Robertus Cæmentarius. *Leland. Itin.* vol. iii. p. 60.—
Berham is supposed to have repaired King John's palace at
Westminster. A writ was likewise directed, " Magistro
Johanni de Gloucester, cæmiterio suo, et custodibus operationum de Westminster." Fitz Otho Aurifex, a German, was
likewise employed, not as an architect but as a carver.—
Walpole's Anecdotes, last edition.

† There were two great colleges in Germany, one at
Cologne and the other at Strasburgh. *Grandidier,* in his
manual relating to the last-mentioned cathedral, attributes the
origin of that masonry to the erection of that celebrated edifice by Irwin von Steinbach, in the thirteenth century. All
the German lodges, when established, considered Strasburgh as
their common parent, and their original statutes are preserved there. The celebrated *Hammer* of Vienna asserts them
to be contemporary with the Knights Templars. — " I defy
all the masons of England, France, Germany, or Scotland—
even those who have attained to the highest degrees in the
society, to prove as much, in spite of Hiram and the temple
of Solomon, and in spite of Phaleg and the tower of Babel.
The cathedrals of Vienna, Cologne, and Lanshut, were all
of them being built at the same time. I believe that the
tower of Strasburgh is a more sensible and certain monument
of the origin of the society, than the brazen columns of

that several architects were employed in both those countries, and perhaps before their own countrymen, both in point of time and preference.* The style denominated " The *Teutonic,* or *German,*" was the invention of this bold and very highly scientific order of architecture,

Jachin and Boaz." This chivalrous challenge is given by an anonymous author, in a letter affixed to *Grandidier's Essais sur la Cathédrale de Strasburgh,* 1782, 8vo. Notwithstanding that this period is so peremptorily fixed as to the confraternities, it is certain that individual German architects were employed in other countries—as Zamodia *(Tedesco)* at Pisa; Lapo, or Jacopo, at Arezzo, 1240; and John and Simon of Cologne, who built the cathedral of Burgos in Spain. The French strenuously contest the claim of the Germans, nor do I find the record of any of their architects who were employed in France or England, excepting Enguerand, or Ingelramme, the master-mason of the cathedral of Rouen, 1244, and of the second abbey of Bec, in Normandy. " The vaults of many very large churches are only from nine to ten inches thick; and the outer walls, though more than sixty feet high, are frequently but two feet thick." *Möller.* — A more complete proof of their consummate skill and proficiency need not be given. Previously to the commencement of Westminster Abbey, Henry III. is said to have had consultations with many master-masons — " convocati sunt artifices *Franci* et *Angli.*" *T. Walsingham, X. Script.*—Upon the introduction of these artificers, the building of the following cathedrals was going on almost simultaneously: Wells, 1212–1230; Salisbury, 1220 ; Worcester, 1218—1230 ; Peterborough façade, 1233–1246; Lichfield, 1235; Durham, 1230; Ely, 1235; Lincoln, 1240; York, 1227. Many of the largest and most sumptuous buildings and abbey churches were likewise contemporary. For such works a great number of these fraternities were indispensable.   * *Dibdin's Tour,* v. iii. *Strasburgh.*

which may be referred to those chosen and selected artists, who have shown themselves, in repeated instances, great mathematicians, and perfectly experienced in mechanics; and who, on assured principles of science, executed some of the boldest and most astonishing works which were ever erected by man.

It has been observed by a celebrated modern architect, that " the incorporation of masons, in the thirteenth century, may have finally brought the pointed arch to that consistency and perfection to which it had not then attained."*

. Two principal colleges were formed, at Strasburgh and at Cologne, by the master-masons of those stupendous cathedrals, who at that period assumed, and were allowed, a jurisdiction over all inferior societies, wherever they exercised their craft. In these conventions regulations were formed, which were religiously preserved under the strong sanction of good faith and secrecy. They were probably very numerously attended, at least by master-masons; and as all communications relative to their art† were delivered orally, the subordinate

* *Archæologia*, vol. xxiii. essay by *R. Smirke.*

† Bishop Lucy, for building his cathedral in 1202, instituted a confraternity of workmen to endure for five years. *Milner's History of Winchester*, vol. ii. p. 14. 4to. — As a fact which has not been questioned, the first complete example of the Gothick style in England is De Lucy's addition to

associates had only the experience which the practice afforded them of applying the principles thus detailed. A difficulty occurs, if it be considered that none but oral instruction was given even to the master-masons, how to account for plans and working-drawings which have been preserved in the archives of so many of the foreign cathedrals. We know the cause of their destruction in England.

It has been asserted, that in the early part of the thirteenth century, " THE COLLEGES OF

Winchester cathedral in 1202. It has been remarked by *Whittington* in his Essay — " That from the first rise of Gothick in the twelfth, to its completion in the fifteenth century, the improvements are owing to the munificence of the Church, and the vast abilities of the free masons, in the Middle Ages. These scientific persons have great claim to our admiration, from the richness and fertility of their inventive powers. By them the eastern style was transplanted into the west ; and under them, it was so much altered and amplified, that it assumed an entirely new appearance." Did they accompany the Croisaders, and learn the Arab architecture for the purpose of adopting it upon their return ? " These immense works produced a host of artificers, out of whom, in imitation of the confraternities, which for various purposes had existed from ancient times, companies were formed, academies, schools, and bodies were established. An oath of secrecy was administered to the noviciates; a veil of mystery pervaded their meetings, which, in an age when many were ignorant, conferred importance. Such institutions, in the infancy of science, were singularly beneficial. By their efforts new lights were elicited, and valuable discoveries extensively diffused."—*Gunn* on Gothick Architecture, p. 60. *Muratori,* Disc. 75.

MASONS," in every country of Europe where
they had assembled themselves, received the
blessing of the Holy See, under an injunction
of dedicating their skill to the erection of
ecclesiastical buildings; and that certain immunities were conceded to them, such as forming themselves into small and migratory societies, under the government of a MASTER of the
craft, with the privilege of taking apprentices,
who, after a due initiation, became FREE AND
ACCEPTED MASONS.*   But it is certain that
such a papal rescript or document has been
industriously sought for in the Vatican library,
and without success. If this indulgence took
place in the first half of the thirteenth century,
as it is said to have done, there were three
popes before 1250.

Some writers on the subject have claimed
for these fraternities a close connexion with the
Knights Templars, from the similarity which
is presumed to have subsisted with respect to
both, of their mysterious rites of initiation.
Be that as it may, it is allowed that they came
into England nearly at one and the same time.
Nor is there decided proof of their alliance,
but a great resemblance in their mysterious

* *Wren's Parentalia.   Archæologia*, vol. iv. 150 ; vol. ix.
110—126. *Shakspeare* has an accurate idea of a master-
mason : " *Chief architect and plotter,*" i. e. the layer of a
foundation.

pretensions. Exclusion was imperatively ordained by both, as the sure guardian of mystery. They adopted the anathema of Eleusis,
"*Procul! O procul este prophani!*"

Yet, in candour, we may allow the assertion,
that these secret meetings of the master-masons,
within any particular district, did not foster
political objects, but were, in fact, confined to
consultations with each other, which mainly
tended to the communication of science, and of
improvement in their art. An evident result
was seen in the general uniformity of their
designs in architecture, with respect both to
plan and ornament, yet not without deviations.

We may conclude that the craft or mystery
of architects and operative masons was involved
in secrecy, by which a knowledge of their practice was carefully excluded from the acquirement of all who were not enrolled in their
fraternity. Still it was absolutely necessary
that when they engaged in contracts with
bishops, or patrons of the great ecclesiastical
buildings, a specification should be made of
the component parts, and of the terms by which
either contracting party should be rendered
conversant with them.* A certain nomencla-

---

* See page 170 to 176. This glossary is confined to such
terms as are known by adducing proofs from contemporary
authorities of the acceptation and definitive sense in which
they occur.

ture was then divulged by the master-masons for such a purpose, and became in general acceptation in the middle ages.

After these preliminary observations, I will attempt an investigation of the three leading points which I have had in view in this discourse:—I. The various designations of master-masons and their associates or operatives, which may be authenticated either from their epitaphs in the magnificent structures where they had sepulture, or from the contracts with their patrons and supervisors.—II. An inquiry into the true claims of ecclesiastics, with respect to their having been the sole designers, or architects, of cathedrals and their parts, exclusively of the master-masons whom they employed, and who were required only to execute plans already allowed them.—III. Of architects who practised in England, during the middle ages, concerning whom documentary evidence is adduced, in a series.

I. In the course of research, I have observed so many memorials of master-masons, with a certain variation in the designation of individuals in their sepulchral inscriptions, that the more remarkable only require to be noticed.*

* MAGISTER was the original term universally applied to an architect, and which, in distinction to his small band of associated masons, was continued to the latest period. *Magister Irvinus de Steinbach.* Maistre Jean de Chelles built the

Where their effigies are engraven in inlaid
brass, as in the cathedral at Rouen, the com-

south porch of Nôtre Dame in 1257. Alexander de Berneval,
maistre des œuvres de maçonrie at the cathedral of Rouen.
Depositor operum, literally, he who lays a foundation or gives
a plan. The generic word was *cæmentarius*, which, or *magister
lapidum*, was used by the earliest Italian writers upon architecture. The French have *tailleurs de pierres*. *L'Anglois*
observes that " it was not before the eleventh century that
churches in France were built entirely of stone, which the
historians distinguish as being *ex cæmentario lapide*. In the
epitaph of the master-mason of the abbey of Caen, in Normandy, he is styled, " *Gulielmus jacet petrarum summus in
arte :*" and in St. Michael's church, at St. Alban's—"*T. Wolvey,
latomus summus in arte necnon armiger Ricardi Secundi,
regis Angliæ, ob. 1430.*" *Latomus*, or *lithotomus*, is, literally,
stone-hewer (*lapicida*), and differs in some degree from
cæmentarius : the first-mentioned, merely a rough-mason ;
the other, who squared and polished the blocks of stone, as
ashler, for the intended walls, or who prepared them for
ornamental carving and statuary, " 𝔤𝔢𝔫𝔱𝔦𝔩 𝔢𝔫𝔱𝔞𝔦𝔩." *Chaucer.*—
Gervase says of William of Sens—" formas quoque ad lapides formandos, his qui convenerant sculptoribus tradidit.
X. Script. In strict alliance with him was the " MAGISTER
CARPENTRARIUS et depositor operum quoad artem carpen-
trarii." The immense and most scientifically constructed
roofs of timber-frame, in the fourteenth century particularly,
were the works of their hands. Such an artisan was called
by Cicero, " *faber tignarius.*" There were still more perfect
discriminations, which have been applied by Chaucer :—

> 𝔄bout 𝔥im lefte 𝔥e no ma𝔠on *(cæmentarius)*
> 𝔗𝔥at coul𝔡 stone la𝔭ne *(depositor)* ne querrour, *(latomus)*
> 𝔥e 𝔥ire𝔡 t𝔥em to make a toure.
>
> *Romaunt of the Rose.*

In contracts we observe plastrarius (*plasterer*); parietor
(*pargetor*) &c. temp. Edw. I.

pass, square, and tablet describing a ground plan, are usually added: at Gloucester, with a square only, supported by a projecting figure, sculptured: at Worcester, in a bas-relief, already mentioned. It was a natural wish, that their bones should rest under the stupendous roofs which they themselves had raised.

It would be inconsistent both with the limits and purpose of this essay, to enumerate the various contracts, which may be still examined; an instance or two may suffice.*

II. It is an inquiry, not without its difficulty, but which may be yet attended with a satisfactory result, — whether a perfect discrimination can be made between the controllers of the works and the master-masons?

---

* In *Rymer's Fœdera, Stow,* and *Dugdale,* they occur at length. Richard de Stowe, in 1306, master-mason of Lincoln cathedral, contracted to do the plain work by measure, and the fine carved work and images by the day. *Rot. Pat.* 3 Edw. Tertii.—Walter de Weston for St. Stephen's chapel, Westminster. *Rot. Pat.* 26 Hen. VI. p. 2. m. 35. — To John Smythe, warden of the masons, and Robert Wheteley, warden of the carpenters, for King's College, Cambridge. The following is a proof of the estimation and rank which a master-mason or architect held in society during the middle ages. The abbot of St. Edmundsbury (13 Hen. VI. 1439,) contracts with John Wood, *masoun,* for the repairs and restoration of the great bell tower " in all mannere of thinges that longe to Free masounry — Borde for himselfe, as a gentilman, and his servaunt as a yoman, and therto, two robys, one for himself after a gentilmanys livery. Wages of masons three shillings a man weekly in winter, and 3 shillings 4 pence in summer."—*Archæologia,* vol. xxiii. p. 331.

Although the number of those who have been styled architects will be considerably reduced by ranking as such only the *magistri ædificantes* and the *latomi*, yet that claim may be authenticated by comparing the several designations by which patrons and contributors only are distinguished from others, who might possibly have given the original designs.*

* This question appears to find its solution in an inscription in the Campo Santo at Pisa : — " *Operario*, (master of the works,) Orlando Sardella; Johanne, *magistro ædificante*." The controller was merely an auditor of expenses, or an executor of some great benefactor, as at Gloucester :—" Tullii *ex onere*, Sebroke Abbate jubente." See p. 178. The common working mason was styled " *opifex*." *Legend St. Gaul.*— If the different phrases used to discriminate the precise share which these superior ecclesiastics had, either in the foundation of cathedrals, or the large rebuilding, or additions to them, their bearing will be found to rest upon grammatical construction. These would not have been so widely varied, but with a specific meaning. 1 insert many, merely as a matter of curiosity, being certain that they will not derogate from the real merit of the master-masons : — " fabricavit," " construxit," " ædificavit," " inchoavit," " fere perfecit," " perfecit," " fecit ædificari," " ædificationes novo genere fecit," " fieri fecit hanc fabricam," " incæpit facere." It would be tedious to enumerate all the instances which have occurred, in examining monkish chronicles.

Any catalogue of practical architects among the ecclesiastics, after a strict scrutiny, will be confined to a very few names, from a deficiency of evidence. Surveyors, controllers, or benefactors, have been improperly identified with the actual builders.

GONDULF, or GUNDULPHUS, a monk of the abbey of Bec, in Normandy, is the first recorded architect of the

We are accustomed to attribute, and justly in many known instances, all the arts of design to ingenious ecclesiastics of the Middle Ages. But this concession must not be exclusively made with respect to professional artists. Proofs indeed abound, that individuals among the higher rank of clergy cultivated and under-stood architecture *theoretically*. We generally

cathedral and keep of Rochester, and likewise of the chapel, at least, in the Tower of London; " *in opere cæmentario plurimum sciens et efficax erat.*"—Angl. Sac. t. i. p. 338.

WILLIAM WYKEHAM, bishop of Winchester. *Bishop Lowth*, in his life of that eminent prelate, asserts that his talents were originally discovered in his knowledge of architecture; and that, at a very early period of life, before he had dedicated himself to the priesthood, he was employed in designing the royal works at Windsor and Queenborough. In the years 1357 and 59, he received patents, with a competent salary, and with powers to impress every kind of artificer. That this knowledge and taste for architecture retained their strongest influence through his whole life, cannot admit of a doubt, and that he was the architect, in fact, *(sciens et efficax,)* of both his colleges at Oxford and Winton. In the decline of his life, his works in the cathedral of the last-mentioned, were solely entrusted to William Wynford, a master-mason of great ability, who had long enjoyed his patronage, and whose future services are commanded in the Bishop's will. " Volo etiam et ordino quod dispositio et ordinatio hujusmodi novi operis fiant per magistrum *Wilhelmum Wynford* et *alios sufficientes*, discretos, et *in arte illâ approbatos* (evidently meaning FREE MASONS,) ab executoribus meis deputandos; ac quod Dominus Simon Membury (a priest) sit supervisor et solutor dicti operis sit, in futurum."—*Lowth's Life of Wykeham*, App. xxxv. Here the office of the master of the works is distinctly marked out.

William,

see in contemporary chronicles, supplied from local registers, the single name of the bishop or abbot recorded, under whose patronage the master-masons were employed, but who are sunk in oblivion in most instances. Although most frequently their plans were executed by ordinary masons, it cannot be fairly supposed, that the erection of many cathedrals could

. WILLIAM REDE, bishop of Chichester, was a consummate geometrician, and discovered eminent talents in buildings at Merton College, Oxford, of which he was a fellow. In 1379 he began his castle at Amberley in Sussex, in which he was employed during ten years. Its construction is upon a plan differing, in material instances, from the system of military architecture and contrivance peculiar to that age. The towers at the angles were built in the base-court, not projecting beyond the skreen walls. — *Dallaway's Western Sussex,* Amberley.

But the pride of ecclesiastics among practical architects was ALAN DE WALSINGHAM, prior of Ely. His great work was the louvre tower in the centre of that cathedral. It forms an octagon with as many arches, in which strength and elegance are alike conspicuous ; and the whole abounds in curious embellishment carved in bas-relief. Consummate skill is shown in the construction of the timber-frame roof :— " Summo ac mirabili mentis ingenio imaginata." Of this most beautiful effort of his genius and science, the conception originated in his own mind. He was neither the imitator of, nor was he imitated by, any other architect. Completed in 1328. Trinity chapel is another example of his superior talent. He was buried at Ely, and in an ancient chronicle is styled, " Vir venerabilis et artificiosus frater." His constant patron, who supplied funds with unexampled munificence, was Bishop Hotham. —*Bentham's Ely,* passim. *Leland's Collectanea.*

have been designed and perfected excepting by eminent professors, exclusively devoted to the study and practice of their art.

It may be found necessary to disrobe several of the prelates and abbots who have so long enjoyed the fame of being the architects of their own churches, in pursuit of this evidence. The parts taken by these great ecelesiastics should be separately considered :—first, as contributors only, or patrons of works; or, secondly, as having designed plans which were communicated to the master-masons for execution by them. They were probably not so well versed in geometrical science as the master-masons, for mathematics formed a part of monastic learning in a very limited degree.

The real obligation of posterity to the founders of these magnificent edifices, which all who are endued with taste or religious feeling will not cease to venerate, in those which have been preserved to the present day, constitutes their true praise. Only let us reflect, upon a comparison with the present value of money, what an expenditure would be necessary to complete even the least considerable of them! Funds, always accumulating, were dedicated solely to those purposes, with a perseverance, and to an extent, of which we can recognise no other example. It would be invidious to attribute the only cause to their superfluous wealth.

But the honour due to the original founder
of these edifices is almost invariably transferred
to the ecclesiastics under whose patronage they
rose, rather than to the skill and design of the
master-mason, or professional architect, because
the only historians were monks. The masons
rejected history, as their system allowed oral
tradition only; and it is from their contracts,
or epitaphs, that we can rescue any individual
name. That the original plan, or the details
of it, was often suggested by one of the more
ingenious of the ecclesiastics, cannot be candidly doubted; but that in more instances the
master-mason had the exclusive execution, is
not less an approved fact.

In the earliest æra of the masonic establishment, a geometrical figure, or canon, was adopted in all sacred buildings, which had an import
hid from' the vulgar. As it had a decided
reference to the Christian religion, it might
have been invented by the Church; but it has
likewise an equal analogy with other mysteries
professed by the first societies " of masons."

This hieroglyphical device was styled *Vesica
Piscis.** " It may be traced from the church of
St. John Lateran, and Old St. Peter's at Rome,

* Observations on the *Vesica piscis* in the architecture of the
Middle Ages, and in Gothick architecture, by *T. Kerrich*, A.M.
Principal Librarian of the University of Cambridge.—*Archæo-
logia*, vol. xvi. p. 292 ; and vol. xix. p. 353.

to the church of Bath, one of the latest Gothick buildings of any consequence in England. It was formed by two equal circles, cutting each other in their centres, and was held in high veneration, having been invariably adopted by master-masons in all countries. In bas-reliefs, which are seen in the most ancient churches, over doorways, it usually circumscribes the figure of Our Saviour." It was, indeed, a principle which pervaded every building dedicated to the Christian religion. But this fact allowed, " it has been exclusively attributed to a knowledge of Euclid, and necessarily involves the construction of the pointed arch. The early architects were certainly not ignorant of Euclid's works, which had been translated from Greek into Latin, by Boethius. Cassiodorus had recommended Euclid to Theodoric king of the Goths."*

There is, as it has been judiciously observed, an evident disparity between several of the ornamental parts of many cathedrals, which will be evident by contrasting the skill of the amateur monk with that of the professional artist.†

III. Offering to our present view such master-masons whose more eminent and ascertained pretensions may have distinguished them

* *Hawkins' Origin of Gothick Architecture*, 8vo. p. 244.
† *Wild's Illustration of Cathedrals*, ut sup.

from others, whose names have been recognised in various documents, I have selected the following only. Such of them who have been employed in military architecture will be noticed with reference to their several works.* The master-masons, and their brotherhood, could have been scarcely ever void of employment, as their labours were not always confined to ecclesiastical buildings. They were employed not only in raising castles, but in inventing military stratagems in their formation, and making engines of war : such had the peculiar name of *Ingeniatores.*† For completing castellated or grand domestic mansions, they were no less in requisition. A very early instance occurs in the reign of Henry III. of Paul le Peverer, in his house at Todington, in Bedfordshire, and of the numerous artificers whom he had assembled.‡

---

* But and he couthe through his sleight,
  To maken up a toure of height ;
  Though it were of no rounde stone,
  Wrought with squere and scantilone. *(square* and *measure.)*
CHAUCER.

† " Fratri Roberto de Ulmo, *magistro ingeniatori*, ad vadia Regis, ix den. per diem," &c. — *Lib. Garderobæ* Edw. Primi, anno 1299, published by the Society of Antiquaries, 1787.

‡ P. 383. *Matt. Paris' Hist.* p. 821, folio. " Operarii namque plurimis annis, ædificiorum suorum, quâlibet septimanâ centum solidos, et plures x marcas, recepisse pro stipendiis, asseruntur."

MASTER-MASONS FROM THE TWELFTH TO THE END OF THE FIFTEENTH CENTURY.

XII. CENTURY.

William Anglus, of whom *see page* 42.

XIII. CENTURY.

Adam de Glapham and Patric de Carlile, " magister cæmentariorum et carpentariorum, cum septem sociis," employed to build Caernarvon Castle.—*Lib. Garderobæ* 26 Edw. I. 1200.

Henricus de Ellerton, " magister operum." 1292.

Michael de Cantuariâ, cæmentarius, St. Stephen's Chapel.

XIV. CENTURY.

Richard de Stowe was the master-mason of Lincoln Cathedral, and Nicholas Walton, magister-carpentarius, *(roof-maker,)* in 1306.

Henry Latomus, from 1300—1319. Evesham Abbey.

William Boyden, 1308—1326.

Walter de Weston.—*Pat.* 4 Edw. Tertii, 1331. St. Stephen's, Westminster, and Windsor Castle, St. George's Hall.

William Wynford.* Nave of Winchester Cathedral.

---

* Will of W. Wykeham: — *Lowth's Life of Wykeham,* p. 195.

Henry Yeveley of London, master-mason;
Robert Wasburn, and John Swallow, and W.
Hall, master-carpenters of Westminster and
Eltham Halls.—*Rymer's Fœdera.*

Robert de Skillington,* master-mason of the
hall in Kenilworth Castle, 1392.

XV. CENTURY.

In the computus of payments (in 1429) of the
cathedral of Canterbury, the names of the masters,
wardens, and masons, are all recited.—*Preston.*

William Horwood. Chapel of the College of
Fotheringay.—*Contract with Richard Duke of
York*, 1435.†

John Wastell, Henry Semerk, master-masons of King's College, 1444.

John Smyth, master-mason; Robert Wes-
terley, master-carpenter for Eton College.—
Rot. Pat. 26 Hen. VI. p. 2. m. 35. 1450.

---

* The great additions made by John of Gaunt to that
Castle were in consequence of a warrant from Richard II, in
1392, directed to Skillington, to impress twenty workmen,
carpenters, &c.—*Dugdale's Warwickshire.*

† " Covenant by oversight of masters of the same craft.
To build the nave and ailes, with the spire, for £300, and if
not performed duly, he shall yelde his bodye to prisoun, at
the lord's will."—*Dugdale's Monasticon*, vol. iii.   The wages
of a free mason at St. George's, Windsor, one shilling a-day.
Grant of arms to Nicholas Cloos, Roger Keys, and Thomas
his brother, by King Henry VI, 1449, 1450 (*Bentley's Excerpta Historica*, 8vo. p. 364):—the above were architects or
supervisors, and not master-masons.

Edward Seamer, or Semerk, master-mason of St. George's Chapel at Windsor, 1480 and 1499. Wages, one shilling a-day.

John Woolrich, master-mason of King's College, 1476.

John Woode, Abbey of St. Edmundsbury.— *See page* 415, *note.*

Roger Keys and John Druet were supervisors of the building of All-Souls' College.

A'Wood gives the names of Hethe, Wrabey, and Balle, as master-masons, 1438.

William Orcheyerde, " master of masonry of Magdalene College, Oxford, 1475."—*A'Wood's Antiquities of Oxford,* p. 310.

XVI. CENTURY.

John Cole, master-mason, tower and spire of Louth, Lincolnshire, 1500—1506. *Archæologia,* vol. x.—*Britton's Architec. Antiq.* vol. iv. 4to.

Robert Vertue, works in the Tower of London, 1501.

Henry Smyth, for works in the palace of Richmond, 1505.

Hector Ashley, at Hunsdon and other palaces, before 1530.

Some of my readers may object to this, as a meagre catalogue, but I proposed to give notices only of actual masons, not of patrons and amateurs among the ecclesiastics, and it is therefore narrowed to positive evidence, as far as I have found it, and, of course, with certain omissions.

In the art of sculpture, at least of carved work, not as confined to architectural embellishment only, but of the human figure, they had attained to a high degree of excellence. They had few opportunities of displaying anatomical science; in bas-reliefs, positively none. In statues, being usually enclosed in narrow niches, their skill could be chiefly shown in draperies or armour; yet in the heads we may often discover great boldness and a freedom of execution; and in the countenances of female saints absolute and characteristic beauty, more especially in that of the Virgin Mary. This is most remarkable before the close of the fourteenth century.* Some of the more ingenious among them were capable of carving the recumbent sepulchral figures, as large as life. These, in numerous contracts, are denominated " marblers."

The political history of the FREE MASONS in England must be the next subject of investigation; and no proof has been as yet adduced

* See *Gough's Sepulchral Monuments; Carter's Ancient Sculpture*, &c. and the *Ancient Sepulchral Monuments*, by the late accurate *Charles Stothard;* folio.

from any chronicle or history of this country, that, as a fraternity or guild, they at any period possessed or held by patent any exclusive privilege whatsoever: all that may be collected from the records is of a contrary tendency.

The statute of the 24th of Edward III, 1351, did not originate in any political jealousy, but in punishment of the contumacious masons whom he had assembled at Windsor Castle, under the direction of William of Wykeham, the comptroller of the royal works (*magister operum*). They refused the ˌwages, withdrew from their engagements, and, at last, openly refused to return. The subjoined penalties were then enacted.* Nor can we collect from the preamble of the second Act, in the reign of Henry VI. that any allusion is made to a political conspiracy, but merely to enforce the restrictions imposed on them by the Statute of

* *Statutes of the Realm*, vol. i. p. 367. Translated from the French. — "If labourers and artificers absent themselves out of their services in another town or country, the party shall have suit before the justices:"—"and if he does not return after three monitions, and for the falsity, he shall be burned in the forehead with an iron made and formed to the letter ꬵ (for false), but may be respited by the justices. No artificer shall take wages on festival days." It is evident that the free masons had, at that period, no exemption from other artificers, nor were endowed with any distinct privileges as a fraternity, nor were they formidable in a political point of view. *Lowth's Life of Wykeham*, p. 17.—*Rot. Pat.* 30 Edw. Tertii, 1356.

Labourers.* They were bound, as before, to obey the royal mandate, or patent to others, when required, and to take the prescribed wages. Preston asserts that they received immunities from that monarch. But, in 1435, he granted a patent to Richard Duke of York to impress masons, who contracted with William Horwood, as master, to build the chapel at Fotheringhay, " who, if the contract be not performed properly, shall yield his body to prison at the lord's will." With due diligence, I have searched the *Rotulus Patentium*, without having discovered *any* granted to free masons by Henry VI, although very frequently given to gilds and fraternities. † The penalties enacted were probably evaded by the proviso

* *Statutes of the Realm*, vol. ii. p. 227, 1425. Translation from the French :—" Whereas by the early combinations and confederacies made by masons in their general assemblies and chapters, the good cause and effect of the statute of labourers be openly violated and broken, in subversion of the law and the great damage of the Commons, our sovereign lord the King has ordained, that such chapters and congregations shall not be held hereafter : and if any such be made, if they be convicted, shall be adjudged felons. And that all other masons that come to such chapters or congregations shall be punished by imprisonment and fine." They were liable to be seized, and retained by the King's order, whenever he designed a palace or an abbey. — *Rymer's Fœdera*, vol. v. p. 670.

† See *Calendarium Rotul. Patent.* in Turri Londinensi; *Calendarium Rotul. Chartarum*, published by authority of Parliament.

made by the master-masons in all great contracts, the conditions annexed to undue performance having been always specified; so that
these two compulsory acts having lain totally
dormant, is a mere assumption.* The fixed
wages, however, were considerably higher than
those of any other mechanics; and if we estimate them by the relative value of money to
what it now bears, sufficiently liberal.† Even
as late as Charles the Second's time, the magistrates of Warwickshire set an assize for them
as for other *artisans.*‡

If the chapters, or assembling of free masons,
had been injurious to the state by fomenting
insurrections, it is scarcely probable that such
fact would have been totally overlooked, not
only by the English historians but in the statutes. It is alleged, that by the Act of the
fifth of Elizabeth (1562) they were exonerated

* Preston alleges that these penalties were never inflicted.
Whether inflicted, or not, it is too late to inquire with any
degree of proof. In Henry the Sixth's will, respecting the
college of Eton, he restricts the fashion of extreme ornament
in masonry, " layinge apart too curious workes of entaile,
and busy mouldinge."—*Royal and Noble Wills.*

† According to Adam Smith, wages are fifteen times
increased since the eleventh century.

‡ Rates of wages, 1684, at the Quarter Sessions held at
Warwick, 1684.—FREE mason, 1s. 4d. without board, 5d.
with: penalty for taking above this rate, twenty-one days'
imprisonment. What becomes, then, of the exemptions declared by the fifth of Elizabeth?—*Archæologia,* vol. xi. p. 208.

from all penalties, which is recited as the opinion of a very celebrated sage of the law.*

When it is said that the Act of Henry VI. was passed at the instigation of Henry Cardinal Beaufort, and that the Bishops Wykeham, Waynflete, and Chicheley, were grand-masters, I must be allowed to prefer evidence to conjecture, but none has been adduced. It admits of a doubt, whether it were then considered as authorized by ecclesiastical constitutions, that its most eminent members could have presided as grand masters, and have been associated with the mysterious brotherhood; or that they could have been so, without the prescribed initiation? If authentic documents were ever in the archives of the fraternity, a modern inquirer would seek for them in vain. But if the mysteries of the brotherhood are considered to be sacred, why is their true history concealed?—or given, as by Preston and his predecessors, without citing any other than obscure authority? Ware, in his Essay in the Archæologia, says that Nicholas Stone destroyed many valuable papers belonging to the society of free masons: and he adds — " Perhaps his master, Inigo Jones, thought that the new mode, though dependent on taste, was independent on science; and, like

---

* *Coke's Institutes*, 5 Eliz. 1562. They were exempted by implication only, for they are not named, as a body corporate, nor, indeed, under any specific denomination.

the Calife Omar, that what was agreeable to the new faith was useless, and that what was not ought to be destroyed."

An important subject of these observations is the examination of several treatises which have appeared in print, one of which is taken from a most curious and early MS. said to have been in the handwriting of King Henry VI, but nowhere extant. A copy taken by Leland, and preserved among his papers, is said to be in the Bodleian Library. This has been recopied, and was first published at Francfort, in Germany, in 1748. There is scarcely a work on Freemasonry in which it has not been reprinted. We are apt to attach an imaginary value to MSS. which have been destroyed, as we are precluded from making a collation of the copy with the original. From an inspection of Henry the Sixth's royal signature, and a letter in the British Museum, it may admit of some doubt whether that was an autograph MS. which Leland copied ; for in that age few men of high rank could write at all legibly, that being the work of regular scribes. This singular treatise is entitled—

* 𝕮𝖊𝖗𝖙𝖆𝖞𝖓𝖊 𝕼𝖚𝖊𝖘𝖙𝖎𝖔𝖓𝖘 𝖜𝖞𝖙𝖍 𝕬𝖚𝖓𝖘𝖜𝖊𝖗𝖊𝖘 to the same, concernynge the Mystery of Maconrye, writtenne by the hande of Kynge

---

* Lives of *Leland, Hearne* and *Wood*, 8vo. 1772. Appendix, No. vii. with Notes by John Locke. It is at least singular, that after a search through the " Catalogus " of the

𝕳enrpe t𝔥e si𝔯t𝔥e of t𝔥e name, an𝔡 fapt𝔥fullp coppe𝔡 bp m̄e 𝕵o𝔥an 𝕷eplan𝔡e, 𝔄ntiquarius, bp commaun𝔡e of 𝕳is 𝕳ig𝔥nesse.*

MSS. of Leland and Bodley in the Bodleian Library, no such MS. is mentioned. See *Catalogus MSS. Librorum*, Oxon. fol. 1697. The copy sent to Locke was from another collection. It was reprinted in England in the Gentleman's Magazine, 1753, from the Francfort edition.

This short treatise is accompanied by the animadversions of that acute and celebrated philosopher, and shrewdly descanted on. The apologists, Preston and others, have asserted that he was afterwards admitted a brother, and, of course, altered his opinion ; but this circumstance is nowhere alluded to, either in his works or letters.

" ' What dothe the masons concele and hyde ? The arte of fynding out new arts, and that for her owne proffytte and preise.' I think that, in this particular, they shew too much regard for their own society, and too little for the rest of mankind." L.

" ' The arte of keeping secrettes, that soe that the worlde mayeth nothinge concele from them.' What kind of an art this is, I can by no means imagine. But, certainly, such an art the masons must have, for though, as some people suppose, they have no secret at all, even that must be a secret which, being discovered, would expose them to the highest ridicule, and therefore it requires the utmost caution to conceal it." L.

" Other concealed arts are, ' the arte of Chaunges *(transmutation of metals)* ; the wey of wynning the facultye of Abrac.' Here I am utterly in the dark." L. — ABRAC, (we, the *uninitiated,* are candidly informed by Preston,) which had puzzled whole centuries as a verbal signal, and no less than the profound Locke, is merely an abbreviation of ABRACADABRA, of cabalistic notoriety, especially when written upon a paper and worn round the neck, as an infallible charm against the ague.

" ' The universal lingage of maçonnes.' If it be true, I guess it must be something like the language of the ancient pantomimes among the Romans." L.

* King Henry VIII.

There is proof that the mind of the imbecile monarch was, in early life, directed to the discovery of " hidden things."   He was a dupe to the possibility of the philosopher's stone, (as his wiser predecessor, Edward III, had been before,*) and gave a patent to the alchemists, having summoned them to display their art before him.† No wonder that he should entertain a similar curiosity to learn the secrets of the craft, and it is more than probable that this examination of them took place before him in council, 1445.

It commences with a *question*—" What mote it be ?"—*Answer :* " Yt beith the skylle of nature; the understandinge of the myghte that ys herynne, and its sondrye werkynges, sonderlyche, the skill of reckonnynges; of wayghtes and metynges ; and the true manere of façonynge all thinges for mannys use, headlie, dwellings and buildynges of all kindes, and all odther thynges that make goode to manne."‡ Farther

* *Rot Pat.* 1329, 2 Edw. Tertii.—*Fœdera*, vol. iv. p. 384. " Johanni Goble, quod possit per artem philosophiæ metalla imperfecta in aurum sive argentum transubstantiare."

† *Rot. Pat.* 23 Hen. Sexti. " To John Rous and W. Dalby to make gold or silver, and to bring their instruments before him.—*Ashmole's Theatrum Chemicum.*"

‡ " What artes have the Maçonnes techedde mankynde ?" The artes Agricultura, Architectura, Astronomia, Geometria, Nume*res*, Musica, Poesie, Kymistryè, Governmente, and Religioune." Locke observes, that what appears most odd

extracts are unnecessary, as the whole is published, and may be readily examined by the
more curious reader.

The first publications dealt principally in
tradition: Jachin and Boaz, and the original
lodge as established at York* in Saxon times.
Of those which are more modern, two are entitled to notice. Preston's Illustrations are
held in high estimation. As the history only
is important to the present inquiry, it must be
observed, that no recital is made of the penalties of either statute above-quoted; and that
in the chapter assigned to an examination of
Locke's notes upon Leland's transcript, such
opinions as impugn the high credit of masonry
are omitted. It offers an elaborate vindication
of the system of Free masonry upon its general

---

is, that they reckon religion among the arts.—" Peter Gower a
Grecian journeyedde yn everiche londe whereas the Venetians
had plauntedde Maçonrye." Could it be suspected that
Peter Gower was Pythagoras, and the Venetians Phenicians?

* The ingenious Dr. Plot, in his *History of Staffordshire,*
(chap. viii. p. 316,) indulges himself in some sarcastic observations, which are indignantly repelled by Preston. The
first general chapter of free masons in England is said to have
been convened at York by Edwyn son of King Athelstan, in
924. This, as it might well be, is ridiculed by Dr. Plot as
being an historical blunder. Athelstan succeeded his father,
Edward the Elder, in 924. He had no son, Edwyn was his
brother, and in that same year conspired against him, and
was deprived of life by his order. — *Turner's Anglo-Saxon
History,* vol. ii. p. 207.

principles and analogies, with few and imperfect references to genuine history: the first compulsory act of Edward III. is not even alluded to.

In the *Encyclopædia Britannica*, vol. xii. 4to. pages 639 to 669 are occupied by "An Essay on Free Masonry," which is an apologetical digest of all that has been written by previous authors, but with a dereliction of several of the more popular traditions. Of this essay the main object is a vindication of Freemasonry from the charge urged against it by Barüel and Robison. However it may have applied to lodges on the Continent, it will be readily allowed that those in the British empire were honourably free from those imputations. The investigation is elaborate. The last-mentioned author speaks of the original connexion, by analogy at least, with the mysteries of Eleusis; the Essenes; of the school of masonry established at Crotona in Magna Græcia by Pythagoras; and lastly, the intimate alliance which subsisted between the Knights Templars* and the Free Masons, with a profusion of useless and inapplicable learning. I hazard this opinion,

---

* It is a conjecture supported by clear deduction from contemporary history, that the bands of masons who followed the later Croisaders were patronized by them on their return to England; and that the model of the Holy Sepulchre at Jerusalem was brought by them into this country, and ap-

under favour, as being merely a common reader.
No mention is made by this inquirer of the
Jewish origin, nor of the establishment, in this
country, before the twelfth century. Both the
lodge held by Edwyn at York, and the penal
statute of Edward III, are totally omitted.
The MSS. of Bode and Mouncer (German authors) are quoted as authorities.

A passage in the Leland MS. seems to
authorise a conjecture, that the denomination
of Free-masons in England was merely a vernacular corruption (by no means unusual) of
the FRERES-MAÇONS established in France.
" Secretes such as do bynde the *Freres* more
strongliche togeddre by the profytte and
commoditye comynge to the *confrerie* ther-
fromme."

But I am not borne out by their appellations
or titles on the Continent.* Yet how un-
founded is the name *free,* when assumed by
our countrymen, who never enjoyed *here* either
privilege or exemption.

Both Jones and Wren were grand masters

---

plied to the Round churches. Nor did the castles built by
Edward I. bear a less near analogy to the military structures
of the great Saladin. The crested towers called macchicolations, from an Arab term, then so universally adopted, have
certainly an Oriental origin.

* Frey-Maureren, *German.* Liberi Muratori, *Italian.*
Fratres Liberales, *Roman.* Franc-maçons, *French.* Fratres
Architectonici, *Modern Inscription.*

of the English lodges ; and it may be observed, that no buildings can shew a further departure from the genuine Gothick of any period than the chapel of Lincoln's Inn, the towers of Westminster, and the Campanile, Christchurch, Oxford.   The science and practice of the Gothick school were entirely abandoned, although in a professed imitation.

In conclusion of this attempt, which I have been induced to undertake with diffidence, and the sole view of discovering historical truth, I disavow any inclination to scrutinize mysteries, concerning which I should be an unauthorized inquirer.   But, in acknowledging with sincere praise, what is conspicuously apparent to all, it must be said, that during the last century the Freemasons of this kingdom have eminently distinguished themselves by their sound loyalty and their widely-extended and useful benevolence.

And so — an eminent brother of the craft will say, after their patron King Henry VI.—

" 𝔥𝔢 𝔈𝔫𝔡𝔰—𝔞𝔫𝔡 𝔪𝔞𝔨𝔢𝔰 𝔫𝔬 𝔖𝔦𝔤𝔫 !"

INDEX.

THE END.

LONDON:
PRINTED BY SAMUEL BENTLEY,
Dorset Street, Fleet Street.

Featured Titles from Westphalia Press

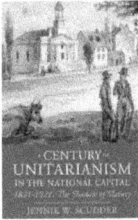

A Century of Unitarianism in the National Capital, 1821-1921
by Jennie W. Scudder

Jennie Scudder's work traces the sometimes controversial history of Unitarianism in the District of Columbia, centering on All Souls Unitarian Church. The account includes the development in the District and surrounding towns in northern Virginia and Southern Maryland.

The Rise of the Book Plate: An Exemplative of the Art
by W. G. Bowdoin, Introduction by Henry Blackwel

Bookplates were made to denote ownership and hopefully steer the volume back to the rightful shelf if borrowed. They often contained highly stylized writing, drawings, coat of arms, badges or other images of interest to the owner.

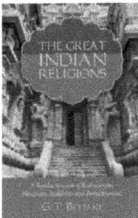

The Great Indian Religions
by G. T. Bettany

G. T. (George Thomas) Bettany (1850-1891) was born and educated in England, attending Gonville and Caius College in Cambridge University, studying medicine and the natural sciences. This book is his account of Brahmanism, Hinduism, Buddhism, and Zoroastrianism

Unworkable Conservatism: Small Government, Free-markets, and Impracticality by Max J. Skidmore

Unworkable Conservatism looks at what passes these days for "conservative" principles—small government, low taxes, minimal regulation—and demonstrates that they are not feasible under modern conditions.

Secrets & Lies in the United Kingdom: Analysis of Political Corruption
Edited by by Fabienne Portier-Le Cocq

Secrets & Lies in the United Kingdom: Analysis of Political Corruption lifts the shroud of secrecy in the United Kingdom in relation to modern freemasonry in Scotland in the late-18th century, the 'Stolen Generations' in Australia from the early 1900s to the late 1970s, and so much more.

Boston Unitarianism 1820-1850
by Octavius Brooks Frothingham

From the author, "Many years ago I proposed writing something in memory of Dr. Frothingham, but abandoned the project on account of the meagerness of the biographical material. Within the twelvemonth, a warm friend and admirer of his asked me to prepare a memoir."

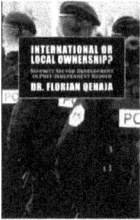

International or Local Ownership?: Security Sector Development in Post-Independent Kosovo
by Dr. Florian Qehaja

International or Local Ownership? contributes to the debate on the concept of local ownership in post-conflict settings, and discussions on international relations, peacebuilding, security and development studies.

The Bahai Movement: A Series of Nineteen Papers
by Charles Mason Remey

Charles Mason Remey (1874-1974) was the son of Admiral George Collier Remey and grew up in Washington DC. He studied to be an architect at Cornell (1893-1896) and the Ecole des Beaux Arts in Paris (1896-1903), where he learned about the Baha'i faith, and quickly adopted it.

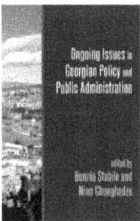

Ongoing Issues in Georgian Policy and Public Administration
Edited by Bonnie Stabile and Nino Ghonghadze

Thriving democracy and representative government depend upon a well functioning civil service, rich civic life and economic success. Georgia has been considered a top performer among countries in South Eastern Europe seeking to establish themselves in the post-Soviet era.

Poverty in America: Urban and Rural Inequality and Deprivation in the 21st Century
Edited by Max J. Skidmore

Poverty in America too often goes unnoticed, and disregarded. This perhaps results from America's general level of prosperity along with a fairly widespread notion that conditions inevitably are better in the USA than elsewhere. Political rhetoric frequently enforces such an erroneous notion.

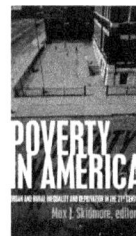

www.ingramcontent.com/pod-product-compliance
Lightning Source LLC
Chambersburg PA
CBHW051410090426
42737CB00014B/2606

* 9 7 8 1 6 3 3 9 1 6 8 3 8 *